ROUTLEDGE LIBRARY EDITIONS:
INTERNATIONAL SECURITY STUDIES

Volume 22

WARFARE IN THE ENEMY'S REAR

T0382658

WARFARE IN THE ENEMY'S REAR

OTTO HEILBRUNN

Routledge
Taylor & Francis Group

LONDON AND NEW YORK

First published in 1963 by George Allen & Unwin Ltd

This edition first published in 2021
by Routledge
2 Park Square, Milton Park, Abingdon, Oxon OX14 4RN

and by Routledge
52 Vanderbilt Avenue, New York, NY 10017

Routledge is an imprint of the Taylor & Francis Group, an informa business

© 1963 George Allen & Unwin Ltd

British Library Cataloguing in Publication Data
A catalogue record for this book is available from the British Library

ISBN: 978-0-367-68499-0 (Set)
ISBN: 978-1-00-316169-1 (Set) (ebk)
ISBN: 978-0-367-71182-5 (Volume 22) (hbk)
ISBN: 978-0-367-71184-9 (Volume 22) (pbk)
ISBN: 978-1-00-314967-5 (Volume 22) (ebk)

Publisher's Note
The publisher has gone to great lengths to ensure the quality of this reprint but points out that some imperfections in the original copies may be apparent.

Disclaimer
The publisher has made every effort to trace copyright holders and would welcome correspondence from those they have been unable to trace.

WARFARE IN THE ENEMY'S REAR

BY

OTTO HEILBRUNN

WITH A FOREWORD BY
LT-GENERAL SIR JOHN WINTHROP HACKETT
K.C.B., C.B.E., D.S.O., M.C., M.A., B.LITT.
Deputy Chief of the Imperial General Staff

London
GEORGE ALLEN & UNWIN LTD
RUSKIN HOUSE MUSEUM STREET

PRINTED IN GREAT BRITAIN
in 11 point Juliana type
BY SIMSON SHAND LTD
LONDON, HERTFORD AND HARLOW

FOREWORD

BY LT.-GENERAL SIR J. W. HACKETT

K.C.B., C.B.E., D.S.O., M.C., M.A., B.LITT.

A need has long been felt for a systematic study of warfare in depth. Different types of operation conducted in different degrees of depth have been investigated often enough. What is the relationship between them, and where do they stand in relation to a coherent whole? That is a question which many of us have been asking since the last war, as we reflect on the big dividends paid by some unorthodox operations and the disappointing results of others, and as we remember the diversity of private armies and the frequent difficulty of co-ordinating their efforts with the main battle. This book takes us a long way on in the search for an answer to this question.

How far do operations in unusual depth or with other special characteristics demand special forces? There can, of course, be no general answer. A sensible approach is to accept the principle that regular types of units should be the norm, and should be used for any task which they can adequately carry out. If an essential task can only be done much less efficiently (or not at all) by a regular type of unit, the creation of a special force can be considered. This is the position taken on this point by the more conservative commanders and is on the whole a good one to start from.

It is possible that we have in Britain, in our military practice, insufficiently explored the variation of regular types of unit, in organization, equipment, technique and training, to meet unusual needs. It would be far from true to say that, in the British army at least, this has been ignored. A problem faced by many commanders in BAOR in recent years has been the reintegration of a unit (an infantry battalion say) into a normal formation, training for full-scale warfare in Western Europe, when the unit came fresh from a tour of operations in the special circumstances of Kenya, Cyprus or Malaya. In those theatres some of the infantry support weapons were put away and techniques of infantry co-operation with guns and armour received scanty attention. The infantry rifleman became the dominant figure once more and Battalion Commanders squeezed out as many riflemen as they could. Dispersed fighting was practised, and dif-

7

ferent forms of patrolling were studied; techniques proper to the terrain and to the methods, equipment and purpose of the enemy were learnt and applied.

On transfer from operations of this sort to a NATO assignment these battalions (never, in my experience, anything but the better for their experiences) lost no time in reactivating those parts of their structure which had been permitted a temporary atrophy. The transition, well prepared at either end of the cycle, was usually quite smooth and provided there were early opportunities to fire weapons and practise other aspects of the relevant techniques it was quite quickly made.

Thus variation of operational method, and even of internal structure to meet changing requirements, is by no means untried. We have, indeed, within fairly close limits, had a good deal of experience of it. What now needs careful study is how far variation in operational demand can be met in this way; how far, that is, the limits can be extended.

In other words, what is a special operation; and when does an operation become so special that only a special force can carry it out? In the search, not so much for answers to these questions, as for a dialectical method by which the answers in any set of circumstances can be found, the preparatory work presented in this book will be invaluable.

Three points seem to me worth making here. First of all, what is at one time special (in the way in which we are using this word) often tends to become normal as time passes. This tendency is far advanced with airborne forces already and also with many aspects of Royal Marine Commando work. In the latter, when the tendency has gone further still, the argument for dropping the term Commando and describing a Marine battalion as such will be heard with added force.

Secondly, in a small regular army, like the British, which has to meet a variety of demands, further attention to variation of structural form and operational techniques within normal units is quite inevitable. We simply cannot afford too many special types of unit.

Thirdly, it is worth reflecting for a moment on the high diversity among the abnormal types of unit mentioned in Dr Heilbrunn's book and noting at the same time as a point of some interest how many of them were of British origin.

The British take very kindly to the oblique approach in war. Some day a competent enquiry will establish why this should be so, making use of the admirable work of Liddell Hart and others in this field, and looking at the question on its sociological and historical background. It is probable that geography, racial mixture and climate will turn out to have much to do with it. The first has been particularly important in its effect on Britain's maritime development. At the same time we should remember a quite common British tendency to conceal highly eccentric personal characteristics under a deceptively conformist exterior. Special forces of one sort or another gave the opportunity to exploit a rich vein of eccentricity in support of Britain's effort in the last war.

This should not be forgotten in considering in principle the adaptation of normal units either to meet abnormal requirements or to seize unusual opportunities. It is often the appearance of the unusual person on the scene which causes the opportunity or the requirement to be first recognized. It is his own proposals which are often seen to be the best (and sometimes the only) way of doing what ought to be done and if he is the best person available to take charge (as he is sometimes the only one) the project is likely to be handled in the way he proposes. This is often how private armies are born.

We sometimes set up forces to make use of a rare talent, which might otherwise find inadequate outlet or none, in doing something which seems to be important at the time. The conjunction of the opportunity and the appropriate person is what then matters most. What often emerges can only be described as a special force, as for example with Bagnold and the LRDG, with David Stirling and the 1st SAS, and with Popsky. This may happen again. For we have even now got nowhere near that degree of adaptability of regular types of unit which would have allowed us to make use of these potentialities in war without raising special forces.

The importance of the single person is often such that it dominates, and even determines, method and organization. In this book the author tells of the reorganization of the SAS in Middle East in the winter of 1942-43, when the Special Boat Squadron was split off and other adjustments took place. This looks like the sort of organizational modification which a responsive organism undergoes to meet changes in circumstances. In a sense it was. But the change in circumstances which had these and other far-reaching results was the capture of David Stirling. He was doing what he was told not to do: trying to join up with First Army from the Egyptian side by way of the Gabes gap on the coast, which was stiff with Germans, instead of going round by a much longer (and safer) inland route through the Shott ed Djerid. Since the SAS had been formed by him and developed into what it was around him no one could take his place. The best proposal the unit could make was to get Bill Stirling out from England to succeed his brother, as someone who knew the trade and was probably as near a real substitute for David as anyone who was not David himself could be. This was no answer and was impossible anyway. The only answer that could be found was to split the SAS up and reorganize it.

There is a clear dilemma here, between the requirement on the one hand to match unusual opportunities with exceptional people in order to make the best use of both, and the need on the other to depart as little as possible from normal procedures and organizations. It is best to face the fact that in the end a theatre commander may find himself compelled, however reluctantly, to raise *ad hoc* forces and use them in special operations. Since full co-ordination with other efforts is essential for the best results (and is very rarely found) those drawing up staff procedures and ordering the training of staff officers should bear this possibility in mind. They do, in fact, in the UK today.

Another difficulty which is likely to persist is that arising from the requirement to co-ordinate between themselves special operations which cannot be easily reconciled with each other. Offensive action, for example, is difficult to reconcile with reconnaissance. The author of this book expresses doubts whether there was a requirement for *both* SAS and LRDG in the desert. But there was then a requirement both for the offensive action which the open flank invited, at which the SAS were very good, and deep reconnaissance, at which the LRDG were unequalled. The superb technique of the LRDG was applied in operations, often of critical intelligence value, which were deft, bold and above all unobtrusive. The SAS, with a splendid combination of ingenuity, economy and violence, used to turn up somewhere like a thunderbolt, leave a score of the enemy's priceless aircraft in blazing ruins on the ground and vanish more or less (but never quite) completely. The index of their offensive value to the Allies was the size of the hornet cloud which then swarmed out from Axis nests to find them. The prime condition of the LRDG's beautiful system of deep intelligence reporting was that the area they worked in should not be stirred up at all. 'For goodness sake,' I can hear Prendergast saying, 'keep the Stirlings away from us!' At one time, near the end of the desert campaign, it was necessary to choose a meridian on the map and give the SAS everything east of it to play in, the LRDG everything west. The SAS of course, did useful intelligence work and the LRDG liked an occasional beat-up; but the principal functions of the two units were diametrically opposed.

The difficulty is still with us. The LRDG, to the regret of many, has gone. The SAS is happily very much alive. But if the functions of troops such as these include deep reconnaissance, offensive action and action in support of partisans, how do you organize, equip and train them? Do you have separate units for each function, or a squadron in each unit specialized in each way, or separate troops in each squadron? What you cannot reasonably ask is that the same small groups become equally proficient in every task, and if you give the same group all three of these functions at once what you *are* asking for is trouble.

There are many other questions raised directly or by implication in this admirable book. Should partisans harass or fight? How far has the helicopter simplified tactical control of our own rear? In the highly fluid conditions of modern war does the rear attack from greater depth, that is, by your own parties operating *towards* your own front, grow more attractive? Is the Stronghold concept dead or only dormant? What is the optimum size of the operating group in different circumstances? When is the point reached at which the effort to survive absorbs so much of an operating group's effort that the group produces no dividend? How can you avoid the segregation of some of the best men, for occasional use only, without risking the loss of the fleeting golden chance? Is there more use to be made of the Brandenburger concept than the Allies in the last war believed? How can the action of special forces best be co-ordinated? Above all, how special should they be?

One thing seems to be almost certain. If nuclear general war becomes less likely lesser forms of warfare become more. These lesser forms are bound to include operations, techniques and organizations whose similarity to those discussed in this book will not be accidental.

It is high time we had a systematic approach to the study of forms of warfare more closely characteristic of the time we live in than almost any others. This book, at last, presents it.

CONTENTS

13

II. CONVENTIONAL FORCES AND THEIR TASKS

III. THE REAR THEATRE OF WAR

CONTENTS

IV. THE FRONT AND THE REAR

CHARTS AND MAP

CONTENTS

IV. THE FRONT AND THE REAR

INTRODUCTION

The forces of the rear with which this study is concerned are the airborne troops, the Special Forces, the partisans, and certain elements of the air forces of the belligerents of the last war.

The war in the enemy rear from 1939 to 1945 was not conducted in accordance with a recognized general doctrine because no such doctrine had then been developed, nor has any attempt been made since to present a study of the theoretical aspects of the war in the rear as a whole and of front and rear warfare as an entity. The present book tries to initiate the search for such a doctrine and to make a contribution towards its formulation.

The war in the rear cannot be comparted: the efforts of the various forces of the rear are often interrelated, or should be so, and the effort of these forces should be co-ordinated with the operations at the front.

The subject matter is complex: so many forces undertake a great variety of tasks with different means and aims, operating too in such widely separated areas that the many aspects of rear warfare hardly seem to have a common denominator. The present study treats the subject by following three guiding lights: (i) each force has a specific task, (ii) the nature of the task is often conditioned by the zone in which the force operates (immediate rear, near rear, far rear), and (iii) the rear operations must be geared with those of the front. Hence the book first discusses the duties assigned to the various—unconventional and conventional —forces of the rear (Parts I and II), then, concentrating on land warfare, tries to find out what type of effort is desirable and possible in the various enemy rear zones (Part III); it subsequently discusses how the rear operations are interrelated with those of the front and outlines the control structure which the integration of front and rear effort requires. It finally deals with the war against the enemy in the rear of one's own forces (Part IV).

CHAPTER 1

THE WAR IN THE ENEMY'S REAR

The Schlieffen Plan, the blueprint of the Prussian General Staff for the defeat of France in the 1914 war, provided that the massed right wing of the German Army in the west should execute a wheeling movement hinged upon Diedenhofen-Metz, sweep through Belgium and, after clearing Northern France of the enemy, press him back against his fortress belt along the French-German frontier from Verdun to Belfort; the French, compelled to fight with their front reversed, would then be totally defeated.

It has been said that the novel feature of Schlieffen's plan was to 'force the factors of space, and, in a sense, time into his service' and enable him by the use of modern methods of transport and communication 'to deploy over an enormous area and endanger his enemy in flank and rear'.[1] This is certainly true, but perhaps more startling than the methods was the hoped-for effect: the main German forces would not only endanger the enemy in his rear but also, and above all, they would seek the decision in his rear.

The Schlieffen Plan was not carried out, and this was also partly the fate of the Manstein Plan for the German campaign of 1940 in the west. Hitler adopted only the first phase of this plan which resulted in the German break-through at Sedan and the turning movement towards Abbéville and the sea; it forced the French and British armies in Belgium facing east also to fight north, south and west. The second unexecuted phase of the plan which bears the Schlieffen imprint provided that the Army Group which had encircled the enemy in Belgium should wheel forward over the lower Somme and envelop him in a battle in the rear of the Maginot Line, again with his front reversed.[2]

It is, of course, an old military concept to engage an enemy in

[1] So Walter Görlitz, The German General Staff. Its History and Structure 1657-1945, London 1953, p. 137.
[2] Field-Marshal Erich von Manstein, Lost Victories, London 1958, p. 126.

his rear. Much of Prussia's rise to power in the nineteenth century was due to successful battles of encirclement, one of the oldest forms of fighting in the enemy's rear. The battle of Leipzig (1814) which paved the way to Napoleon's abdication, the battle of Königgrätz (Sadowa) which sealed the fate of the Austrians in 1866, and the battles of Metz and Sedan in which the Imperial French Army was defeated in 1870, were all battles of encirclement, as were many of Germany's battles in World War II. But while in an encirclement part of the battle is fought in the rear, the rear would have been *the* final battlefield, had Schlieffen and Manstein had their way. Because the enemy front was secured by a fortress belt or line, both generals wanted to fight and defeat him in the rear. That a war in the rear could be waged for much smaller stakes than a strategic or operational decision, merely for the purpose of harassing the enemy on his lines of communication, was not acknowledged by the German General Staff until shortly before the outbreak of World War II, and that the enemy could do so on a large scale was overlooked.

Yet armies had greatly added to their vulnerability in their rear when they became increasingly dependent on bases for supplies. Nobody realized this more clearly than Napoleon and nobody suffered in the last century more from the consequences than he. In 1807 he defined the secret of warfare as the art of maintaining one's own communications and gaining possession of the enemy's. Irregular forces were quick to apply his precepts against him and with so much effect that he himself authorized the formation of irregular units for the defence of France when she was invaded in 1814.

In his *Essay on Partisan War* General Davidov, one of the commanders of Russian formations in the French rear, has analysed this type of warfare; his work became a classic of Russian military literature. General Davidov's partisans were not a motley collection of patriots, brigands and adventurers but a Cossack unit of the type which in French and German terminology is referred to as Freecorps, that is to say a light force of irregulars and armed peasants under military leadership. He makes clear in his essay that partisan warfare aims neither at inflicting pinpricks on the enemy, such as kidnapping an isolated sentry, nor at achieving a decisive victory by a frontal attack on his main force. This type of warfare 'is concerned with the entire area which separates the

enemy from his operational base', and its objectives are 'to cut
the communication lines, destroy all units and wagons wanting
to join up with him, inflict surprise blows on the enemy left without food and cartridges and at the same time block his retreat.
This is the real meaning of partisan war.'[1]

Thus the rear is designated as the proper battlefield for irregular formations. Yet other irregular forces of the last century did
not operate in the rear but carried out frontal attacks on the
enemy main force. When Austria declared war on Napoleon in
1809 and Prussia, occupied by the French, was unable to come
to Austria's support, a Prussian officer, Major von Schill, rallied
a freecorps of 5,000 hussars and set out to expel Napoleon's
brother, King Jerome, from Westphalia. At Wittenberg the freecorps was turned back by Jerome's forces, it unsuccessfully
attacked Magdeburg and then moved on to the fortress of Stral-
sund where it was annihilated. Fifty years later another freecorps
leader, Garibaldi with his 1,000 Redshirts, equally engaged in
frontal attacks, taking cities and clearing the country of the
enemy, and was victorious.

It must be realized, though, that General Davidov was outlining his tactical rules for a partisan force that operates in support of a regular army, as his own unit did, and not for a movement that fights on its own, as von Schill's and Garibaldi's freecorps did. But even the Spanish guerrillas (1808-14) did not
always observe those rules when they fought in association with
the British. Wellington decided to co-ordinate the activities of
the guerrillas with the British; he sent a liaison officer to advise
them, and the Army and Navy furnished them with supplies.
They blocked roads, carried out raids, intercepted couriers, and
especially in the north managed to cut off the French garrisons
from each other, from Madrid and from France. They not only
engaged in combined frontal operations with a force of Marines
landed by the British Navy[2] but also attacked on their own; they
took towns and blockhouses from which the French tried to
pacify the country, engaged regular forces two or three battalions
strong, and cleared large parts of the country of the enemy. Ob-

[1] General Denis Davidov, *Essay sur la guerre de partisans*. Traduit du russe.
1841, p. 7.
[2] Cf. Charles Oman, A *History of the Peninsular War*, vol. v, Oxford 1914,
pp. 551 f.

viously, since the French had garrisons and blockhouses all over
the country, the distinction between the enemy rear and front
was blurred and, as a result, so was the borderline between
regular and irregular warfare which General Davidov had sought
to establish. Still, where the guerrillas felt strong enough they
fought a regular war.

Clausewitz, writing in the 1820s, also stressed that the people
in arms should not fight against strong enemy formations. The
partisans are meant 'not to crack the nut but only to gnaw on the
surface and the borders'. Partisan detachments, stiffened by some
regular troops, may venture to engage in larger operations and
attack garrisons, but they must never make a determined stand
because the enemy will rout them and their morale will suffer;
if the enemy has broken through they must disengage, disperse
like a nebulous vapory matter and stage a surprise attack elsewhere.

Clausewitz seems to agree that the partisans' field of operations
is the enemy rear. The movement should first be raised in places
on the flank of the war theatre which will not be occupied in
any great strength by the enemy, and then spread like a fire
behind him when he advances, catching his lines of communication and endangering his life thread.

Partisan operations, Clausewitz pointed out, can only succeed
if the theatre of operations is vast, the terrain favourable and the
people's character lends itself to this type of warfare. As a result
of their operations the enemy's morale will be weakened and his
forces will be tied down because he must dispatch many small
parties in order to safeguard his convoys and depots, the mountain passes and bridges.[1]

On the whole, Clausewitz has added little to the theory of
partisan warfare but the emphasis on the importance of morale
—the people's and the enemy's—in partisan warfare gives his
ideas a very modern ring.

Colonel Mosby, of American Civil War fame, was a partisan
leader who fully understood the purpose of his mission. He
operated in the rear and on the flank of the Federal Army aiming
at Richmond. He attacked with a small force, never sought battle
but constantly harassed, striking quickly at railways, wagon

[1] General Carl von Clausewitz, *Von Kriege*, Berlin 1832, Part II, vol. 6, Chapter
26, pp. 374 f.

trains and depots and dispersing his force at once afterwards. He often took on small parties of the enemy, and one of his best-remembered exploits is the kidnapping of General Stoughton. He obtained his Intelligence from the population and prisoners, and this enabled him to strike surprise blows and remain elusive himself. The Spanish guerrillas had managed by their operations to pin down twice their own numbers;[1] Colonel Mosby is generally credited with a much higher rate.

The role of the French francs-tireurs in the Franco-Prussian War was never clearly defined and this was certainly one of the reasons why French hopes in this force were not fulfilled. A few months after the outbreak of war the francs-tireurs were placed under orders of the commanders in the field, and a number of them were incorporated into the Army, while others kept their separate existence. It was not surprising, then, to find the former frequently performing front-line duties. On a number of occasions German units fought against a combined force of French hussars and francs-tireurs or Garde Nationale Mobile and francs-tireurs; the advancing German troops encountered them frequently; a force of 1,000 francs-tireurs encircled German troops at Châtillon sur Seine and another force took part in the defence of Châteaudun. But the francs-tireurs also carried out a fair number of raids against supply convoys and trains, blew up an important bridge over the Moselle and interrupted traffic for ten days; and they incessantly attacked the German rear during and after the attacks on Strasbourg and Pfalzburg fortress. When the Germans advanced on Paris the francs-tireurs became so active that they required the attention of a *Landwehr Division*. However, on the whole they were a nuisance but hardly ever more than that.[2]

If we restrict the survey to irregulars operating in conjunction with a regular army, we find that they had no clearly defined battlefield. The Russians and American Confederates struck in the rear and the Spanish and French often at the front, while in the First World War Lawrence's Arabian force was active on the flank. Where there was a sustained effort in the rear it was not made by regular forces but by partisans. When regular troops fought in the rear, they confined their activities to the

[1] Cf. Charles Oman, *op. cit.*, vol. iii, Oxford 1908, pp. 491-2.
[2] Cf. Michael Howard, *The Franco-Prussian War*, London 1961, pp. 249 f and throughout for an excellent account of francs-tireurs activities.

immediate rear. World War II brought two important developments with it: soldiers, enlisted in Special Forces, were dispatched to the far rear for prolonged action, and the guerrillas'
theatre of operations was no longer in the front line but only in
the rear. The entire rear was thus recognized as a theatre of war
for sustained operations by soldiers and civilians.

One might have thought that when the concept of total war
was born, the extension of the battlefield to every corner of the
enemy's rear was accepted as its logical concomitant, but this is
not so. Before World War II, total war was not as a rule thought
of as a war in which the civilian should or might have to take up
arms and in which the rear in occupied country would become
the scene of land warfare. Total war implied only that Armed
Forces and civilians alike would have to contribute their utmost
towards victory, the Armed Forces by fighting and the civilians
in every other sphere. 'Every able-bodied man is destined to be a
warrior, every man and woman able to work assists with hands
or brain in the purposes (sic) of war to which the entire life of the
nation is geared, not only politically or militarily, but also
economically, financially, in trade policy, propaganda, etc.' Only
in this limited sense was it accepted that 'the entire territory
becomes a war zone'.[1] Total war also meant, as General Ludendorff has pointed out in his book *Der totale Krieg*, that 'not only
the armies but also the peoples are subjected to direct war operations, although to a different degree, and they are also indirectly
affected by blockade and propaganda'.[2] Paradoxically enough, this
philosophy of war excluded one area from hostile land operations,
and that was the rear in occupied country—as long as the occupation army was not driven out by the opposing forces—because
the inhabitants of the area were not supposed to act against the
interests of the occupier and least of all take up arms against him.
Article 43 of the Hague Convention on Land Warfare provided,
in fact, that executive power is vested in the commanding general

---

[1] *Handbuch der neuzeitlichen Wehrwissenschaften*, ed. by General-Major Hermann Franke, vol. i, Berlin und Leipzig, 1936, pp. 173-4. Stalin and Mao
Tse-tung had a clearer conception of the meaning of total war. Cf. for Stalin
'Report of the Central Committee of the Communist Party of the Soviet Union'
(1934), in *Socialism Victorious*, London, n.d., p. 15, and for Mao 'Interview with
the British Correspondent James Bertram' (1937), in *Selected Works of Mao
Tse-tung*, vol. ii, London 1954, pp. 91-2.
[2] München 1940, p. 5. The book was written in 1937.

of the occupying army and he would, of course, forbid the population to engage in any such activities.

It was only to a small extent due to the concept of total war that rear warfare came into its own during World War II. The rear had by then become an even more profitable theatre of war since the armies now depended almost entirely on the rear for a sustained effort; also the extension of the lines of communication and the battlefield itself provided the forces in the rear with an abundance of targets. Aircraft developments made large-scale strategic bombing, parachute jumps, air lifts and supplies to the rear possible, contact could now be kept by wireless, and many rear operations became feasible which could not have been carried out in earlier wars. But it must not be overlooked that large guerrilla forces formed up before the new mechanics of warfare had been tested, and Special Forces moved first into action with little benefit from this new potential. To some extent the war in the rear was fought so extensively from 1940 on not because it had become more feasible but because it had become more necessary. The reasons, though, were different for the British and Germans.

In World War I both sides were so evenly matched that neither thought of employing on a large scale unconventional means by which, as Karl Marx once said, 'a weaker force can overcome its stronger and better-organized opponent' and 'a small nation can hope to maintain itself against an adversary superior in numbers and equipment'.[1] Before the Germans started their attack in the west in World War II, both sides in the contest again appeared more or less equally powerful, and this again is probably one of the reasons why nobody on the Allied side seems to have taken much interest in exploring, let alone introducing, unconventional warfare methods—apart from propaganda. There is a further reason. Unconventional warfare stands for initiative and aggressiveness. While it was therefore unsuited to the defensive state of mind which dominated the French Army, it was perfectly attuned to the Blitzkrieg mentality; what is more, the successful conduct of Blitzkrieg operations often depends on unconventional

[1] Karl Marx, in Neue Rheinische Zeitung, No. 161, of April 1, 1849. Quoted in F. O. Miksche, Secret Forces, The Technique of Underground Movements, London 1950, p. 25. Marx was speaking of mass uprisings, revolutionary methods and guerrilla warfare.

preparations, such as securing bridges or road crossings behind the enemy lines or weakening his will of resistance. Hence there was this time a certain readiness on the German side to employ unconventional warfare methods right from the start of the war, while the British and the Free French turned to them only after the fall of France.

Germany had other reasons for paying attention to unconventional warfare. Hitler, in his rise to power, had known the importance of agitation and insurrection, and the Civil War in Spain had made the value of a fifth column evident. Furthermore, during the Sudeten crisis of 1938, German elements in that area had been charged with carrying out espionage, sabotage and securing landing grounds behind the Czechoslovak fortifications in case of war, and the assistance which would thus have been given to the Wehrmacht was considered so useful that the idea for the creation of Special Forces for just such purposes was conceived.[1] In August 1939, some days before the start of the campaign against Poland, several hundred lightly-armed German civilian agents, dressed as miners and white collar workers, went into Poland a few hours before the invasion in order to occupy a number of important industrial undertakings; the agents prevented their destruction and the factories could immediately start working for the German war industry.[2] Also a few days before the outbreak of hostilities the first German raiding forces crossed the frontier into Poland, where they temporarily occupied the important Jablunka Pass on the southern invasion route— unaware, as it happened, that Hitler had postponed the invasion by six days[3]—and others later destroyed enemy communications in his rear and delayed his troop movements. It was the success of these actions which led in October 1939 to the formation of the first commando force, the 'Brandenburgers', followed later by the Special Task Battalion 100 and *Sturmbannführer* Skorzeny's SS Special Formation.[4]

[1] Cf. Paul Leverkuehn, *Der geheime Nachrichtendienst der deutschen Wehrmacht im Kriege*, Frankfurt am Main 1957. p. 23.
[2] *Ibid.*, p. 24.
[3] Cf. Major Herbert Kriegsheim, *Getarnt, Getäuscht und doch Getreu, Die geheimnisvollen 'Brandenburger'*, Berlin 1958, Part II, p. 294, contributed by an anonymous German senior officer.
[4] For Soviet Russian unconventional warfare against the Allies prior to the fall of France, cf. Otto Heilbrunn, *The Soviet Secret Services*, London, second edition 1957, New York 1956, pp. 56-74.

Great Britain engaged in the war in the rear because, after Germany's conquest of much of the European continent, it was in fact for a time the only war on land which Great Britain could fight there at all. 'When so much was uncertain, the need to recover the initiative glared forth,'[1] and it was almost inevitable that she at once organized guerrilla-type amphibious raiding forces for action against the German-held coast of Europe. On June 4, 1940, the Admiralty had announced that Operation Dynamo, the code name for the evacuation from Dunkirk, had been completed. On that very same day two people, both in close touch with Sir John Dill, the then Chief of the Imperial General Staff, but unbeknown to each other, were inspired to put their thoughts on the formation of amphibious guerrilla forces to paper: the one was the Prime Minister, the other Colonel Dudley Clarke, Military Assistant to the CIGS.[2] The CIGS acted at once, and less than three weeks later No. 11 Commando went into action on the French coast.

Already before the fall of France, the British Prime Minister had envisaged that she should maintain a gigantic guerrilla force. When Italy entered the war the British organized an Ethiopian partisan force. In Europe, Britain was at first more interested in establishing a network of Intelligence agents than guerrilla movements but she soon took the lead in organizing, supplying and guiding them.[3]

Paratroops, another almost essential element of the *Blitzkrieg*, were first employed with spectacular success by the Germans, and the various strategic air forces set out to inflict maximum damage on the enemy's operational base itself while tactical air forces frequently supplied formations in the rear with arms and equipment. The Navy played its part in transporting Special Forces to and from their target areas and giving them artillery support, and in Britain it also provided the Royal Marine Commandos.

The rear had thus become the scene of orthodox land, air and sea warfare and of unconventional warfare as well, the latter

[1] Sir Winston Churchill, *The Second World War*, London 1949, vol. ii, p. 213.
[2] Minute of the Prime Minister, Sir Winston Churchill, dated April 4, 1940, in his *The Second World War*, op. cit., p. 214; Brigadier Dudley Clarke, *Seven Assignments*, London 1948, pp. 205 f; and Hilary St George Saunders, *The Green Beret*, London 1949, p. 21.
[3] Cf. for this and the factors promoting resistance, Otto Heilbrunn, *Partisan Warfare*, London 1962, New York 1962, etc., pp. 171 seq.

waged by soldiers of the Special Forces and civilians in partisan movements and the Resistance. But it was perhaps inevitable that this sudden outburst of activity in the enemy rear should have caught the military planners by surprise. German preparations for anti-partisan warfare were entirely insufficient and unrealistic, especially in Soviet Russia.[1] On the Allied side the new concept of the war in the rear was not based on a preconceived plan and there was no grand strategy for its conduct. Some of the forces emerged sporadically as was often the case with guerrilla movements and Special Forces. At times Special Forces were employed in the rear only if they could be spared from the front, and the rear area selected for operations was not always the most suitable one. Sometimes various forces operated in the same area and did not know of each other's existence, and the activities of the agencies which were employed in the same rear theatre frequently overlapped. While there is usually a clearly-established chain of command for the front-line troops and their own rear services, there was often little of it in respect of the units engaged in the enemy's rear. If the experiment is worth repeating under the conditions of a future war, structural and organizational improvements are obviously called for.

No clear pattern evolved for the conduct of the war in the rear. The rear was not divided up into a combat zone in the near rear and a harassing zone in the far rear: Tito's partisans fought large-scale engagements in the far rear, while those in equally far-away Greece restricted themselves to harassing. Nor was combat an exclusive task for soldiers and harassing reserved for partisans. Airborne troops were, of course, mostly employed as combat formations but the Russians also used them as partisan reinforcements for harassing activities, and the Second Chindit Expedition had both a harassing and a combat assignment. Special Forces had had mostly harassing tasks but the Commandos, Rangers and Marauders were often or always used as combat forces. And so, as we already said, were the partisans under Tito.

It is, of course, evident that where numerically strong forces are active in the enemy's rear, he will have to attack them and large-scale fighting will ensue—unless their field of activity is so badly selected that their presence will not disturb the enemy or

[1] Cf. C. A. Dixon and O. Heilbrunn, *Communist Guerrilla Warfare*, London, third edition 1961, New York fourth edition 1962, pp. 99 f.

will do so very little. But in suitable areas such forces will tie down large numbers of the enemy. On the other hand, small forces in the rear, if skilfully deployed, can—or could formerly —achieve similar results: Colonel Mosby hardly ever took more than a few hundred men on his raids and yet neutralized 50,000 of the enemy. The maintenance of large forces in the rear creates a manpower and supply problem which does not exist with small parties.

This is another of the yet unsolved problems, the optimum size of units in the rear, measured in terms of capability and cost. Should the far rear be exclusively a harassing zone and combat be restricted to the near rear? Should the missions be assigned differently as between soldiers and partisans and, as far as soldiers are concerned, as between the conventional and unconventional forces? Are the forces of the rear meant to operate on the axis of advance, the lines of communication, or wherever the terrain is favourable? Can the forces of the rear in certain circumstances replace the formations which hitherto broke through the enemy front or moved round the flank into the rear? How can they assist them? What can we learn from the performance of the rear forces of other nations? What structure is required for the efficient direction of the fight in the rear? Should control be unified and, if so, under a rear forces commander, the theatre commander, or an even higher authority? These are some of the questions which we try to answer in this book.

An inquiry of this nature presupposes that there is still scope in a future conflict for war in the enemy rear. It seems that there is, even under nuclear conditions.

World War II has made the importance of the rear war evident; it has shown what Special Forces and guerrillas, the air force, paratroops and air landing troops can do. On the whole their usefulness in a future war should not therefore be in doubt. Political allegiance to a possible future enemy might deprive the West of some partisan support which it enjoyed in the last war, but other partisan formations might then willingly take over instead.

In anti-guerrilla operations and in a Korea-type war the conflict can therefore be carried to the rear. The same applies to a war in which nuclear weapons might be or have been used. Partisans may be available only if the attacker will move out of his own country and occupy part of his opponent's territory. As for the other forces of the rear, they can go where the enemy can go, and the combat forces of the rear can fight him in the same way as hitherto. As far as the harassing forces of the rear are concerned, they will find even more targets; since the enemy troops will be more widely dispersed, their installations must also be more widely dispersed and there will be more of them. The forces in the rear will be comparatively safe from nuclear attack since the enemy is unlikely to endanger his own hinterland by exploding nuclear weapons there.

Air defences have, of course, been greatly improved since the end of the war and the air contribution to the war in the rear may be curbed but not eliminated in the near future.

It therefore appears that the war in the rear, as it developed in World War II, was not a unique phenomenon but is likely to become a permanent feature of modern war.

I. UNCONVENTIONAL FORCES AND THEIR TASKS

CHAPTER 2

THE GENESIS OF SPECIAL FORCES

The British Commandos, as we have seen, owed their formation
to Sir Winston Churchill and Colonel Dudley Clarke.

Colonel Clarke had been a Staff Officer in Palestine in 1936
and he had seen how a handful of rebels could harass a British
regular force of two divisions. He therefore conceived the Commandos as uniformed guerrillas on amphibious raiding operations
in occupied Europe.

Sir Winston Churchill drew on a different experience. He also
considered that these 'Striking Companies', as he originally
called them, should be raiding forces which would help to turn
'the passive resistance war' into 'a vigorous, enterprising and
ceaseless offensive'.[1] But he had an additional task in mind for
them. He had always been greatly impressed by the performance
of German 'Storm Troops' in 1918 and then by their successors
in France in 1940, 'an incredibly small number of highly
equipped élite, while the dull mass of the German Army came
on behind, made good the conquest and occupied it'.[2] Commandos
overseas should also fulfil the tasks of the Storm Troops.[2]

In the defence of the United Kingdom, threatened with invasion, the Commandos were supposed to serve in yet another
capacity: they were to act as highly mobile reserve and pounce
in 'leopard' fashion on any enemy lodgments on the British coast.[3]
But they were not supposed to fight as partisans behind the
enemy lines. This task was assigned to the so-called Auxiliary
Units, Britain's own guerrilla force. The idea for its formation
came from General Andrew Thorne. The units were made up of
officers, selected Home Guard personnel and civilians, men and
women, and they were trained in the use of high explosives. They
were to go into action if the enemy should succeed in breaking

[1] *The Second World War, op. cit.*, p. 217.
[2] *Ibidem*, p. 413.
[3] *Ibidem*, pp. 251-2, and Index Reference 'Commando' p. 661.

C 33

out from the coast, and they had to harass his advancing columns and sabotage his water, food and petrol supply routes.[1] By 1942 a very considerable organization numbering many thousands had been built up, and we have it on General Denning's authority that 'the ingenuity used in planning such action was of a high order, perhaps higher than that ... used by the Russians'.[2]

The Commando idea was soon taken up by the Dominions. In Australia, late in 1940, Independent Companies were trained on Commando lines by British officers. Even before the outbreak of hostilities with Japan the Independent Companies were scattered round important Australian outposts; these units were to stay behind after a Japanese invasion and carry on guerrilla warfare.[3] New Zealand, too, formed Independent Companies, while Canada and the United States jointly activated the Special Service Force early in 1942. This force first received parachute training for operations in Norway and when these were cancelled, it was transformed into an amphibious unit. It fought, in a Commando role, in August 1944 on the islands near Toulon.[4]

Finally, the Rangers were America's Commandos. Their formation in June 1942 was also inspired by the British example, they were first trained by British Commandos, they continued their training with them and, like the Commandos, they were raiders.

The Commandos and Rangers were, of course, not the only British and American Special Forces. There was, on the British side, Phantom, the first of the private armies, which collected and transmitted information in most theatres of war. Soon afterwards the Long Range Desert Group was formed; it contained a New Zealand squadron. The LRDG owed its inception to Brigadier (then Major) Ralph Bagnold, who had in pre-war days acquired

---

[1] Cf. Colonel Peter Fleming, *Invasion 1940. An Account of the German Preparations and the British Counter-Measures.* London 1957, pp. 269-71; and Basil Collier, *The Defence of the United Kingdom. History of the Second World War.* London 1957.

[2] C. A. Dixon and O. Heilbrunn, *Communist Guerrilla Warfare,* London, third ed. 1961, New York, fourth ed. 1962, p. vi, Paris 1956, p. viii, Frankfurt am Main 1956, p. vi.

[3] Cf. Dudley McCarthy, *Australia in the War of 1939-1945,* Series One, vol. v, 'South-West Pacific Area—First Year'. Canberra 1959, pp. 84 f.

[4] Colonel C. P. Stracey, *The Canadian Army, 1939-1945, An Official Historical Summary.* Ottawa 1948, pp. 296 f.; Robert D. Burhans, *The First Special Service Force,* Washington 1947.

an unrivalled knowledge of the Libyan desert and its transport problems. When Italy came into the war, the Major immediately received permission to form the first patrols which, from the summer of 1940, carried out raids deep behind the enemy lines and brought back valuable information.[1]

In the following year SAS, the Special Air Service, was formed in the same theatre. Early in 1941 the British Commandos in North Africa, known as Layforce, had been disbanded; they had been designed to approach their target from the sea and the Navy could no longer spare the ships to transport the men; they were also needed to strengthen the front line, especially against Rommel. Colonel (then Lieutenant) David Stirling, a member of the disbanded Layforce, became convinced that a much smaller number of men, dropped by parachute, could profitably carry out sabotage tasks behind the enemy lines, and SAS was born.[2] The Special Boat Service—SBS—soon followed. Out of units of the LRDG, SBS, the Holding Unit Special Forces, the Greek Sacred Squadron and Kalpaks, still another special detachment, Raiding Forces, was formed in 1943 for raids on German-held islands in the Dodecanese, Aegean and elsewhere.[3] And, also, there were Popski's Private Army, for obtaining intelligence and raiding in the enemy's rear, and F Squadron, a small force of Italians who fought after the armistice with the Allies and reconnoitred and ambushed small German parties behind the lines.[4]

Another British officer, Major-General (then Captain) Wingate, had, like Colonel Clarke, served in Palestine, and he too applied the lessons learned there to World War II. He had in 1938 initiated, organized and led the Special Night Squads, recruited from the Jewish supernumerary police with a stiffening of British officers and men, in order to stop Arab raiders. In 1940 he thought of organizing auxiliary units,[5] but whereas those originated by General Thorne were to go into action behind the

[1] Cf. Michael Crichton-Stuart, G-Patrol, London 1958, pp. 7-9 of the Introduction by Brigadier Sir Bernard Fergusson.
[2] Cf. Virginia Cowles, The Phantom Major, The Story of David Stirling and the SAS Regiment. London 1958.
[3] Cf. Raiding Forces, The Story of an Independent Command in the Aegean 1943-1945. Compiled from Official Sources and Reports by Observer Officers of No. 1 Public Relation Service, MEF. Edited by Captain G. W. Read; and W. E. Benyon-Tinker, Dust Upon the Sea, London 1947.
[4] Cf. Carlo Bonciani, 'F' Squadron, London 1947.
[5] Cf. Christopher Sykes, Orde Wingate, London 1959, pp. 227 f.

German lines, Wingate's special units were to fight behind the British lines against enemy penetration—by tanks, parachutists or airborne troops—and against German Fifth Column agents. In 1941 he led the Gideon Force, with partisan support, to victory over the Italians in Ethiopia. In 1942, now a colonel, he took command of all guerrilla operations in Burma. In 1943 he led 77 Brigade in the First Chindit Expedition deep behind the Japanese front in Burma. The success of this Long Range Penetration Group inspired the Americans to form in the same year a similar force, known as Merrill's Marauders, who operated in north Burma and spearheaded General Stilwell's advance. The Second Chindit Expedition by 3rd Indian Division got under way in February 1944; in March, General Wingate was killed in an air accident and no further Chindit expedition was mounted.

Also in the Far East, the Small Operational Group was formed in 1944, for tasks similar to those of the LRDG, particularly reconnaissance.

Of the other Allies, the Free French had their own Commando groups from North Africa which took part in the capture of the island of Elba and the landing on the coast of Provence. French soldiers also formed a unit of the British No. 10 (Inter-Allied) Commando, as did Belgians, Dutchmen, Norwegians, Danes, Germans, Austrians, Hungarians and Czechs. Frenchmen and Belgians also served with SAS; there were at first two French Parachute Battalions and later Régiments de Chasseurs Parachutistes with SAS, and there was also a Belgian Parachute Company and subsequently a Belgian SAS Regiment.

Soviet Russia had less need for Special Forces than her Allies. Her war was fought on land, and although she mounted amphibious operations they had nothing like the significance for her which similar operations had for Britain and America.[1] As a rule the Soviets relied on their guerrillas for executing the tasks of Special Forces behind the enemy lines. For assignments beyond partisan capabilities, such as certain interdiction and intelligence missions, the Soviets sent NKGB (secret police) and Red Army

[1] For amphibious landings by Soviet Marine Infantry in the German rear, mostly on undefended or weakly defended coast, cf. Jürg Meister, 'Die sowjetrussischen amphibischen Operationen 1939-45', in *Marine Rundschau*, Heft 4, 1955, pp. 124 f.

men.[1] For sabotage work in areas where there were no partisans, the Soviets sometimes dropped small parties of paratroops; on one occasion, in the Smolensk area in July 1941, they moved an entire paratroop brigade on foot through the German lines to the rear, where it carried out partisan operations.[2]

On the whole the partisans were well qualified to carry out their missions.[3] Even amphibious operations could be executed with partisan support if the objective was on Russian soil. When approximately 700 Red Army soldiers landed at Eupatoria in the Crimea in January 1942, about an equal number of local partisans joined in the attack. For land operations, partisans were usually available for what would otherwise have been a Special Forces' task because, particularly from 1943 on, Soviet strategy was directed towards forming continuous, solid partisan areas,[4] which were selected in accordance with military needs. Sometimes partisans were reinforced by Red Army paratroops if stiffening was required.[5]

Even after the Red Army had liberated Soviet Russia and advanced westward, it could still draw to some extent on partisan support: there were the communist partisans in Poland; Czechoslovakia was supplied by Soviet Russia with officers with guerrilla experience and about 400 partisans; there was an underground movement in Bulgaria, and in Yugoslavia close co-operation with Tito and his forces had been established long before the Red Army approached her border.

The Japanese Army employed Flying Columns in China. Composed of infantry, cavalry and sometimes tank forces, they attacked enemy lines of communication and laid ambushes deep behind the front. They also occupied key positions ahead of their advancing main force.

These columns proved so valuable that the Japanese proceeded to form Raiding Units of a similar character for the war in the Pacific. These raiders not only disrupted lines of communica-

[1] Cf. Raymond L. Garthoff, *Soviet Military Doctrine*, Glencoe, Illinois 1953, p. 401.
[2] Cf. General-Leutnant Walter Schwabedissen, *The Russian Airforce in the Eyes of German Commanders*, USAF Historical Division, Study No. 175, Research Studies Institute, Air University, Alabama, June 1960, p. 156.
[3] Cf. Dixon/Heilbrunn, *Communist Guerrilla Warfare*, op. cit., throughout.
[4] Cf. Major Edgar M. Howell, *The Soviet Partisan Movement 1941-44*, Department of the Army Pamphlet, Washington 1956, p. 179.
[5] On Soviet airborne Commandos formed after the war, cf. below Chapter 3.

tion, but they also acted as assault troops and attacked fortified positions, tank concentrations and other special objectives. However, it appears that these forces were not established on a permanent basis, and their members often returned to their original units after completion of their special tasks.[1]

In Manchuria the Japanese formed guerrilla units of indigenous veterans under Japanese command. These were attached to the various armies and they were to conduct partisan warfare if Soviet Russia attacked and overran the Japanese positions in their area.[2]

In the last war, Special Forces sometimes co-operated in the field with partisan units. In the Far East, P-Force raised Karen Levies in Burma, Kachins of Dagforce worked with the Chindits, Commandos were assisted by V-Force, and Merrill's Marauders were supported by Kachin guerrillas. In Europe, Special Forces usually linked themselves with the partisans if they fought in partisan territory, as they did on the Dalmatian islands, in Albania, in France and in Italy, although the link in France was rather loose.[3]

The Brandenburg Division was the only Special Force in World War II which also fought against partisans, and Brandenburg units were so employed in Soviet Russia and Yugoslavia. The Brandenburgers were also engaged in political warfare. The Indian Legion under Subhas Chandra Bose, attached to Brandenburg, was supposed to land by parachute on the Khyber Pass and incite the mountain tribes to revolt, but the undertaking never got past the planning stage. Attempts to provoke a popular rising in Afghanistan were equally condemned to failure, and a plan for the invasion of Iraq was also abandoned.[4] Only Operation Shamyl, a parachute landing by Brandenburgers and Caucasians in the Caucasus, was carried out, but while they succeeded

[1] Cf. War Department, Technical Manual, Handbook on Japanese Military Forces, Washington, October 1, 1944, p. 81.
[2] Cf. Japanese Preparations for Operations in Manchuria, January 1943-August 1945. Prepared by Military History Section, HQ Army Forces Far East, 1953, p. 62.
[3] Instances of co-operation of the Army—as distinct from Special Forces in the field—with partisans during World War II are numerous. Cf. Otto Heilbrunn, Partisan Warfare, London 1962, New York 1962, Paris 1963, and Frankfurt am Main 1963, Chapter 7.
[4] Cf. Major Herbert Kriegsheim, op. cit., Part II, pp. 301 f, and Paul Leverkuehn, op. cit., p. 177.

in gaining some local partisan support and drawing the attention of large Soviet forces upon themselves, they failed to organize the popular revolt against the Soviets which was the principal objective of their mission.[1]

There was one air commando in the last war, Colonels Coch-ran's and Alison's No. 1 Air Commando, which closely co-operated with the Second Chindit Expedition. It consisted of fighters, light bombers for close support, transport aircraft, gliders, and light planes for the evacuation of wounded. It was the invaluable air wing of the Chindits and we shall later refer to it as the component of a Special Force rather than as a Commando of its own.

In addition to the amphibious forces already mentioned, a number of special formations operated from and in the sea. The Italians were the first to employ Special Underwater Raiding Forces which attached limpet mines to enemy shipping and did considerable damage to British battleships in Alexandria harbour. The Royal Marines' Boom Patrol, the British Special Boat Section —a unit within the Commandos—and the Special Boat Service— temporarily an SAS unit until it regained its independence— subsequently performed similar tasks and damaged the *Tirpitz*. The Special Boat Service did also much sabotage work in the desert and southern Europe. The Japanese used Special Boat Units, small amphibious commando teams, and suicide swimmers who interfered with Allied landing craft. Very late in the war the Germans organized their K-Men, viz. frogmen and midget-submarine crews, whose objectives were the ships of the invasion fleet, bridges and harbours; they also engaged in pirate warfare in the Adriatic and in operations against the Russians in the Oder river.[2]

The British Small Scale Raiding Force was another Commando unit which carried out sabotage raids against coastal positions. The British also had the Combined Operations Pilotage Parties for beach reconnaissance and the Underwater Swimming Unit for demolition work. The Americans formed the Underwater Demolition Team. They also activated Amphibious Scouts, who

[1] Cf. Major Kriegsheim, *op. cit.*, pp. 90 f, and P. Leverkuehn, *op. cit.*, p. 137.
[2] Cf. C. D. Bekker, *K-Men, The Story of the German Frogmen and Midget Submarines.* London 1955. For another German formation, the Coastal Hunter Company, cf. Chapter 3 below.

were employed in all major Allied landings in the Mediterranean for obtaining information on beach obstacles, beach conditions and the nature of the terrain inland, and the Alaska Scouts, who collected similar technical data in the South Pacific in advance of the landings. The Soviets formed their Assault and Underwater Swimmer Detachments only after the war.[1]

In the post-war period the SAS Regiment went into action in Malaya and Oman, and the New Zealand Squadron of the SAS in Malaya. US Rangers and British Commandos fought in Korea and French Commandos in Indo-China. British Commandos also fought as an anti-guerrilla force in Malaya and Cyprus, and British and French Commandos were in action at Port Said.

Also in the post-war period the Americans have formed a new Special Force for guerrilla and anti-guerrilla roles. This Special Force consists of detachments of usually two officers and ten men each with the mission to form, organize, train and direct a guerrilla unit of up to 1,500 men in wartime. This new establishment thus takes care of the tasks which were tackled in World War II by way of brilliant but sporadic experiments: by American officers in the Philippines and by the US Office of Strategic Services in Europe and Burma; by the Australian Z Special Force in Timor, and by the British in 101 Special Training School, operating on an island off Singapore; by Force 136, first based in Singapore, P-Force in Burma, the Bush Warfare School, also in Burma, and 204 Mission in Chungking (China); by V-Force, defending India's eastern frontier, the Operational Centres in Khartoum, and Special Operations Executive and SAS elsewhere. Different from its predecessors, the new American Special Force has also a peace-time, or rather cold-war, function: it will assist friendly governments, on their request, in anti-rebel operations.[2] In this book we are subsequently concerned only with the Special Force missions in an international war.

No uniform terminology for all these operations—political warfare, partisan warfare, and Special Forces operations—has so far been adopted and the present classifications and usages of some terms do not always commend themselves. All these opera-

[1] Cf. Jürg Meister, loc. cit., p. 136.
[2] Cf. Brigadier-General William P. Yarborough, 'Special Warriors in the US Army', The Airman, November 1961, pp. 42 and 43, and Special Warfare US Army, prepared by Office, Chief of Information, Department of the Army, Washington DC, 1962, throughout.

tions have in common that they are unorthodox or unconventional; some of the operations are non-military, others have a military character. It appears, therefore, convenient to classify all operations as either military or non-military, under the common heading 'Unconventional Warfare', as shown on the following chart.[1] Only the larger Special Forces are listed there.

[1] In the US Army terminology for operations in a cold war, 'Special Warfare' is used as a term to embrace all the military and paramilitary measures and activities related to unconventional warfare, counter-insurgency and psychological warfare. Unconventional Warfare comprises Guerrilla Warfare, Evasion and Escape, and Resistance, while Counter-Insurgency includes Counter-Guerrilla Operations and Civic Action. Cf. *Special Warfare US Army*, op. cit., pp. 8 and 9.

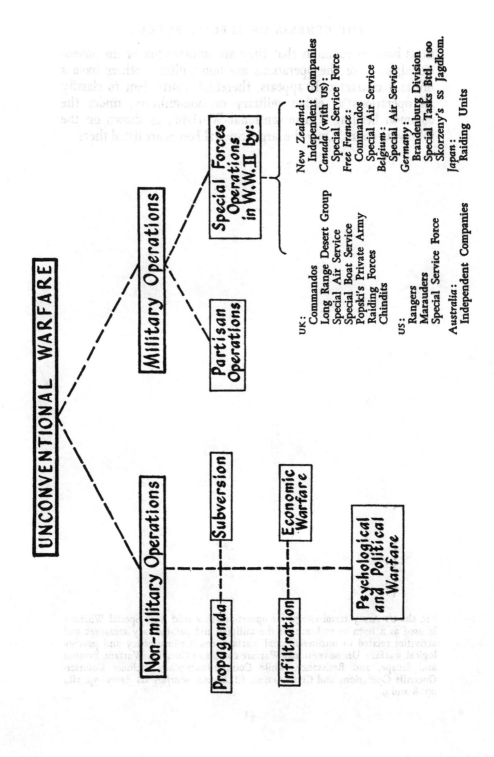

CHAPTER 3

THE SPECIAL TASKS IN THE WAR IN EUROPE, AFRICA AND THE PACIFIC

The appearance of Special Forces in World War II was not everywhere welcome. In Britain, the opposition felt that regular troops could do the special jobs just as well, and it resented the enlistment of some of the best regimental officers and men for special duties. There were other grounds for antagonism: some feared for the prestige of the regular troops if only Special Forces were considered good enough for the execution of certain, sometimes spectacular, tasks, some envied their reputation, and others disliked their leaders, whom they regarded as prima donnas and suspected of being treated as such in high quarters. The Royal Marines had another grievance against the Commandos; they considered that the Army Commandos were usurping a task for which they, the Royal Marines, had been created and which they had always performed in the past.

Three of Britain's most famous field marshals have voiced serious doubts about the usefulness of Special Forces. Viscount Alanbrooke, Sir John Dill's successor as Chief of the Imperial General Staff, writes in his *Notes on My Life* that he 'remained convinced till the end of the war that the Commandos should never have been divorced from the Army in the way they were. Each division should have been responsible for maintaining a divisional battle patrol capable of any Commando work that might be asked of it.'[1] Viscount Slim, of Burma fame, fully shares these views: 'Any well-trained infantry battalion,' he states, 'should be able to do what a Commando can do; in the Fourteenth Army they could and did.'[2] Field Marshal Earl Wavell has voiced similar thoughts.[3]

---

[1] Quoted in Sir Arthur Bryant, *The Turn of the Tide, Based on the War Diaries of Field Marshal Viscount Alanbrooke*, London 1957, p. 255 ftn. 2, on p. 256.
[2] Field Marshal Sir William Slim, *Defeat Into Victory*, London 1956, p. 547.
[3] 'The Soldier as Citizen', *Sunday Times*, August 26, 1945.

It is apparent, though, that the CIGS was not opposed to all the Special Forces. In August 1943 he met the then Colonel Wingate, just back from his First Chindit Expedition, and the colonel requested for his Second Expedition 'the cream of everything, the best men, the best NCOs, the best officers, the best equipment and a large air-lift'. In his record of this meeting, the CIGS goes on: 'I considered that the results of his form of attacks were certainly worth backing within reason,'[1] and back them he did even before Sir Winston Churchill and President Roosevelt gave their wholehearted approval to Wingate's plans at the Quebec Conference.

On the other hand Lord Slim, under whose command and in whose area the Second Chindit Expedition operated, has reservations about this Special Force too. He considers the First Expedition an expensive military failure, though justifiable on psychological grounds[2]—it greatly helped to raise Army morale. He is also critical of the Second Expedition. The Chindit force assembled for this purpose consisted of six brigades, viz. 3 West African Brigade, 77 and 111 Indian Brigade, and three brigades which had formed 70 British Division. 'I was convinced,' he says, 'that a battle-tried, experienced, well-knit British division, like the 70th, would have more effect against the Japanese than a special force of twice its size.'[3]

But Field Marshal Slim's objections to unconventional forces went even further than that. We have already mentioned a number of such forces operating in the Burma theatre. Some of them were under headquarters of their own. 'Such was the secrecy and mutual suspicion in which they operated,' the Field Marshal states, 'that they sometimes acted in close proximity to our troops without the knowledge of any commander in the field, with a complete lack of co-ordination among themselves, and in dangerous ignorance of local tactical developments.'[4] He drew the lesson and it ought not to be forgotten: he instituted a system of co-ordination and sometimes control under a Staff officer of the commander of the area, and as a result 'confusion, ineffectiveness and lost opportunities were avoided'. And he

[1] Sir Arthur Bryant, op. cit., p. 691.
[2] Field Marshal Sir William Slim, op. cit., p. 162.
[3] Ibidem, p. 216.
[4] Ibidem, pp. 548-9.

insists that Special Forces should undertake only such tasks as are beyond the normal scope of warfare in the field.

The Brandenburg Division was received with even less enthusiasm by the German military. It was originally a company and expanded by stages into a battalion, a regiment and then a division. It was formed by Admiral Canaris, the chief of the German Counter-Intelligence; it was at the disposal of Counter-Intelligence but its units were also under the operational control of the army groups and armies in whose areas they operated. This double subordination proved fatal for Brandenburg, because it gave the commanders in the field the decisive say over its employment and many of them were sceptical about, or disdainful of, isolated operations in enemy uniform, sometimes far from the battlefield. The Brandenburgers were not helped either by the rather curious designation of their unit; before it was raised to a division it was called 'Training Company (Battalion, Regiment) for Special Tasks 800', and this led to frequent confusion with the 'Penal Battalion 500' and the 'Penal Battalion 900'. As the war progressed, more and more Brandenburg units were used as ordinary infantry formations until in the autumn of 1944 the Division ceased to exist as a Special Force.[1]

Are there, then, tasks which can or should only be executed by Special Forces? The last war saw so many Special Forces on such varied missions in so many theatres of operation that a review of these activities should supply the answer.

Commandos and Rangers

The first British Commandos were provided by the Army. Since they carried out amphibious raids, the choice may seem surprising; we have already mentioned that the Royal Marines had always had the function to provide detachments for amphibious operations. That the Royal Marines were not much in evidence as a raiding force in 1940 and 1941 was due to two reasons. In the first place, as long as Britain was threatened with invasion, the Royal Marines, who had not been disorganized in the débâcle in France, were indispensable for Britain's defence and therefore not available for other duties.[2] Secondly, the Royal Marines carry

---

[1] Only one regiment remained in existence as a Special Force, viz. Regiment Kurfürst.

[2] Cf. Hilary St George Saunders, op cit., p. 149.

out sea and land duties. The sea duties of the Royal Marines serving afloat take precedence over military training, and it was therefore difficult to maintain the highest standard of military efficiency required to fight a well-trained enemy in a heavily fortified area.[1] The gap was filled by the Army Commandos. When later on the Royal Marines became available, they too were employed in amphibious actions. But this task was not assigned to their infantry division, but to specially formed, trained and equipped Royal Marine Commandos. They amalgamated with the Army Commandos to form the Special Service Group. Royal Marine and Army Commandos kept their separate identities but fought together in the same brigades—there were two Royal Marine and two Army Commandos in each of the four Special Service Brigades—in identical tasks under a combined Army and Royal Marine Headquarters.

In one respect the Americans were confronted with a similar problem: their Marine Raider battalions could and did take care of Royal Marine Commando tasks, even though a Marine battalion is the nucleus of a landing team while a Royal Marine Commando carries out independent duties. But the Marine Corps was largely tied up in the Pacific and with the invasion of Europe still far off, amphibious raids by Rangers seemed in 1942 an effective way of making America's presence in the war against Germany and Italy felt. While the British Army Commandos and Royal Marine Commandos were at the earliest possible moment amalgamated, the Rangers and the Marine Corps remained under different commands.

The tasks carried out by Commandos and Rangers were manifold. There were, in the first place, the many amphibious operations, executed by Rangers in Algeria and Morocco, Sicily, Salerno, Anzio, Normandy, New Guinea, Leyte and Luzon, and by Commandos against the Lofoten Islands, Spitzbergen, Vaagso, Maaloy, Bruneval, St Nazaire, Crete, the Libyan coast, the Channel Islands, Diego Suarez, Arakan, Rangoon, Myebon, Singapore, Dieppe, Sicily, Salerno, Normandy and Walcheren. There were also innumerable missions on land, such as crossing a river as the leading assault unit, clearing out strongpoints, attacking fortified positions, neutralizing enemy coast defences,

[1] Cf. General Sir Dallas Brooks, lecture on 'The Royal Marines', reprinted in *Royal United Service Institution Journal* 1948, vol. 93, p. 260.

seizing a pass by a coup de main, and infiltrating into the enemy's rear. But many ordinary infantry tasks were also assigned to Commandos and Rangers, such as relieving infantry in the line, preparing defences, occupying ground, patrolling, straightening the front line, searching a village, clearing a forest, securing the flanks, guarding headquarters, acting as mobile reserves or reinforcing divisions for a frontal attack. On occasions they also took over parachutists' tasks. Sometimes Commandos and Rangers provided a stiffening. When the Army was hard pressed they were often used to fill the gaps. For example, when 1 Special Service Brigade was briefed for Operation Overlord, it was given to understand that it would be withdrawn from the beachhead after seven days and then carry out further operations along the coast,[1] and equally, when after seven days in France one of the Commandos of 4 Special Service Brigade made appeals to England for supplies and reinforcements, it was informed that its return to the United Kingdom was imminent.[2] In the event, pressure of manpower always proved too great and both brigades stayed on, except for a four months' spell of 1 Brigade in England.

It is this plethora of tasks with which Commandos and Rangers were saddled that makes it difficult to discern their proper missions. That the Commandos' role in amphibious operations apparently underwent several changes during the war, adds to the complications.

In their first amphibious missions the Commandos were the beach assault and raiding and demolition parties. But while they continued to carry out all these functions right to the end of the war, they soon were no longer the only, or the leading, assault units to go ashore. In the Dieppe raid, in August 1942, the main assault was made by Canadian battalions while the Commandos assaulted only on the flanks. At Normandy the beach defences on 1 Corps front were to be mopped up by its own infantry units while Nos 41 and 48 Royal Marine Commandos were expected to land behind them unopposed.

The Commandos and Rangers were still given the most diffi-

[1] Cf. *The Story of 45 Royal Marine Commando*, written by the officers and published privately, 1946, p. 33.
[2] *48 Royal Marine Commando. The Story 1944-46*, published privately, 1946, p. 27.

cult tasks: it was believed by the planners of Overlord that the American landings could not succeed unless a German battery on the steep cliff of Point de Hoc could be silenced,[1] and the Rangers were entrusted with the mission to capture it. When the Scheldt Estuary had to be cleared, Walcheren presented the most hazardous task in view of its strong defences, and the Commandos were selected for this job. But the capture of Bresken island was a hard task too; it also involved an amphibious landing, and it was successfully carried out by a Canadian brigade. Again, the assault on the defended coast of Madagascar, in May 1942, was mounted by a Royal Marine detachment, three infantry brigades, and one Commando whose tasks were not much different from those of the other units.

One could possibly draw up an impressive list of coastal operations in which Commandos and Rangers did not take a leading part. Such incidents in particular led to the widespread belief that Commandos had no special function to perform.

It is obvious that Commandos and Rangers were first designed for amphibious operations and, when the Allied Armies landed in enemy occupied territory, they also had to carry out special—as well as ordinary—land warfare duties. It is also obvious that they were not an invasion army, nor was it their task to conquer islands.

When the Commandos went on their first exploits, Sir Winston Churchill described them as 'nimble forces'[2] and this implied three things: the Commandos would rely on surprise, they would be lightly equipped and, as a result, once they had landed their radius of operation would be limited. They were to strike a lightning blow and then quickly retreat. They were not a Long Range Penetration Force.[3] Nor did they become one when they subsequently fought together with the Army on land.

Two characteristics, then, marked Commando and Ranger operations throughout the war: their task was to carry out a *coup de main*, and their field of operation was close to the enemy front line. They were therefore never acting as guerrillas who as a rule operate deep in the enemy's rear, are stationed there

[1] Cf. Samuel Eliot Morison, *The Invasion of France and Germany 1944-45, History of US Naval Operations in World War II,* vol. xi, London 1957, pp. 125 f.

[2] *Op. cit.,* p. 413.

[3] The 1,200-miles raid towards Tobruk in September 1942 was a rare exception.

more or less permanently, and frequently require a base or at least a camp from which they carry out their sallies against the enemy. This holds even true for the Commandos on the Dalmatian Islands who co-operated there with Tito's partisans; these Commandos and partisans were not stationed behind the enemy front.

Two questions must therefore be answered, viz: (1) what sort of *coups de main* did Commandos and Rangers carry out, and (2) can these tasks be equally well performed by divisional units?

(1) We must differentiate at the outset between amphibious assaults (coastal warfare) and land warfare operations. The amphibious assaults were staged, as we have seen, in order to strike a surprise blow followed by immediate withdrawal, while the land warfare operations, often also launched from the sea, had normally as their aim to gain and hold an objective until the arrival of regular troops. The purpose of the first type of operations is to smash, grab and run, and of the second to assist in gaining ground from the enemy.[1]

Amphibious raids may be undertaken in order to:

— raise morale at home or in enemy-occupied countries—this was the aim of the first operations in World War II—and promote resistance against the occupying enemy;

— undermine enemy morale by making him jumpy. Most raids have this side effect; some were particularly designed for this purpose, such as the Channel Island raid on Sark where unsuspecting German soldiers suddenly found themselves taken prisoner;

— carry out reconnaissance. Many small raids throughout the last war were made in order to obtain general and technical intelligence; before D-Day underwater obstacles on the French coast were examined;

— destroy military, naval or war-economic targets. Often German and Italian coastal batteries were attacked; at St Nazaire the only dry dock on the Atlantic coast suitable for the *Tirpitz* was put out of action, and at Vaagso oil factories and at Glomfjord, also in Norway, a plant for the production of aluminium were demolished;

— gain invasion experience. This was the purpose of the

[1] Airborne Commando operations can be of either type.

D

Dieppe raid. Commandos acted there as a support force;
— bind enemy forces and prevent their employment else-where. Indeed, the Germans thought to discover in the Com-mando raids a pattern of reconnaissance missions which would disclose the probable invasion front, and in the beginning of 1943 German Counter-Intelligence believed to have found a number of possible invasion-front 'centres of gravity' along the French coast.[1] They were nothing of the kind; it was only at this time that the Allies first set up an inter-Service Staff for the prepara-tion of an invasion plan. Yet the Germans considered even Bordeaux an invasion possibility.[2] By wrongfully guessing Allied intentions they must have squandered some of their occupation forces.

All these missions were carried out by Commandos, but never by regular troops. Two further facts stand out: whenever cliff landings were called for in the last war, Commandos and Rangers were entrusted with the mission, and it fell to them, as a rule, to execute a particularly tricky task, such as clearing almost inaccessible enemy coast defences within a strict time limit, and thereby assuring the success of a larger operation.

Those were their special coastal warfare tasks.

What were the land warfare tasks of Commandos and Rangers?

Whatever these special tasks may have been, Commandos and Rangers were not meant to act as Storm Troops. On occasions they came near to this role. They often led the way. They fre-quently silenced an enemy battery, captured high ground or a bridge and made the advance possible by their action. The success of the main attack was due to, or facilitated by, their success. But precisely because they rarely carried out the main attack them-selves and, brushing aside all enemy resistance, broke the enemy front, they were not Storm Troops. Being the nimble forces they were, a frontal attack of theirs would not normally have had the necessary weight.

But because they were nimble, they could attack from a dif-ferent direction, and by infiltrating the enemy's lines take him

[1] Cf. Paul Leverkuehn, op. cit., p. 92.
[2] Ibidem. Referring to the period from 1942 on, Dr Leverkuehn states (on p. 91) that 'it was clearly realized on the German side right from the start how dangerous were these British Commando operations'.

by surprise from the rear. Throughout the last war, in the earlier and later operations, in coastal and land warfare, wherever infiltration was resorted to, Commandos and Rangers were selected for this mission if they were at hand.

The first of these infiltration raids was made in July 1941 on two hills held by an Italian force besieging Tobruk. It was decided to attack the Italian position; the Commandos should filter at night through the Italian forward position and their main defensive lines, then turn, move to the rear of the hills and attack from there while an Indian Cavalry Regiment mounted a frontal attack. The raid was a perfect success. The next infiltration raid, in November 1941, was made from the sea: a Commando force of about sixty officers and men was to land by submarine behind the enemy lines and assault Rommel's headquarters, but the operation, which was carried out with the utmost dash, failed: the house selected for attack had never been the German Field Marshal's command post.

Soon after the Americans came into the fight, the Rangers moved out on night infiltration marches, one of them against Sened Station.[1] Rangers and Commandos carried out their first joint infiltration in the Bizerta area. This time British and Americans, making up the Commando, were ordered to support the advance of 36 Infantry Brigade by turning the enemy's flank from the sea and cutting his lines of communication. They succeeded in holding one road junction for twenty-four hours and another one for three days and denied the use of the road to the enemy.[2] At Salerno, on the Italian mainland, Commandos and Rangers were ordered to go ashore, move inland, seize the defiles of La Molina and Nocera and hold them until the main force could move through. At Termoli Commandos and the Special Raiding Squadron landed and seized the town, harbour and a road junction on the axis of the Allied advance.[3]

On the day of the Normandy landings Commandos made

[1] For a description of the raid see Captain Leilyn M. Young, 'Rangers in a Night Operation', *Military Review*, vol. xxiv, July 1944, No 4, pp. 64 f.
[2] Cf. Hilary St George Saunders, op. cit., p. 139.
[3] Cf. Lt.-Col. Peter Young, *Storm from the Sea*, London 1958, pp. 125 f.; Brigadier T. B. L. Churchill, 'The Value of Commandos', *Royal United Service Institution Journal*, 1950, vol. 95, pp. 87-8; and Brigadier John Durnford-Slater, *Commando*, London 1953, pp. 156 f.

another infiltration raid. At Port-en-Bessin the Germans had specially prepared for the defence of the harbour against attacks from the sea. The Commandos therefore landed far off from the harbour and after a twelve-mile approach march they attacked from inland; after a second attack the German garrison surrendered.[1] Many more night infiltration marches, 'which were to become such a feature of the (Commando) Brigade's campaign in Germany',[2] followed. They were not always successful; the Germans had sometimes evacuated the area before the Commandos reached their position,[3] and sometimes surprise was lost on the way. But often they succeeded and then the damage done to the enemy was great because he had been unexpectedly struck in his most vulnerable point, his rear.

Probably the first inland night infiltration in brigade strength was made by 1 Special Service Brigade on August 20, 1944. Moving in single file, it chose a difficult route in order to avoid detection, and just over five hours after its start it took a German headquarters by surprise. The Commandos were through the lines and half an hour later they dug in on high ground in their allotted area. When the Germans became aware of the position they at once attacked in strength but were beaten back. The Commandos, in turn, began to open their supply route while the Germans continued until the end of the afternoon with a series of attacks against the flank and rear of the Commando position. The attacks failed and at midnight the Germans had to withdraw from the area.[4] The Rangers, too, continued with their infiltration missions. On one occasion, on the Irsch-Zerf road across the Saar, they managed to stay for nine days in the enemy's rear and denied him the use of the road for reinforcements.[5] Commandos carried out an assault crossing of the Weser river, followed it up by a night infiltration march and attacked the village of Leese from the rear, and they seized a road bridge over the

[1] Cf. Brigadier Sir Bernard Fergusson, The Watery Maze, The Story of Combined Operations, London 1961, p. 348.
[2] The Story of 45 Royal Marine Commando, op. cit., p. 38.
[3] Cf. the operation described in 48 Royal Marine Commando, op. cit., pp. 35-42.
[4] The Story of 45 Royal Marine Commando, op. cit., pp. 38 f. Cf. also Brigadier Derek Mills-Roberts, Clash by Night, London 1956, pp. 128 f.
[5] Cf. Henry S. Glassman, Lead the Way, Rangers—5th Ranger Bn., 1945, pp. 59 f.

Aller river in similar fashion.[1] These infiltration missions, it should be noted, were never carried out in German uniforms.

The object of these missions varied. They were executed in order to gain a favourable position for attack or deprive the enemy of a favourable position for counter-attack; or to gain a bridge or road, or to deny a bridge or road to the enemy for reinforcements or retreat; or to remove an obstacle in the way of the advancing troops, such as coastal batteries and strongholds, or to launch a surprise attack on an enemy-held position. The target for the attack was always a key point, it was on the axis of advance and as a rule relatively near to the front. The Commandos did not aim at encircling the enemy.

After the war the Army Commandos were dissolved[2] and it is now left to the Marine Commandos to carry on the tradition. Their post-war duties in Malaya, Korea, Cyprus and Port Said gave little scope for infiltration missions, and it appears that these missions are no longer regarded as one of the Commandos' special tasks. During the emergency in Malaya the Royal Marine Commandos of 3 Commando Brigade took over an operational area and were employed on infantry work; they assisted in the squatter resettlement, they went on patrols and they fought against guerrillas for two years. In Korea, the Royal Marine Commando was hardly employed on infiltration tasks. It mounted three large-scale amphibious attacks in the enemy rear against the railway lines near the east coast and also went on small and medium-sized amphibious raids in the rear, ambushed troops and convoys, blew up some more railway lines and reconnoitred the beach. Apart from these duties it became an additional reconnaissance company when it joined 1 US Marine Division, and fought on land as an ordinary infantry unit.[3] So did the Rangers.

In Cyprus, the Commandos were also employed on antiterrorist missions, such as search operations, screening, raids and so on. At Port Said, two Commandos made a seaborne assault after British and French paratroops had dropped in areas around the town. The Commandos had to secure the beachhead, clear

[1] Cf. Bryan Samain, *Commando Men*, London 1948, pp. 153 f., 160 f.
[2] And so were the Marine Raider battalions in the US where it is held that any Marine battalion can carry out a beach assault.
[3] Cf. Lt.-Colonel D. B. Drysdale, '41 Commando', *Marine Corps Gazette*, August 1953, vol. 37, pp. 28 f.

the waterfront and a number of buildings, and then link up with the paratroops. Another Commando landed in helicopters from two light fleet carriers in beachheads previously established by the two other Commandos; it cleared a street and secured the flank of a brigade. The French Commandos employed in this operation had similar tasks; they seized the outer harbour and canal installations and assaulted a coastal battery.

Indeed, the Royal Marine Commandos have now reverted to the role in which Royal Marines were traditionally used by Great Britain in wars with continental nations. In 1948 the then Commandant-General of the Royal Marines, General Brooks, defined a Commando 'as a lightly-equipped infantry unit with a minimum administrative detail, trained for cliff and assault landings on different natures of beach. They may be employed in raids, on special tasks in a major assault—such as the capture of a flank coastal battery, as at Dieppe—or in the seizure of a port.'[1] He went on to say that because of their lightness they can easily be moved in peace-time for policing,[2] that they must be highly-trained infantrymen, and have at least one special qualification, as cliff climbers, parachutists, or small boat experts. No mention is made that Commandos must be trained as an inland infiltration task force.

The fact, then, is that the United States still has a Special Force, the Rangers, whose land duties are shallow infiltration and attack against key points in the enemy rear, be it from inland or from the sea. In Great Britain, however, the Commandos no longer perform this function and no other Special Force has taken their place.

(2) No one, at least no one in Britain, will deny the Royal Marine Commandos a leading role in cliff and assault landings. But are Commandos and Rangers indispensable in land warfare for infiltration and rear attack, or can this task be equally well performed by divisional units, that is by forces raised by each division out of its numbers and trained by it?

There would be a simple answer if the British and Americans had trained such divisional units in the last war and sent them out on infiltration missions; their performance could then be compared with that of the Commandos and Rangers on identical

[1] Cf. Lecture by General Sir Dallas Brooks, reprinted loc. cit., p. 261.
[2] As they were in Brunei in 1962.

missions in the same theatre. But there were no such divisional units and, moreover, infiltration never played a large part in Allied tactics. Nor does the practice of the other belligerents show whether or not Commando-type troops were more skilful in infiltration than regular forces; in particular no conclusions can be drawn from Japanese experience because their soldiers are born infiltrators.

One of the best qualified judges, Lt.-Colonel Peter Young, himself a former Commando officer, has stated that 'any infantry can do our job; only we, the Commandos, can do it in the time allotted', and the historian of the Commandos, Hilary St George Saunders, agreed with this dictum.[1] On the other hand, Viscount Alanbrooke considered the Commando training much too stereotyped to meet all possible operational requirements; 'still thinking much too small in all our plans'.[2] However, he did not want more Commandos to receive still more specialized training, as might be thought, but preferred, as we have seen, that each division should train its own battle patrol. Colonel Darby, of Rangers fame, has stated that if he had to do the job again, he would select a unit for a particular job and give it the special training and equipment required for that task.[3]

There is no doubt that battle patrols, and also reconnaissance squadrons, can infiltrate too—they have done it often enough. It is hardly possible to decide if the swifter strike claimed for the Commandos would justify their retention as a Special Force. We must therefore approach the problem from a different angle.

We have seen that Commandos mounted infiltration attacks against key points in brigade strength[4] and such moves, especially against a strong enemy, must sometimes be made on this or even a larger scale if they are to succeed. It is obvious that a division cannot possibly train a battle patrol of that size. It is doubtful whether a corps could do it; but if it did, the battle patrol, or rather group, would be frittered away in pure infantry tasks because no corps can afford to keep a sizeable part of its total

[1] Op. cit., p. 350, where Colonel Young's remark is also quoted.
[2] Cf. Sir Arthur Bryant, op. cit., p. 255, ftn. 2.
[3] Cp. Colonel R. C. Williams, Jr, 'Amphibious Scouts and Raiders', Military Affairs, vol. xiii, 1949, p. 157.
[4] Rangers operated only in battalion strength in the last war. There were altogether six Ranger battalions, as against four Commando brigades.

strength indefinitely together for special—and in the corps area possibly infrequent—tasks without using it some of the time or most of the time in the same way as any other of its brigades. The result would be that at the critical moment the brigade could not be spared for the special job or that it would be under strength and unable to do it.

It is more than anything else this requirement of numbers and the availability in any sector at any time that call for a Special Force for infiltration attack and justify its existence. But if this is so, the Rangers should be reorganized along the Commando model. Commandos—and Rangers—were always under control of the higher infantry, tank or parachute formation to which they were attached, and the Commandos were sometimes, and the Rangers as a rule, split up in battalion strength over a number of such formations. But as far as the Commandos are concerned, their organization, different from the Rangers, made it possible to withdraw the various Commandos (corresponding to battalions), form up as a Commando brigade and thus provide the numerical strength necessary for larger operations.

As for Britain, the Royal Marine Commandos could, of course, be assigned the task of inland infiltration, but this seems unlikely. The close links between Royal Navy and Royal Marines rule their Commandos out for such assignments. However, the infiltration task could well be assigned to the airborne forces, and they seem, indeed, most suitable for this task.

In the first place they fulfil the requirements of numbers as well as availability. Furthermore, they usually fight in the rear. Thirdly, as we shall see in Chapter 8, they were in the last war employed on Commando missions, and on occasions airborne troops and Commandos fought on the same battlefield. Only their way of approach to the rear battlefield was different: once the campaign on the European continent was under way, the Commandos usually went through the enemy lines on foot while the airborne troops were flown over them. There is no reason why the airborne troops could not be trained in ground infiltration tactics and a number of good reasons why they should. As it was, the airborne forces of all belligerents were underemployed and they were frequently assigned infantry duties in the line. By taking over, as foot soldiers, the Commando infiltration role in addition to their present assignment, they would more often carry out the task for which they were designed, viz. to fight in the enemy rear. The time needed for planning an operation, though, must be adapted to Commando speed.

As far as other nations are concerned, the Belgians have decided to carry on the Army Commando tradition. After the war they formed a Commando Regiment, the nucleus of which was composed of wartime members of the British No. 10 (Inter-Allied) Commando. The tasks of the Commando Regiment include attacks against the enemy rear.[1]

The post-war Viet-minh Commandos in the Indo-China war were not Commandos in that sense. They too infiltrated but their targets were French airfields and transport planes on the ground.[2] They were saboteurs and used in an SAS-type role. So were the FLN Commandos in Algeria.

The Soviet Russians, however, have raised after the war proper Commando units. In 1956 Soviet Russia was supposed to have ten airborne divisions of about 10,000 men each. In each division there is one special regiment designed to carry out Commando raids and what is called extremely difficult tasks. In addition it is also trained for sabotage missions.[3]

Brandenburgers

The Germans thought of the Brandenburg Division as their Commando, as indeed it was to some extent. It was designed and trained to operate in the enemy's rear. Its battlefield was, according to the *Gesamtanweisung*,[4] where fighting did not yet take place or was over. When the German troops advanced it had to act as spearhead and infiltrate through the enemy lines, and when they retreated it had to stay put, allow itself to be overtaken by the enemy and halt or delay his advance. It had little opportunity to function in that latter capacity because it had almost

[1] Cf. 'Régiment Commando', *L'Armée, La Nation*, November 1947, vol. 2, p. 14.
[2] Cf. Otto Heilbrunn, *Partisan Warfare*, op. cit., pp. 138-9.
[3] Cf. Colonel-General Kurt Student, 'Airborne Forces', in *The Soviet Army*, edited by B. H. Liddell Hart, London 1956, p. 381. Cf. also J. M. Mackintosh, 'Soviet Airborne Troops', in *The Soviet Air and Rocket Forces*, edited by Asher Lee, London 1959, p. 167. Cf. also Bruno Maurach, 'Die sowjetischen Luftlandetruppen', *General Military Review*, October 1962, about the future employment of Soviet airborne troops against nuclear bases and similar targets.
[4] The General Directives for the Brandenburg Division.

ceased to exist as a Special Force when Germany had to relinquish her conquests, but was all the more prominent during the German thrust through Europe.[1]

The Brandenburg concept therefore differed from that of the Commandos: Brandenburg was exclusively to operate in the enemy's rear. Hence inland infiltration missions were the recognized task for which it was designed. But it was by accident rather than design that infiltration marches—and rear attack— 'were to become such a feature of the (Commando) Brigade's campaign in Germany'; as the reader will remember, the Commandos were meant to be recalled to England after the landing in France and then be employed on coastal operations.

Also different were the Brandenburg methods of infiltration. Commandos and Rangers moved under the protection of night through the enemy lines, the Brandenburgers sought protection by donning 'camouflage' uniform. That does not mean that Allied troops did not on some occasion also wear enemy uniform or insignia; Skorzeny owes his acquittal to the fact that they occasionally did. By contrast, the Brandenburgers very frequently wore enemy uniforms in their raids, except when they came under Rommel's command, who forbade this practice. The Germans differentiated between 'half-camouflage' and 'full camouflage', the first meaning that only one or two pieces of enemy uniform, such as a steel helmet or overalls, were worn, while full camouflage was the term for wearing full enemy uniform.[2] Half-camouflage was discarded before the start of the actual attack, while in full camouflage 'the confusion, caused in the enemy by

[1] From mid-1944 on, preparations were made for the formation of *Streifkorps*, composed of foreign language speakers of the Brandenburg Division and indigenous personnel, in regions still occupied by the Germans in the Baltic countries, Slovakia, the Balkans, Italy and France; the formation of a *Streifkorps Biscaya*, with Spanish-speaking legionaries, was also envisaged: the Germans considered an Allied invasion of Spain possible. The *Streifkorps*, under the command of a captain or lieutenant, were to act as stay-behind parties and prepare their regions for small-war activities and active resistance by the population, while other Brandenburg formations would subsequently infiltrate into these regions, exploit the situation and, presumably, return with the *Streifkorps* to the German lines. These plans were not executed; personnel selected for the *Streifkorps* was transferred to the SS.
[2] Cf. Paul Leverkuehn, *op. cit.*, p. 29.

the fire of his "own" troops, was used for executing the mission by way of surprise'.[1]

The Brandenburgers adopted another element of camouflage: many of their members were ethnic Germans who had been born abroad or who had lived there and spoke foreign languages fluently; there were Germans from Poland, the Sudetenland, the Baltic countries, Roumania, South-West Africa, Palestine and elsewhere,[2] and they could speak and act the part which they had to play in foreign uniform. There were also legionary troops of Ukrainians, Persians, Indians and others attached.

The Brandenburgers therefore tried to infiltrate by deceiving the enemy; Commandos and Rangers infiltrated by outmanoeuvring him. But Allied and German Commandos differed in still further aspects, as a survey of Brandenburg operations will show.

Denmark was attacked on the morning of April 9, 1940. The Brandenburgers' task was to prevent the blowing up of important bridges. Before the start of hostilities they went over the frontier in small detachments.[3] Their main objective was the bridge over the Belt, which they reached in time.[4] The mission was carried out in camouflage uniform[5] and was successful. The Brandenburgers were also the first to set foot on Norwegian soil.[6] On this occasion they 'probably dressed themselves in Norwegian uniform, or disguised themselves in some other way'.[7] Again, these missions were carried out by small parties.

On May 10th, Holland, Belgium, Luxembourg and France were invaded. In the attack on Holland the Brandenburgers shared their duties with the Battalion for Special Tasks 100. This detach-

---

[1] Ibid. The theory may have been also to discard full camouflage before actual fighting started, and this impression is conveyed by Die Geschichte des Panzerkorps Grossdeutschland, III. Band, collected and assembled by Helmuth Spaeter, ed. by Dr Wilhelm Ritter von Schramm, Duisburg-Ruhrort 1958, p. 40, but this was not, or not always, the practice: cf. P. Leverkuehn, loc. cit., p. 137, and Major Herbert Kriegsheim, op. cit., pp. 48, 119, 305 and throughout.
[2] Many had foreign nationality.
[3] Cf. Louis de Jong, The German Fifth Column in the Second World War, London 1956, p. 160.
[4] Die Geschichte des Panzerkorps Grossdeutschland, vol. iii, op. cit., referred to in future as Geschichte, p. 45; Major Herbert Kriegsheim, op. cit., p. 308.
[5] Major Herbert Kriegsheim, ibidem.
[6] Cf. Geschichte, p. 45.
[7] Louis de Jong, op. cit., p. 180.

ment, led by 'false Dutchmen',[1] tried to secure the bridge across the Maas to Maastricht, but while the Germans succeeded in occupying it, they could not prevent its destruction.[2] To the Brandenburgers fell the task of securing the bridge near Arnhem.[3] The attack also failed; the Dutch agents had supplied the Germans with false information[4] and the defenders spotted in time the cardboard helmets and odd—Dutch—uniforms of the Brandenburgers.[5] But a Brandenburg platoon[6] succeeded in securing the Maas bridge at Gennep and thus opened the way for the Panzerdivision held up at Maastricht. At Gennep the Germans, 'guarded' by three of their Dutch agents dressed up as Dutch frontier police, posed as PoWs; they were in Wehrmacht uniform, with greatcoat unbuttoned; they carried machine-pistols concealed under their armpits and had pistols, hand-grenades and wire-cutters in their pockets.[7] They occupied the bridge, still before H-hour,[8] and secured it, as a German participant says, by 'ruse, surprise and firearms'.[9] Further Brandenburg tasks included the seizure of four bridges over the Juliana Canal by one company. 'All these missions,' says the History of the Panzerkorps Grossdeutschland, 'were designed to save the blood and life of the attacking German units.'[10] Or, as a notable Dutchman puts it, 'a number of Dutch soldiers was treacherously shot down in all these attacks'.[11]

In preparation for the invasion of Luxembourg the Brandenburgers had to take and secure a number of objectives along the frontier and thus keep the way to the Ardennes open for the Panzer breakthrough. They crossed the River Oub, which forms the frontier, six or eight hours before H-hour;[12] at H-hour they

[1] Paul Leverkuehn, op. cit., p. 73.
[2] There is some doubt about when these formations slipped over the frontier. L. de Jong, p. 185, gives as date May 9th, while P. Leverkuehn says that the departure was in the early morning hours of May 10th.
[3] Geschichte, p. 46.
[4] Ibidem.
[5] L. de Jong, op. cit., p. 185.
[6] Major H. Kriegsheim, op. cit., p. 308.
[7] Geschichte, p. 46; P. Leverkuehn, op. cit., p. 73; Major H. Kriegsheim, op. cit., p. 308.
[8] P. Leverkuehn, op. cit., p. 74.
[9] Geschichte, p. 49.
[10] Geschichte, p. 46.
[11] L. de Jong, op. cit., p. 185.
[12] Geschichte, p. 58.

had arrived at their objectives. In Belgium a squad of Brandenburgers, this time dressed in Belgian berets and greatcoats,[1] was
ordered to take bridges at Nievport and prevent the inundation of
the Yser district—it had been flooded in 1915—by securing the
floodgates. In a Belgian bus and guided by French-speakers, they
passed through Belgian troops without arousing suspicion. On
the bridge they came under fire from a British unit opposite but
succeeded in carrying out their mission.[2] Other detachments, disguised as refugees and mingling with Belgian civilians, carried
their arms in prams and trucks;[3] their task was to seize other
bridges.

The Brandenburgers were only on a few occasions employed
in France, near Abbéville, Reims and Paris.[4] Again, some of their
usual activities were carried out there by the Battalion for Special
Tasks 100. Then Brandenburg was ordered to prepare itself for
Operation Sea Lion, the landing in England. Altogether two and
a half companies were to take part.

The German Army Staff had initially planned that troops were
to land along the coast from Dover to Lyme Bay. The best part
of one company of Brandenburgers was to make a parachute
descent on Dover jetty and harbour, in 'camouflage' uniform.[5]
This plan seems to have undergone several changes; first it was
decided to land by gliders, then by barges. The objectives were
to prevent the blockage of the harbour, where a British ship was
standing by for this purpose, and to seize the coastal batteries on
the cliffs.[6] But this plan was abandoned when the German
Supreme Command decided towards the end of August 1940
that Dover was to be captured from the landward side. Another
half-company of Brandenburgers received orders to go ashore
with the first wave west of Hastings and form a bridgehead at
St Leonards, then advance on motor bicycles inland and seize the
coastal batteries of Beachy Head from the rear. This half-company
consisted for the most part of English-speaking oversea Germans;
the uniform to be worn for the occasion is described as

[1] Ibidem, p. 51.
[2] Ibidem, pp. 49 f.
[3] L. de Jong, op. cit., p. 198.
[4] Major H. Kriegsheim, op. cit., p. 308.
[5] Ibidem, p. 308.
[6] Geschichte, p. 62.

'Ueberwurf-Uniform'[1] and seems to indicate half-camouflage, to be discarded if and when fire is exchanged.[2] A further company was assigned to land on another part of the coast.[3]

Brandenburg was in action in Yugoslavia, where part of a battalion, in co-operation with other units, crossed the Danube in the early morning of April 6, 1941, secured the Yugoslav side of the Iron Gate and prevented the blockage of the river.[4] From the following June on, Brandenburgers were also active in North Africa, first on reconnaissance, then in infiltrating agents behind the British lines,[5] and in sabotage operations against a railway bridge over the Wadi el-Kbir, a bridge north of Kasserini and another bridge over the Wadi al-Melah.[6] Allied troops suffered practically no discomfort from these activities and in the desert campaign they were not even noticed. Brandenburgers also took part as an assault unit in Rommel's big attack against the US II Corps south of Fonduk in February 1943.[7]

In the first half of the campaign against Soviet Russia and especially during the first days of the invasion, Brandenburgers had the mission to seize and hold bridgeheads, roads, railway tracks, tunnels and military depots ahead of the German advance, to eliminate enemy artillery and to carry out sabotage; all objectives were in the enemy's rear. The Brandenburgers approached their objectives on foot, skis, in boats, gliders or by parachute; their favourite method of infiltration was to join a retreating Red Army unit in captured military trucks, with Russian-speakers in front and in the rear. On most occasions Soviet uniform, in part or in full, was worn during the approach to the objective. Indeed, one Brandenburg unit, 'dressed as Russian soldiers, operated for weeks in the Russian rear, captured a divisional staff and returned later to the German line'.[8]

Once the German attack got under way, Brandenburg opera-

---

[1] Ibid., p. 63. Ueberwurf means a loose outer garment or cloak.
[2] For the operation planned against Gibraltar in 1940, Spanish Foreign Legion uniform was to be worn. Cf. P. Leverkuehn, p. 104.
[3] Geschichte, p. 62.
[4] L. de Jong, op. cit., p. 232; Geschichte, p. 65.
[5] Geschichte, pp. 68 f. The Germans, too, had a multitude of Special Forces in this theatre. In addition to Brandenburg there were Special Unit 287, Special Unit 288 and a Legionary Force 505.
[6] Major H. Kriegsheim, op. cit., pp. 311-12.
[7] Geschichte, p. 76.
[8] P. Leverkuehn, op. cit., p. 137.

tions became less frequent. The reason is not far to seek. 'With the quick advance of the German armies eastwards and far into the depth of enemy country, further Brandenburg operations are, as a rule, no longer required. The element of surprise is now mainly exploited by the Panzerdivisions and their armoured advance units, the number of targets diminishes, they can be taken only by larger-scale combat operations.'[1]

The foregoing survey shows that apart from their political warfare missions[2] the Brandenburgers, like the Commandos and Rangers, usually operated in close contact with the regular units and close to the front line.[3] But the Brandenburg range of activities was more restricted. They never occupied and held a hill, town, or any larger area in the enemy rear, and there was therefore no need for them to operate in battalion strength, as the Rangers did, or in brigade strength, as did the Commandos. Nor were the Brandenburgers meant to take their objectives by the use of arms, which they even kept hidden on occasions: the reader will remember the 'disarmed' German PoWs who crossed the Maas bridge under Dutch 'guards', and when later Brandenburgers took the Dwina bridge in Latvia they were disguised as wounded Red Army men. The Brandenburgers were supposed not only to gain, but also to hold their objectives by ruse and stealth; they were often too weak a force to fight it out. Nor could they have held their objectives for more than a very short time. Their job in securing a bridge was almost done if they succeeded in removing the explosive charges.

Finally, amphibious raids played only a small part in Brandenburg operations. No raids were carried out against the coastline of Britain or Allied-occupied Italy. There were a number of reasons for this German reticence: in the earlier stages of the war Germany had no need to raid in order to raise home morale; nor could she later encourage resistance in Allied-occupied countries by this or any other means. Furthermore, Germany is a land power and most of her campaigns were fought on European land, accessible to her by land. Where naval strategy should have taken precedence over military, as in the Mediterranean

---

[1] So *Geschichte*, p. 83.
[2] Cf. above Chapter 2.
[3] The sabotage raid against the Murmansk railway in August 1942, about 120 miles in the enemy rear, is one of the exceptions.

theatre, her leaders failed to grasp the significance of amphibious operations until it was too late.

The amphibious Brandenburg raids were carried out by the Coastal Hunter Company. Its first field of operations was on the Black Sea and Sea of Azov coast, where it had to clear the beach for an unopposed landing by German infantry, destroy a land-based searchlight battery which illuminated the German crossing from the Crimea to the mainland, and board a disabled Soviet ship whose artillery fire harassed the Germans. The raid succeeded.[1] After one or two minor operations in the same theatre, the Company fought against partisans and, trying to surprise them, landed from the sea on the coast of France, the Adriatic and Mediterranean. The company also participated in the operations against Rhodes.[2] The significance of all these raids has been described by a former German counter-intelligence officer as small because the German Navy did not favour such undertakings.[3]

Practically the last Brandenburg operations of the commando type were at Maikop, where the German advance in the east came to a final halt. The division's subsequent infantry role in various theatres ended when it was transformed into a Panzer-grenadier Division in the autumn of 1944. Its members were then asked to join Skorzeny's Waffen-SS and 1,800 officers and men did so.

There is no successor to the Brandenburg Special Force in the post-war West German order of battle. However, the East Germans are reported to have recently formed a unit of 2,000 men, to be known as Reconnaissance Troops. They are to wear West German uniform and are meant to operate in the NATO rear. Their training covers close combat fighting, demolition, sabotage, enemy weapons and lessons in English. They can be used as paratroops.[4]

---

[1] Cf. Major H. Kriegsheim, op. cit., p. 309; Geschichte, p. 110. Part of the operation was commanded by the then First Lieutenant Kriegsheim and is described on pp. 114 f of his book. After the searchlight crew had been surprised and taken prisoner at gunpoint, the Brandenburgers discarded their Soviet blouses which they had worn over their German uniforms. Cf. op. cit., p. 121.
[2] Geschichte, p. 111.
[3] P. Leverkuehn, op. cit., p. 35.
[4] From a report in the Social Democratic Parliamentary Press, reprinted in Deisler und Weserzeitung, March 4, 1961, and translated in Mars & Minerva, vol. 1, No. 6, December 1961, p. 11.

Skorzeny's Special Formation

Skorzeny's missions differed from those hitherto discussed: only on one occasion did his Special Formation operate in conjunction with the army and close to the front line, and that was during Hitler's Ardennes counter-offensive in December 1944. In this operation an assault force under Skorzeny's command was to act as Storm Troops, and a small commando force as a fifth column. Both groups were to wear American or British uniform and use American arms, vehicles and equipment; it was only due to the shortage of these items in German hands that German equipment, suitably adjusted, had mostly to be used in this operation.[1]

Skorzeny's orders were to seize three bridges over the Meuse behind the Allied lines with his assault force and create confusion and despondency in the Allied rear with his commandos. As his assault force he assembled an armoured brigade consisting of twenty tanks, thirty scout cars, three motorized infantry battalions, artillery and AA batteries; altogether there were 3,300 men. This brigade did not operate as a Special Force; it had only one unorthodox feature: it gave itself the appearance of an Allied formation. The commando force for this operation was merely one commando company. Skorzeny's assault force did not seize its objectives and, the German thrust having broken down long before the Meuse was reached, it was used in battle like any other conventional unit. But the commando company did achieve limited success. Operating in small parties, it cut telephone lines, blew up ammunition dumps, removed signposts and passed on false information to those American units it met on the way. Though it did little physical damage, it exploited the element of confusion already created by the counter-offensive. Out of all proportion to its numbers was the nervousness aroused among the Allies, and its greatest achievement was that Allied soldiers became over-suspicious on a number of occasions.[2] It was even

---

[1] Before the operation Skorzeny had a talk with a German colonel of the Legal Branch, who informed him that international law merely forbade a soldier in enemy uniform to use his arms. 'Naturally, I decided to follow this advice' for the assault, says Skorzeny in his book, *Skorzeny's Secret Missions*, New York 1950, p. 225, but in his *Skorzeny's Special Missions*, London 1957, p. 150, he merely states: 'I welcomed such advice, coming from an expert.'
[2] Cf. *Kriegstagebuch des Oberkommandos der Wehrmacht (Wehrmachtsführungsstab)*, vol. iv, Eingeleitet und erläutert von Percy Ernst Schramm, Erster Halbband, Frankfurt Main 1961, pp. 448-9, and Skorzeny's own books, *op. cit.*

believed that General Eisenhower was to be kidnapped by Skorzeny himself; in fact, Hitler had expressly forbidden him to move beyond the German front line.[1]

Skorzeny's Special Force had its origin in the rivalry between Canaris's Military Intelligence organization and Himmler's Reich Main Security Office which concerned itself, among other things, with political and later also with military Intelligence. Because Canaris had the Brandenburgers as his private army, Himmler's Office formed, early in 1943, a similar unit, at first of company strength, and Skorzeny was appointed to its command.[2] It grew to battalion strength (called Friedenthal Special Formation and then Battalion 502) and from the later half of 1944 on it consisted of six battalions. In view of its origin it is not surprising that some of its missions had a strong political flavour: the dramatic rescue of Mussolini, the plan to occupy Vichy and remove Pétain if he were to take up contact with General de Gaulle, and the seizure of the citadel of Budapest, the seat of the Regent, Admiral Horthy, which led to the formation of a new pro-German government in Hungary. Units under Skorzeny were also used to maintain order in Berlin after the July 1944 attempt on Hitler's life. In Mussolini's rescue, commandos played the decisive part but the *coup de main* against the citadel of Budapest was carried out under Skorzeny's orders by two parachute and one motorized infantry battalions, two tank companies, glider troops and only one commando battalion; its success was due to the force by which it was backed.

Skorzeny's other special missions were to be executed far from the front line. Shortly after the force had been formed it received orders to interrupt the British supply lines in Iran, including the supply lines to Russia, by inciting the mountain tribes to revolt. This operation failed; after a few months the tribes handed over to the British the few commandos who had landed in Iran. Next came plans to attack Soviet power plants far in the Russian rear; the plans were shelved. It was then envisaged to sabotage oil pipelines in Irak, but no action was taken. A further plan, to kidnap

---

[1] Why the assault force was put under Skorzeny's command is not quite clear; in the event, the commandos carried out their task without the assistance of the assault force.

[2] While a number of Brandenburgers joined Skorzeny's force, others reacted bitterly against him. Cf. for a Brandenburg colonel's sharp criticism, Major Herbert Kriegsheim, *op. cit.*, p. 305.

Tito, also remained in the planning stage. But late in the war two commando attacks against bridges behind enemy lines succeeded. The force also tried to extricate a German infantry unit of 2,000 men which was left far behind in the Minsk area during the Red Army advance. Skorzeny dispatched for this purpose twenty men, twelve of them Russians, in Red Army uniform, but the attempt failed. Skorzeny was finally, in January 1945, given command of a regular division with some commando elements; it had to defend a bridgehead over the Oder river against the approaching Russians.[1]

Skorzeny's own idea of his special troops was that of 'a self-contained, effective force capable of carrying out an offensive operation, at any rate on a small scale',[2] obviously, as one must add, behind the enemy lines and, probably, independently of the regular army. Since his unit was formed when Germany's retreat from the outposts of her conquests had already begun, he had little chance—apart from his Ardennes mission—of employing it on the Brandenburg model in the fight where fighting did not yet take place. All he could do was to fight where fighting no longer took place. Hence, possibly, his insistence on the nature of the force as a self-contained one and the stiffening of his force by regular units.

As far as the published accounts go, Skorzeny's force seems to have been much underemployed. It is, however, not unlikely that a number of missions were never recorded because the men, fighting on as partisans in isolated pockets of resistance,[3] did not return to tell the tale. Skorzeny himself did not confine his activities to land warfare; he also tried his hand in sea warfare by taking the K-Men[4] under his wing, and he experimented with manned V1 to be released from aircraft. The assignments for the force came direct from Hitler or Himmler, and the unity of purpose which strongly permeated the Allied Special Forces and Brandenburg was somewhat lacking.

SAS
The British Special Air Service (SAS), whose activities we shall

[1] Cf. for the above, Skorzeny's books, op. cit., and also Charles Foley, Commando Extraordinary, London 1954.
[2] Otto Skorzeny, Skorzeny's Special Missions, op. cit., p. 126.
[3] Cf. Major H. Kriegsheim, op. cit., p. 273.
[4] Who sabotaged Allied shipping and so on; see Chapter 2 above.

briefly discuss now, was for a time in its career employed on strict Commando tasks, in close contact with the Army and near the front line. This was during the initial stage of the Italian campaign when SAS was known as Special Raiding Squadron. In the assault on Sicily the Squadron landed at Capo Murro di Porco and put the coastal defence batteries out of action before the Allied invasion fleet moved in. It then occupied the naval base at Augusta which had been by-passed by the Army. At Catania it was to pass through the Commando beachhead and seize the dock area but this plan was abandoned. It landed on the mainland with the task to seize and hold the town of Bagnara until the arrival of the main forces. It landed at Termoli with the Commandos and was ordered to move inland and seize a bridge on the axis of the Allied advance. In the German counter-attack there it fought in the line.[1] All these activities were but an interlude; SAS soon found itself once again pursuing the activities which it had first performed in North Africa.

The SAS had been trained to approach its targets by parachute, submarine, trucks and later jeeps. In the North African desert its favourite targets were enemy aircraft which it destroyed by the hundreds on the ground. It ambushed convoys and coastal railways and raided headquarters. Its route of approach was usually by flank infiltration from the south. It also undertook very successful amphibious operations against Crete. When the Allies landed in French North Africa, the 2nd SAS Regiment was formed and operated there.[2]

After their commando activities in the Italian campaign, small SAS parties went on harassing missions very far behind the enemy lines in Italy, France and Greece, often working together with partisans for whom they provided leadership, stiffening, arms and supplies. In Italy they infiltrated by jeep and boat, cut enemy communications and shot up enemy patrols. In France where they were dropped by parachute they travelled by jeep and blew up enemy transport, roads, petrol dumps and railways; they killed and captured enemy personnel; they reconnoitred for the

[1] Cf. D. I. Harrison, *These Men Are Dangerous. The Special Air Service at War*, London 1957, pp. 29 f.
[2] While still in Africa, 1st SAS Regiment was split up into Special Raiding Squadron and Special Boat Service. Special Raiding Squadron later formed part of SAS Brigade, composed of 1st and 2nd SAS Regiment, two French parachute battalions and one Belgian parachute company.

Army and indicated targets for the Air Force. Their sabotage parties were dropped behind the lines in Belgium and Holland, and in the last stages of the war they attacked in Germany any target that offered itself.[1] They were frequently supplied by air and, in France, sometimes received their orders through a BBC transmitter.

It might appear that because targets were often selected at random or just happened to be where the SAS teams happened to be, their missions lacked effectiveness. But that is not so. If they had no special target they always operated on the axis of Allied advance or the enemy's lines of communication and, by making things generally unpleasant for the enemy, softened up resistance and smoothed the way for the regular troops.

After the war the SAS was dissolved and then reactivated. In Malaya, where one SAS Regiment was in operation from 1951, it fought in deep jungle in an infantry role. It took part in a number of parachute operations, went on reconnaissance and fighting patrols, destroyed rebel camps and prevented the establishment of new ones, and had its fair share of killings. In Oman two SAS Squadrons took the leading part in a brilliantly executed operation against rebels on a mountain, and a detachment is at present employed in an infantry role in Brunei.

In spite of these rather orthodox post-war activities their special task in any future employment remains the same as in the last war. The SAS is trained to carry out, in small parties of from three to fifty men, long-range penetration and long-term raiding operations in enemy-held country. Their operations include reconnaissance, ambushes, sabotage, raids on headquarters, kidnapping, and creating alarm and despondency. They approach their targets on foot, in vehicles, or by sea, parachute or helicopter.[2] A boat section, for operations from the sea, once again forms a part of SAS, and so does a section of frogmen.

A number of other countries have also activated SAS troops. As the reader will remember, French and Belgian SAS had formed part of the British SAS Brigade. The French SAS was disbanded after the end of the war, but soon afterwards a half-brigade of SAS Parachute Commandos was formed for the war in Indo-China

[1] Cf. D. I. Harrison, op. cit., pp. 120 f., and Major Roy Farran, Winged Dagger, London 1948, pp. 155 f.
[2] Cf. Mars and Minerva, vol. i, No. 7, March 1956, p. 19.

and later merged with the Brigade de Parachutistes d'outre Mer. The Belgian SAS Parachutist Regiment was amalgamated with the Commandos. The New Zealand Squadron of the SAS Regiment fought in Malaya. Australia has an SAS Company, and it is designed not only to act as spearhead in an advance but also to defend an area until it is relieved.[1] There is finally a Rhodesian SAS Squadron.

Japanese Raiding Units

The Japanese Raiding Units of the last war were conceived on lines somewhat similar to the SAS. They too were saboteurs, and they executed their missions behind the enemy lines in very small parties. But they approached their target always on foot, their penetration was often shallow, and they stayed behind the lines only for a short period. Their task was to destroy enemy matériel and personnel.

The first Raiding Units in the Pacific theatre seem to have been formed in August 1943 during the fighting at Salamaua.[2] They were at first employed only sporadically, but subsequently they were used more and more methodically and their attacks were co-ordinated among themselves and also with the Army. A large number of teams of two or three men would try to infiltrate at night from many directions and over a wide front. Their main targets were tanks and artillery as well as headquarters. They had to stay in the infiltrated area for one or two nights and, having ascertained the best time, attack in waves. At Luzon they tried to penetrate deeply, and they included airfields and ammunition dumps in the list of their objectives, while at Leyte they also tried to demolish bridges, their infiltration teams there being up to twenty men strong. They avoided contact with the enemy and were expected to return to their own lines after completion of the tasks. Similar Raiding Units were encountered in Burma. Equipment generally included explosives, magnetic mines and bangalore torpedoes for the destruction of wire obstacles.[3]

[1] Cf. *Mars and Minerva*, vol. i, No 5, June 1961, p. 17.
[2] Cf. 'Combat Methods of Small Raiding Parties', *Intelligence Bulletin*, vol. iii, No. 11, July 1945, Military Intelligence Division, War Department, Washington, DC, pp. 6 f.
[3] Cf., *ibid.*

Independent Companies

The Australian Independent Companies were first trained, on Commando lines, before the SAS had been formed in the desert. This may explain why they are often referred to as Commandos although they were actually employed in SAS-type operations. Like the SAS they had to harass enemy personnel and destroy his equipment, deep in enemy-held country. Like the SAS they drew on local support. The SAS parties were often guerrillas in uniform; the Independent Companies were always so.

Australia had eight Independent Companies during the last war. Before the Japanese occupied the outlying islands, they were the forward observation line, and when the islands were invaded they provided a thin defensive screen. 2/1 Independent Company was spread over a 2,000 miles long chain of islands, stretching from the Admiralty Islands to the New Hebrides; few of these men returned but they had been able to supply valuable information. 2/3 Independent Company carried out successful harassing raids in the Wau area. Others protected the near-coastal areas.[1] 2/2 and later 2/4 Independent Companies fought in Portuguese Timor.

With the help of natives 2/2 Independent Company, a little over 300 men, fought against 1,000 and later 6,000 of the enemy. In thirteen months' fighting they killed about 1,500 for the loss of forty of their own men, and harassed the Japanese to such an extent that they brought in a division as further reinforcement. At no time had a guerrilla force or guerrilla-type force in any theatre of World War II withstood for so long such a superior force with such telling results.[2] Herein lies one distinction between the operations of SAS and Independent Companies in the last war: the roving SAS Squadrons would leave the enemy no time to concentrate sufficient troops for hunting them; they would not even try to tie down superior enemy forces for any length of time. The more stationary Independent Companies, operating in Australia's threatened outposts, were almost bound

---

[1] For the raiding and ambushing activities of 2/5 Independent Company on New Guinea cf. Jack Boxall, *A Story of 2/5 Australian Commando Squadron*, n.d.

[2] Even in the most active theatres of guerrilla warfare in the last war the partisans did not tie down much more than half as many troops again. Cf. Otto Heilbrunn, *Partisan Warfare*, London 1962, New York 1962, Paris 1963, Frankfurt am Main 1963, Chapter 12.

to do so. This does not mean, however, that the SAS could not equally have performed this job in suitable areas; it only underlines the fact that guerrilla-type troops will bind superior enemy forces if they operate long enough in a sensitive area. The other difference between the forces is that Independent Companies operated on ground lost and the SAS on ground to be gained.

2/2 Independent Company went out on patrols even before the Japanese had landed, and the knowledge of the terrain thus gained proved the greatest asset in its subsequent exploits. When the Japanese came to the island, the Independent Company set up in inaccessible spots a series of hide-outs as its operational bases, rest and storage centres.[1] Having thus established themselves in typical guerrilla fashion, the Australians now fought like guerrillas. They maintained constant reconnaissance patrols and laid ambushes when the opportunity was favourable. They, with natives as their guides, always knew where the enemy was but he could not find them. They were in no hurry to attack. 'We considered it much better to kill five or ten Japanese and suffer no casualties ourselves than to attempt to kill more and suffer casualties.'[2] They never thought of holding ground and they thus solved the task 'for a company to exist where complete forces had failed, and when everywhere else there was surrender'.[3] Soon the Independent Company spread out over a line sixty miles long, observed every enemy move, harassed him on his lines of communication, and raided an important town. To counter these activities, the enemy set up posts, and these were attacked in turn after their routine had been carefully studied. The supply position of the force was eased when it managed to establish wireless contact with Australia; it also received some air support from then on.

When the inevitable Japanese drive against the force began in the form of an eight-pronged move, the force evaded the enemy long enough until he decided to retire. The Japanese operation was obviously aimed at encircling the force; dangerous though it was, the net was cast much too wide and the starting lines were too far from each other and the operational area of the force.

[1] Cf. for the following the account by Lt.-Col. Bernard J. Callinan, *Independent Company*, London 1953.
[2] *Ibid.*, p. 92.　　　　　　　　　　[3] *Ibid.*, p. 64.

But it was clear that it could not hold out for ever against such odds. First it was reinforced by 2/4 Independent Company, and when the Japanese managed to extend their area of control and win over parts of the population, both companies were evacuated in December 1942 and January 1943.

The special element about these Independent Companies stands out clearly: it was their capability to survive and continue for so long as an effective harassing force. Their record is all the more impressive when compared with that of the regular Australian unit stationed in the Dutch part of the island. It consisted of a battalion and was confronted by 14,500 Japanese, including parachute troops.[1] The ratio of Japanese superiority, the features of the country and the character of the population were more or less identical in both parts of the island. Yet the regular force, through no fault of its own, was soon forced to surrender: like practically all regular troops in the last war, it had not been trained, and did not operate, as a guerrilla force.

Other Special Forces
New Zealand had already in 1941 decided to disband its Independent Companies. The Independent Commandos of New Zealanders and Fijians were meant to act as guerrilla forces instead, should the Japanese land in Fiji, and they received their initial training from former officers of the Independent Companies. When it became clear that the enemy would not invade Fiji, one of the Independent Commandos was absorbed into the newly formed First Commando Fiji Guerrillas, as they were officially called in New Zealand, or South Pacific Scouts, under which name they appeared in the US order of battle, and transferred to the Solomon Islands. Here again they were not used as guerrillas; they carried out numerous reconnaissance and fighting patrols, often behind the enemy lines, and acted as battle guides to US units. Before they were disbanded in May 1944, Second Commando Fiji Guerrillas had taken their place.[2] Their duties were not different from those of regular reconnaissance units.

[1] Cf. Lionel Wigmore, *Australia in the War 1939-1945*, vol. iv, *The Japanese Thrust*, Canberra 1957, p. 466. Cf. also Dudley McCarthy, *op. cit.*, pp. 598 f.
[2] Cf. Colin R. Larsen, *Pacific Commandos, New Zealanders and Fijians in Action*, Wellington 1946.

The British No 1 Demolition Squadron, better known as Popski's Private Army, operated in the desert and Italy. In the desert it carried out long-range sabotage jobs, such as laying mines, blowing up dumps, destroying vehicles and raiding landing grounds. Its unofficial designation as a private army was thoroughly justified in the desert; in view of Popski's special sources of information there and the co-operation he received from the Senoussi Arabs, it was thought appropriate to give him an even freer hand than is usual with Special Forces. In Italy the force went on reconnaissance, in jeeps and on foot, seized a number of towns and cleared large areas of the enemy. Altogether it did not stay very long behind the enemy lines—for a month in Africa and for three weeks in Italy.[1] Most of its objectives are now recognized SAS targets.[2]

The purpose of all the forces discussed so far was strictly offensive, and the same applies to the Special Boat Service. Its operations may be considered as typical for those of all amphibious raiders.

The SBS approached its targets by submarine, surface craft including canoes, and also sometimes by parachute. SBS squadrons were occasionally used almost like regular troops as when they helped to liberate Greece; in Yugoslavia they engaged in guerrilla work like the SAS; a Commando role was assigned to them in the plan for the capture of Rhodes where they were to seize and hold various strong-points so that a regular division could land unopposed and occupy the island, but the plan was abandoned. As a rule their special task was sabotage; their targets were usually inland. In the desert they laid bombs on enemy trucks; in the Tobruk raid of September 1942, in which the SAS, LRDG and a few regulars also took part, they destroyed a wireless station and captured strong-points; in Sicily and Italy they mined railway tracks and destroyed bridges, blew up store dumps and disrupted lines of communication; in Sardinia they raided an aerodrome; in Rhodes and Crete, which they visited twenty times, they destroyed petrol dumps and aircraft on the ground; on other islands in the Aegean they sought out enemy shipping, power and telegraph stations, landing strips and radio

[1] So John Willet, Popski, London 1954, p. 122.
[2] Cf. also Lt.-Col. Vladimir Peniakoff ('Popski'), Popski's Private Army, London 1950, and Park Yunnie, Warriors on Wheels, London 1959.

transmitters; in Greece they moved in when the German retreat had begun, landed unopposed by parachute on an airfield and by boat on the coast, took up the pursuit, mined, ambushed, seized half of Greece from the Germans and engaged in street fighting against Greek communists, and they then went on to the Northern Adriatic and North Italy where they fought their last action and captured four islands in Lake Commachio.[1]

The Long Range Desert Group and Phantom were employed by the British in a different capacity; their task was primarily not offensive; they supplied Intelligence.

The LRDG carried out reconnaissance deep behind the enemy lines. It was equipped with special trucks and later jeeps, wireless transmitters, and plenty of automatic weapons. This group, too, operated in the desert on the southern flank, from three bases. Small patrols kept a road watch for months on all Axis traffic on the main coastal road. The LRDG also transported SAS parties and Popski's men to their target areas and carried out occasional raids on airfields. After the conclusion of the African campaign, though, it took on an amphibious role and formed part of Raiding Forces.[2] Its special task during its employment in Africa stands out: it was strategic reconnaissance.

Phantom, whose official designation was at first GHQ Liaison Regiment, collected and transmitted battle information by wireless to General Headquarters. It operated through small mobile parties in the Allied front line or in the enemy's rear. It served as a small mission in France and Belgium before the French capitulation, and afterwards, as No 1 GHQ Reconnaissance Unit, in Greece, North Africa, Italy, France and Germany.[3]

Somewhat similar missions were carried out on the German side by the Intelligence Units of the Brandenburg Division.

[1] Cf. for the above John Lodwick, *The Filibusters. The Story of the Special Boat Service*, London 1947.
[2] Cf. Captain M. Crichton-Stuart, 'The Story of a Long Range Desert Patrol', *The Army Quarterly*, vol. xlvii, Oct. 1943, pp. 70 f., Jan. 1944, pp. 197 f.; Michael Crichton-Stuart, *G-Patrol*, London 1958; W. B. Kennedy Shaw, *Long Range Desert Group*, London 1945; Lt.-Col. David Lloyd-Owen, *The Desert, My Dwelling Place*, London 1957; *New Zealand in the Second World War*. Official History by R. L. Kay, War History Branch, *Long Range Desert Group in Libya, 1940-41*, Wellington 1949, and *Long Range Desert Group in the Mediterranean*, Wellington 1950. See also *Raiding Forces, The Story of an Independent Command in the Aegean, 1943-45, op. cit.*
[3] Cf. Lt.-Col. R. J. T. Hills, *Phantom Was There*, London 1951.

There were eventually three companies which transmitted orders from Berlin to front-line units, kept in contact with the front during an engagement and supplied it with reconnaissance results.[1] The need for a Special Force of this type is not obvious.

Before we discuss the activities of the Chindits and Marauders —which we shall do in Chapter 4—and of the Special Forces working with guerrillas—which will be examined in Chapter 5— it seems appropriate to sort out the special tasks surveyed so far.

The two obvious principal assignments of all these Special Forces were reconnaissance and offensive missions.

The reconnaissance—and intelligence—tasks were assigned either to amphibious or to land forces, and required either shallow or deep infiltration. In addition to the forces whose primary task was reconnaissance there were others on occasional missions of this type.

The offensive missions were directed against coastal and inland targets. Both types of operation were either carried out in conjunction with operations by regular forces, mostly in order to gain ground, or they were independent actions, usually in the form of raids, ambushes or full-scale guerrilla war.

All land warfare operations were based on infiltration. Some Special Forces stayed only for short and others for extended periods behind the enemy lines.

Infiltration was not the prerogative of the Special Forces and infiltration as such is not a special task. It was only special for the Commandos and also the Rangers because they filtered through a strongly-held enemy front in greater numbers, even brigade strength, than regular troops would normally do in such circumstances. For the other Special Forces it was the nature of the task behind the enemy lines which made it special: it was often of a guerrilla character, almost always unconventional and therefore not within the normal scope of regular warfare.

It is evident, though, that the border line between the normal and the special scope of warfare is not rigidly fixed. Mountain warfare troops and ski troops are not usually considered Special Forces, and neither are parachute troops because the armed forces have come to regard these tasks as normal. What is normal or special, may even be differently interpreted by different countries: the role of the post-war Royal Marine Commandos

[1] Cf. *Die Geschichte des Panzerkorps Grossdeutschland, op. cit.,* p. 61.

is filled in the United States by the Marine Corps. The latter is not a Special Force while the former might be still so regarded, because they carry on the war-time Commando tradition and keep the Commando spirit alive.

CHAPTER 4

THE SPECIAL TASKS IN THE BURMA CAMPAIGN

Before the First Chindit Expedition was launched, there were three separate fronts in the Burma theatre: the front on the west coast, with its flank resting on the Bay of Bengal, was called the Arakan or southern front; here was the gateway to Calcutta which the Japanese hoped to reach. Further to the east the central front provided the last barrier in the way of the Japanese advance into Assam; if they were to conquer it, British rule in India would be jeopardized. The third and most easterly sector was known to the British as the northern front and to the Americans as Northern Combat Area Command. In this part of the country General Stilwell had started to build his Ledo Road; here Merrill's Marauders would operate; in this region was Fort Hertz, and on the other side of the Japanese front, deep in the rear, there would be the terminus of the First Chindit Expedition and the operational theatre of the Second Expedition.

The opposing armies in that country, much of which was mountain jungle, depended on roads, rivers and railways for their supplies. In General Wingate's words, 'the vulnerable artery is the line of communication winding through the jungle. Have no line of communication on the jungle floor. Bring in the goods like Father Christmas, down the chimney.'[1] General Wingate therefore proposed that his force should be supplied by air. With his own supply line immune from attack he could move far into the enemy's rear; there he could inflict telling damage on the enemy. This the First Chindit Expedition set out to do. Its needs determined its size: it had to be large enough to strike and small enough to vanish.

The Chindit operation was originally considered as part of a concerted frontal and rear attack against the Japanese central

[1] Quoted in Lt.-Col. Frank Owen's *The Campaign in Burma*, prepared for South-East Asia Command by the Central Office of Information, London 1946, p. 35.

and northern fronts. The Chindits were to pass through the front of British 4 Corps in the centre, cross the Chindwin river, cut the Burma Railway in the enemy's rear, harass the enemy in the Shwebo area and, if possible, cross the Irrawaddy river and interrupt Japanese supply lines to the northern front. While the Chindits operated in the rear of the central sector, 4 Corps would attack in front, and while they operated in the rear of the northern sector, General Stilwell's two American-trained Chinese divisions in the Ledo area and the Chinese Expeditionary Force from Yunnan would threaten the Japanese front in those theatres.

The role of the Chindits was clear: they would harass the enemy in guerrilla fashion, they would weaken him by destroying his supply dumps and supply lines, and they would tie down his forces which would have to protect their communications and dumps and hunt the intruders. The job of the Allied forces on the other side of the Japanese fronts would thus be made easier.

The concept was fascinating. Guerrilla wars, especially in the post-war years, have shown again and again that it is easier for a resolute guerrilla force to attack vulnerable points than it is for the occupying power to defend them, and that far larger forces are required for the defence than for the attack since the defence, not knowing where the next blow might fall, has to deploy many of its men over a wide area on guard duties. General Wingate was convinced that the diversion of his brigade to the rear would therefore do more damage to the enemy there than if it would be employed at the front.

But the original plan was drastically changed. When it became clear that neither the British nor the Chinese frontal attack would be forthcoming, Sir Archibald Wavell nevertheless gave permission to the Chindits to carry out their part of the operation. He realized that it would no longer bring any strategical profit but he thought it worthwhile to test this novel form of warfare.[1]

The test, however, could only be a limited one. The Japanese,

---

[1] Cf. Field Marshal Wavell's Foreword in Charles Rolo, *Wingate's Raiders*, London 1945, p. 7, and Major-General S. Woodburn Kirby (with C. T. Addis, J. F. Meiklejohn, M. R. Roberts, G. T. Wards and N. L. Desoer), *The War Against Japan*, vol. ii, London 1958, pp. 309 f.

free from worries at the front, could concentrate larger forces against the Chindits and inflict greater losses on them, and that without unduly suffering themselves since they would have time to repair the damage. The test could not show how profitable the tying-down operation would be: it could not demonstrate whether the Penetration Group would tie down the same number again or more or less and whether a larger group would achieve a higher or lower rate of return *against an enemy engaged at the same time at his front.* This proved unfortunate later on because the decision on the optimum size of the Second Expedition could not be based on experience and it still remains a matter of acute controversy.

However, the test could, and did, show that relatively large forces could infiltrate into the enemy's rear and that, with wireless communication, they could be supplied by air.[1]

This first Long Range Penetration Group—77 Brigade—of 3,000 all ranks consisted of a British battalion, a battalion of Gurkha Rifles, a battalion of Burma Rifles, the 142nd Commando Company—this was the designation given to the men of the Bush Warfare School—and a signalling and an RAF section. 142 Commando Company was distributed throughout the brigade, the signalling section was responsible for communications with brigade headquarters and within the column, while the RAF section had to keep wireless contact with the base and arrange supply drops. After intensive jungle training the brigade moved out in February 1943, in eight columns. Mules and oxen carried some of its supplies; the bulk was brought in successively by the RAF. The first part of the Chindit mission was speedily carried out; the force crossed the Chindwin and, in spite of enemy opposition, laid many successful ambushes and cut the Burma Railway line over seventy-five times, but shortly after crossing the Irrawaddy river General Wingate decided not to carry on with the second part of his assignment: air supply had become difficult, the endurance of the brigade had declined, and there was now every possibility that it would be cut off and wiped out. It split up; most groups walked back to the Chindwin while one group marched on into China. The Chindits had been on the expedition

[1] The success of the expedition also brought about a change in Japanese military thinking. Cf. hereto Major-General S. Woodburn Kirby, *op. cit.,* pp. 328 f.

for over ten weeks, they had infiltrated to a depth of two hundred miles, and most of them had walked about 1,000 miles.

General Wingate has claimed that the expedition arrested a Japanese threat to the north and occupied many times its own number of enemy troops. Others have pointed out that Wingate's losses were high—the force lost one third of its strength—and that the railway had been interrupted for only four weeks. In view of the limitations of the test, claims and counter-claims are equally irrelevant.

The force assembled for the Second Chindit Expedition, 3rd Indian Division, consisted of six brigades with 12,000 officers and men as its fighting component and 11,000 support troops; it was now officially referred to as 'Special Force'. Its theatre of operation was astride the Irrawaddy and the railway near Indaw; the Japanese supply lines to the northern front ran through here, and one of the supply lines to the central front touched the southern boundary. One brigade was subsequently withdrawn; four brigades would be flown into the area, beginning on March 5th; the one remaining brigade, starting a month earlier, would march in from the north and secure on its way General Stilwell's right flank.

Again, as it happened before, there was a grand plan for a concerted frontal and rear attack which was not carried out. This plan provided for a British corps to attack on the southern front, for another British corps to attack on the central front, and for the Chinese Expeditionary Force from Yunnan to attack in the north-east. None of these offensives was forthcoming. What remained from the original plan, apart from very limited operations elsewhere, was this:

General Stilwell's two American-trained Chinese divisions would continue to press against the Japanese northern front;[1] the right flank of this column would be secured by one of the Chindit brigades, the left flank by US Marauders, reinforced by Kachin guerrillas, and still further to the left by the force of Gurkhas and Kachin levies from Fort Hertz. General Stilwell's troops would occupy the enemy's attention at his front while the Chindits would do so in the rear. General Wingate's orders, issued by the Army and Air Force Commanders on February 4, 1944, were in the following order of importance: to help the advance of

[1] These Chinese forces were subsequently increased by stages to five divisions.

Stilwell's forces to Myitkyina by drawing off and disorganizing the enemy troops opposing them, to create a favourable situation for an advance by the Chinese Expeditionary Force, and to inflict the maximum confusion, damage and loss on the enemy forces in Northern Burma.

Since neither the Chinese Expeditionary Force would attack in the north-east nor the British corps on the central front, the efforts of the Second Chindit Expedition at inflicting 'the maximum confusion, damage and loss on the enemy' would have just as little strategic value as those of the First Expedition had had—unless, that is, the Chindits could remain in their general area of operation until the Allied offensive would take place—which they could then support—or alternatively the Japanese would launch an offensive—which they could then impede. As a matter of fact the Japanese did attack on the central front on March 8th, a few days after the first Chindits had arrived in their area. What is more, General Wingate had now devised the means for the Chindits to hold on, by basing their operations on a system of defended 'strongholds'.[1]

The Second Chindit Expedition was not only more ambitious than its predecessor on account of its greatly increased size but also with regard to the scope of its activities. There was to be no longer a series of small raids by lightly-armed men against communications, but a self-contained force, equipped with anti-aircraft and 25-pounder guns for the defence of their bases, would undertake large-scale operations. While the First Expedition had to be withdrawn after a time from its operational theatre, successive relief forces would now garrison defended bases for an unlimited period. The force and its equipment would be flown in by the American No 1 Air Commando, working in conjunction with the Anglo-American Troop Carrier Command. Supremacy in the air would be established by intensive attacks on enemy airfields, starting well in advance of the fly-in. Clearings, a hundred miles behind the lines and supposed not to be occupied by the enemy, would be selected as landing grounds for the troops. The first wave would secure the clearing, the second would build an airstrip, and then guns, jeeps and other equipment would be flown in. Troop Carrier Command would handle the bulk of the force's supplies while No. 1 Air Com-

[1] For a discussion of this concept see below Chapter 11.

mando would evacuate the casualties and, briefed from the ground, give close battle support.

In general the plan was at first adhered to. In a few nights the main party of two brigades was brought in by glider and aircraft; the Japanese were taken by surprise and strongholds were established. The road and railway communications to the northern front were cut, in the face of opposition. Chindit columns marched towards Mawlu, the Wuntho-Indaw and the Mandalay-Bhamo communications, and the brigade on foot was approaching Indaw. By the middle of March three brigades of 12,000 Chindits were within fifty miles of Indaw, cutting Japanese supply lines and destroying their dumps.

By April 12th five Chindit brigades were in action. On May 10th a Chinese Expeditionary Force of four divisions started its advance from Yunnan into Burma. General Wingate did not live to see these developments, but outwardly it appeared that the Chindits were now fighting under the exact conditions for which their leader had designed them. But, as will be seen, they never were.

Many of the leading figures, connected in some way or other with the Second Chindit Expedition, have committed their views on its campaign to paper. 'Despite the havoc they caused,' notes Sir Winston Churchill, 'the Japanese withdrew nothing from the Imphal (central) front and only one battalion from Stilwell's (northern front).'[1] But in spite of this disappointment, Sir Winston considered the expedition fully justified, and so do its former commanders. Admiral Earl Mountbatten, the Supreme Allied Commander South-East Asia, speaks in his post-war report to the Combined Chiefs of Staff of 'the considerable contribution which the force as a whole had made to the general campaign'.[2] The British Official History comes to a different conclusion. It stresses that the Chindits never managed to contain more than about two-fifths of their own strength.[3] It would therefore have been much better to have kept the three Chindit brigades, which

[1] *The Second World War*, vol. v, London 1952, p. 502.
[2] *Report to the Combined Chiefs of Staff by the Supreme Allied Commander South-East Asia 1943-45*, London 1951, p. 74. The Report points out that the contribution would have been greater, had it been made in co-ordination with normal formations.
[3] The Japanese assembled altogether about seventeen battalions against the Chindits.

had previously formed 70 British Division, on the central front where they would have made a decisive victory easier to attain, and limited the Chandits to two brigades. These two brigades, the Official History assumes, would have seriously interfered with the Japanese communication lines and contained as many of the enemy as the five Chindit brigades did.[1] The Official History thus supports the views which Field Marshal Sir Claude Auchinleck expressed at the time in his capacity as Commander-in-Chief; he wanted to restrict the Second Expedition to two or three brigades and preserve 70 Division for the front.[2] The Army Group Commander, General Giffard, has stated that 'the results achieved did not prove commensurate with the expenditure in manpower and material'.[3] Field Marshal Slim, the Army Commander, is, as we have seen, of the opinion that 70 Division would have been much better employed at the front than in the rear. Lord Alanbrooke, the Chief of the Imperial General Staff, had misgivings of his own: 'I am not a bit happy about the final plans (for the Burma campaign),' he noted in his diary on February 22, 1944; 'there is no definite objective and large forces of Long Range Penetration Groups are being launched for no definite purpose.'[4]

As long as the battles of the last war are fought out again by generals and historians, the Second Chindit Expedition will be a favourite subject for disputation. After all, the conception was so novel, the figure of General Wingate so controversial, the heroism and sacrifices so great, that agreement on the Chindits' achievement could only be expected if the results had been more conclusive, one way or the other. Yet although much has been said in the discussion about the commander and the force, its size and composition, its purpose and engagements, all too little consideration has been given to its battlefield, and we propose to concentrate on this aspect.

The main object of the Chindit mission was, as the reader will remember, to support General Stilwell's northern front. But when the Japanese advanced on the central front immediately after the Chindits' arrival in Central Burma, a new situation had

[1] Major-General S. Woodburn Kirby, op. cit., vol. iii, London 1961, p. 445.
[2] Christopher Sykes, op. cit., pp. 458 f.
[3] John Ehrman, Grand Strategy, vol. v, August 1943-September 1944. London 1956, p. 416.
[4] In Sir Arthur Bryant, Triumph in the West. Completing the War Diaries of Field Marshal Viscount Alanbrooke, London 1959, p. 152.

arisen. General Stilwell, naturally worried about his right flank, was thought at the time to have slowed down his own advance in the opposite direction. The Chinese Expeditionary Force had not yet moved from its base in Yunnan, and the concentration of the Chindits on the Japanese supply lines to the northern front and on the promotion of a favourable situation for an eventual advance by the Chinese seemed of doubtful value at a time when the Japanese were pressing hard on the central front.

General Wingate had his plans ready to meet the new situation. He wanted to change the Chindits' battlefield. In his 'Forecast of Possible Developments of Operation Thursday' (the code name for the Chindit Expedition), dated March 13, 1944, he envisaged that more brigades be installed south of Indaw in order to block all Japanese routes to Imphal on the central front.[1] On March 21st he discussed with Field Marshal Slim a revised plan for disrupting all the Japanese communication lines to the central front;[2] it was not acted upon. General Wingate showed his 'Forecast' or the revised plan to one of his subordinate commanders, Brigadier Calvert, who, in his own words, 'remonstrated and said that surely we were going beyond our object, which was to help get Stilwell along'. General Wingate 'smiled and said: We have got to help the 14th Army' (on the central front).[3]

In spite of General Wingate's representations the Chindits were kept to their previously allotted battlefield. However, the help they could give from this theatre of operation was restricted. The Japanese had three supply lines to the central front but actually used only two, the southern route from Mandalay-Shwebo-Kalewa and the northern route via Indaw-Homalin. The northern route was cut by Allied bombing and Chindit raids, and supplies had to be brought instead over the more difficult Chindwin river communication to Sittaung since the southern route was already congested. But this southern route was the most important one, *it was out of Chindit reach* and it remained untouched.[4]

---

[1] This plan had obvious shortcomings; cf. Major-General Kirby, *op cit.*, vol. iii, p. 185.
[2] *Ibidem*, pp. 208-9.
[3] Brigadier Michael Calvert, *Prisoners of Hope*, London 1952, p. 61.
[4] Cf. Appendix IV, 'The Japanese Testament', to Brigadier Calvert's book, *op. cit.*, pp. 288 f. This route is hardly ever mentioned in the literature. Cf. also p. 99 of Brigadier Calvert's book.

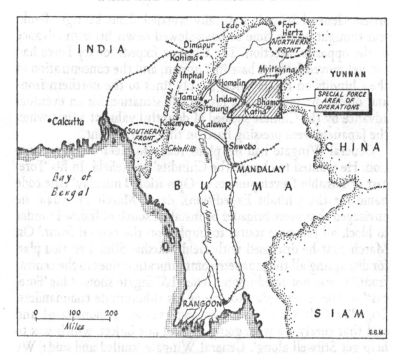

BURMA: BATTLEFIELDS MARCH 1944

It is therefore understandable why the Japanese did not denude their central front of troops in order to hunt down the
Chindit force: their supply position, although uncomfortable,
was not vitally affected.[1]

By contrast the Chindit operations in the rear of the northern
front made the position of the Japanese troops there precarious;
their supply routes were severely affected. But this front was of
only secondary importance to the Japanese because they intended
to reach the town of Dimapur in their advance on the central
front and there to cut the road and rail communications which
maintained General Stilwell's forces: they would thus be compelled to retreat.

Hence a battlefield had been chosen for the Chindits which

[1] The Japanese 53rd Division which fought the Chindits was to have reinforced the central front. Cf. Charles F. Romanus and Riley Sunderland,
Stilwell's Command Problems, Office of the Chief of Military History, Washington 1956, p. 222. Cf. also *Report to the Combined Chiefs of Staff*, op. cit., p. 60,
and Brigadier Calvert, op. cit., p. 303.

proved unsuitable for affecting operations on the vital central front and, well sited though it was for supporting General Stilwell's advance on the northern front, Chindit activities there could not worry the Japanese overmuch because they intended to beat Stilwell elsewhere, at his supply lines behind the central front.

For this reason the Japanese continued with their central front offensive as planned, for this reason the Japanese reaction against the Chindit threat was relatively mild, the Chindits tied down only 8,000 or 9,000 of the enemy, and the enemy did not denude his fronts to engage the Chindits: brilliantly as they fought, they fought in the wrong place.

Yet the supreme importance of the central front had never been out of Wingate's mind. On August 10, 1943, on his way to the Quebec Conference, he had completed a memorandum for the British Joint Planning Staff and he spoke there of a likely Japanese offensive on the Assam front.[1] What is more, he proposed in this memorandum that one of the three Long Range Penetration Groups, whose formation he suggested, should cut communications leading to the northern front, while the second Group should operate from the Chin Hills against the Kalewa-Kalemyo communications and the third from north of Tamu against the Shwebo-Indaw-Myitkyina railway. These operations would have effectively cut all communications to the central front. Again, on January 16, 1944, he sent an appreciation to Lord Mountbatten in which he submitted 'cogent evidence that the Japanese move forward was the preparatory stage of an offensive against Assam. . . . He warned that the offensive would be strong and damaging'.[2] However, the northern battlefield had been assigned to General Wingate and his Chindits as a sequel to the Quebec Conference.

The Americans felt that Japan could not be defeated without Chinese help and that this help would not be forthcoming unless land communications with China could be reopened. Failing this, and the delivery of massive Allied supplies over the land route, China might not be able to stay in the war. The task of reopening the land route was assigned to General Stilwell; his Ledo Road builders would construct the land link with China.

[1] Christopher Sykes, op. cit., pp. 452-3.
[2] Ibid., p. 495.

On the way to the Quebec Conference the British Chiefs of Staff 'got Wingate to come in and discussed what could be done with the Long Range Penetration organization, and finally arrived at a line of action with which to take on the American Chiefs of Staff and prove to them that we are in no way neglecting the operations in Burma'.[1] And so it was agreed at Quebec that the main effort in Burma should have the object of 'establishing land communications with China and improving and securing the air route'. Both targets had a close connection with the northern front: a considerable part of the Ledo Road would be on the axis of General Stilwell's advance, and Myitkyina, the only all-weather aerodrome in Northern Burma and on the direct route to China, was one of his major objectives. It was also approved at Quebec that the Chindits should capture the Katha-Indaw area.[2] While they could from there interfere with most communications to the northern front and one supply line to the central front, it was left undecided which front should be their primary target.

However, the rear of the northern front soon became their main, and subsequently their sole, area of operation. In his report to the Combined Chiefs of Staff, the Supreme Allied Commander, Lord Mountbatten, has stated: 'It was considered that (General Stilwell's) advance would be possible only if the main Japanese forces were contained elsewhere, and if we could cut the lines of communication of 18 Japanese Division, opposing Lieut.-General Stilwell's forces. It was consequently decided that Major-General Wingate's Special Force should at the appropriate moment be brought in to cut the enemy rail and road communications to his northern forces, while the main Japanese forces were to be contained by 4 Corps on the central front.'[3] By November 1943, South-East Asia Command had drafted the following plan for 1944:

'(a)—(c) . . .

'(d) An advance by Stilwell's three divisions on the northern front, supplemented by

[1] Lord Alanbrooke, Diary entry of August 8, 1943, in Sir Arthur Bryant, *The Turn of the Tide, op. cit.,* p. 694.
[2] Cf. 'Despatch by General Sir George J. Giffard on Operations in Burma and North-East India from November 16, 1943, to June 22, 1944', *Supplement to The London Gazette,* March 13, 1951, No. 39171, p. 1352.
[3] *Op. cit.,* p. 34.

'(e) an advance by the Chinese Expeditionary Corps

'(f) operations in support of (d) and (e) by Wingate's Long Range Penetration Groups.'[1]

This plan was approved by the Combined Chiefs of Staff[2] and, as we have seen, orders to this effect were given to General Wingate on February 4, 1944. When in March 1944, just before General Wingate's death, the battle at the central front was at its most critical stages, Field Marshal Slim decided against diverting the Chindits to the central front and ordered them to give, as hitherto, all possible assistance to General Stilwell as their main task; the Supreme Allied Commander and the Army Group Commander fully agreed with this decision.[3] On April 9th the Supreme Allied Commander, together with Field Marshal Slim and Wingate's successor, General Lentaigne, decided that the sole task of the Chindits was from now on to assist General Stilwell's advance on the northern front.[4]

Field Marshal Slim has later admitted, with that magnanimity typical of him, that his decision was mistaken. 'The second and greater problem was,' he writes, 'whether I should change Wingate's main object from helping Stilwell to helping 4 Corps, now hard pressed about Imphal. The alteration had obvious advantages, as it would use the Special Force in direct tactical co-ordination with the main battle. . . . However, I decided to adhere to my original plan, and the Special Force continued to direct its efforts to the north rather than to the west. In this I think I was wrong. Imphal was the decisive battle; it was there only that vital injury could be inflicted on the Japanese Army, and I should have concentrated all available forces to that end. I fear I . . . persisted in a plan which should have been changed.'[5]

But the outcome was not only that with Chindit help victory would have been easier to attain at the central front, but also— and this point needs emphasizing—that they were relegated to a

---

[1] *Ibidem*, p. 27, and John Ehrman, *op. cit.*, p. 153.
[2] Report to the Combined Chiefs of Staff, *op. cit.*, p. 28.
[3] *Ibid.*, p. 60.
[4] Major-General Kirby, vol. iii, *op. cit.*, p. 281. Six days before, the Jorhat Conference, at which General Stilwell was present, had decided to have two Chindit brigades operate against the second of the three Japanese supply lines, if that was feasible; it was, however, discovered in time that this was the disused line. Cf. Major-General Kirby, vol. iii, *op. cit.*, pp. 247 and 281.
[5] Field Marshal Sir William Slim, *Defeat Into Victory*, *op. cit.*, p. 268.

battlefield where the results of their operations could not possibly prove commensurate with the effort.

The verdict on the Second Chindit Expedition must then be this:

On the chosen battleground the Chindits achieved all that was possible. But the battleground was ill-chosen, and success on a strategic level was therefore denied to them.

Little need be said about the Chindit campaign after General Wingate's death on March 24th. Indaw West airfield was taken by the Chindits after a prolonged struggle. In view of the battle on the central front, no relief for the Chindits was possible. It was thought undesirable to let them stay through the monsoon period and it was also held that the air-strips would become untenable.[1] One brigade was flown out at the beginning of May, but the others stayed on and came under General Stilwell's control on May 17th. From then on the Chindits fought in the forward area. At the end of May a Chindit brigade assaulted the fortified town of Mogaung, one of the two main objectives of General Stilwell, and, assisted by Chinese troops, captured it at the end of June. General Wingate's ideas had long been abandoned, and his troops had not been equipped to fight large-scale operations against well-organized forces. The Chindit casualty list reads: 1,500 killed, 2,500 wounded, 7,000 sick; most of these casualties were suffered during the last stage.

The Chindits' special task was to support simultaneous or immediately subsequent Army operations on the enemy front by operations in the rear, aimed at drawing off, binding and disorganizing enemy forces. Whether this task could best be fulfilled by harassing and evading the enemy, or by fighting him, will be discussed in Chapter 11. The point is controversial; in General Wingate's view the Long Range Penetration Groups must fight.[2]

And what are the lessons of the Second Chindit Expedition?

1. Allied air superiority, the geographical conditions of the country, and the disposition of the Japanese troops thinly spread

---

[1] For a criticism of this reasoning, cf. Lt.-Colonel P. W. Mead, 'The Chindit Operations of 1944', *Royal United Service Institution Journal* 1955, vol. 100, pp. 258 f.
[2] General Wingate's Memorandum, August 1943, written during the Quebec Conference and quoted in Christopher Sykes, *op. cit.*, p. 460.

on the ground[1] allowed fairly large Special Forces to land un-opposed. Lack of communications made it possible to deprive the enemy of supplies by cutting a relatively small number of road, rail and river supply lines.

2. A Special Force must not be employed independently but only in order to support the frontal attack of its own troops or impede a frontal attack by the enemy, and

3. The battlefield of the Special Force must be behind the most *sensitive* enemy front—*seen with the enemy's eyes*—and so located that the enemy supply lines—and that means all of them —can be cut and kept cut.

Under such conditions the Special Force will tie down more than its own numbers, especially if its own air superiority pre-vents large-scale enemy supply drops to his front-line troops.[2]

Air operations in support of the Special Force were never seriously affected by Japanese interference. Their aircraft were mostly operating over the main battle front and their airfields and railways had been subjected to frequent Allied air attack even before the Chindits had been flown in. Japanese anti-aircraft guns made themselves more felt but they usually did only minor damage. The Allied air supply system worked on the whole smoothly. Since each brigade was composed of eight columns,

[1] In 1943 the Japanese had five divisions of altogether 135,000 men in Burma; by January 1944 their forces were eight divisions and one brigade, some 200,000 men altogether.

[2] Cf. for Chindit literature in addition to the sources already mentioned: Brigadier Sir Bernard Fergusson: *Beyond the Chindwin*, London 1945, *The Wild Green Earth*, London 1946, *The Black Watch and the King's Enemies*, London 1950, and 'Behind the Enemy Lines in Burma' (lecture), *Royal United Service Institution Journal* 91, Aug. 1946, pp. 347 f. Lowell Thomas, *Back to Mandalay*, New York 1951; Philip Stibbe, *Return Via Rangoon*, London 1947; Roy McKelvie, *The War in Burma*, London 1948; John Connell, *Auchinleck, A Biography of Field Marshal Sir Claude Auchinleck*, London 1959; John Howard Denny, *Chindit Indiscretion*, London 1956; and W. G. Burchett, *Wingate's Phantom Army*, Bombay 1944.

Also on the air aspect: General H. H. Arnold, 'The Aerial Invasion of Burma', *National Geographic Magazine* 86, Aug. 1944, pp. 129 f.; Dr Joe G. Taylor, *Air Supply in the Burma Campaign*, USAF Historical Division, Study No. 75, Research Studies Institute, Air University; Colonel T. F. Van Natta, 'Airdrop Supply', *Infantry Journal* 62, May 1948, pp. 20 f.; J. R. L. Rumsey, 'Air Supply in Burma', *Army Quarterly* 1947, No. 55 (October), pp. 33 f., and 'Despatch by Air Chief Marshal Sir Richard Peirse on Air Operations in South-East Asia, November 16, 1943, to May 31, 1944', *Supplement to The London Gazette* of March 13, 1951, No. 39173.

supplies were requested on a column basis, each column sending its requests to brigade rear headquarters and indicating the dropping zone. Supplies were usually flown in by night. We have mentioned before how the air missions were divided up between No. 1 Air Commando Group and Troop Carrier Command; a Transport Squadron was also assigned to these operations. Whether a 'special' air force—in the form of No. 1 Air Commando—should have been allocated to assist Special Force is a matter of controversy. No. 1 Air Commando was a highly valuable token of American support for General Wingate's operations at a time when the pilots and aircraft could hardly have been found in the theatre, but as a rule conventional air forces and their organization are well fitted to look after all air requirements of a Special Force.

While the Chindits were a Long Range Penetration Group, Merrill's Marauders—5307th Composite Unit (Provisional) in the American order of battle and Galahad in the official code—were used as a Medium Range Penetration Group. They had been trained with the Chindits in India and then came under General Stilwell's command on the northern front. Their task was not to harass the enemy, cut communications far behind the line and destroy dumps, but to fight as infantry combat teams. By fighting behind the enemy lines they had to help the main force to gain ground. While this main—Chinese—force would press on in a more or less straight line, the Marauders would carry out wide outflanking movements to the east and set up roadblocks behind the Japanese lines on the axis of the Chinese advance. The Marauders' operations were therefore closely co-ordinated with those of the main force. Their last operation against Myitkyina did not conform to the pattern: reinforced by Kachin guerrillas and Chinese troops, they swiftly advanced and, without waiting for the arrival of the main force, took the airfield by surprise. By then the Marauders were physically exhausted and the Japanese managed to hold on to the town; it was finally captured, with the Marauders assisting, two and a half months later. According to official figures the force of 3,000 Marauders suffered 424 battle casualties and 1,970 disease casualties. They were disbanded in August 1944.

During their operations the Marauders were supplied by a Troop Carrier Squadron; they did not have a special air component as did the Chindits.[1]

The special task of the Marauders was closer to that of the Rangers than to that of the Chindits. The Americans had created this unit during the Quebec Conference because they were impressed by what they heard there from General Wingate about the success of the First Chindit Expedition and the potentialities of Long Range Penetration Groups in future operations. But since the Marauders were not used as a Long Range Penetration Group, they should not have been formed as a Special Force at all: the existence of Special Forces of this type can create the myth that outflanking movements can be carried out only with their help. This would be a dangerous trend and one that must be discouraged. If the Chinese troops under General Stilwell needed stiffening, regular troops should have done the job.

The essential difference between Commando, Ranger and Brandenburg operations on the one hand, and Marauder missions on the other, is this: the first seize key points in the rear, the latter outflank the enemy. But outflanking moves have always been and must remain a task for regular forces. And while the dividing line was perhaps not always observed in the last war by forces of the first type, it should be strictly adhered to in the future. The Chindits had a special task; the Marauders, who fought with equal valour, had not.

But did the Chindits' special task require a Special Force to carry it out? It certainly did at the time, because there was no trained regular—or irregular—force to execute it. And what of the future? Special Forces are suspect if they are very small —because there seems little need for them—or very large— because they are then a private Army with a capital A. Yet since guerrilla warfare is their speciality, it will remain a Special Force mission because guerrilla warfare is not within the scope of regular warfare, at least not at present. That it should be is obvious, if only because it enables regular troops overrun by the enemy to hold out and survive in guerrilla fashion against odds.

[1] For Marauder literature, cf. Historical Division, US War Department, *Merrill's Marauders (February-May 1944)*, Washington 1945; Charlton Ogburn, *The Marauders*, New York 1956; Charles F. Romanus and R. Sunderland, *Stilwell's Command Problems*, US Army in World War II, Office of the Chief of Military History, Washington, 1956; *The Stilwell Papers*, ed. by Theodore H. White, London 1949; Lt.-Colonel W. L. Osborne, 'Shaduzup', *Infantry Journal* 66, April 1950, pp. 13 f.

During and after World War II, Britain and America have had so much experience with guerrillas that the value of troops trained to fight like guerrillas has become obvious. The odds are that regular troops will do the job and Special Forces of the Chindit type will no longer be required in future.

In addition to the Chindit Long Range Penetration Groups and the Marauder Medium Range Penetration Group, a Short Range Penetration Group also operated in the Burma theatre; this was the one Chindit brigade which had been withdrawn from the Chindits and diverted to the Kohima battle. It was sent into the Japanese rear with the mission to stop enemy infiltration towards the railway and cut enemy communication lines west of the Chindwin. It was used in a Commando role.

Other Special Forces in Burma were the Special Boat Section and the Small Operational Group which we have mentioned before; both were primarily concerned with collecting Intelligence. There was finally 3 Commando Brigade. The Commandos carried out a series of small operations along the west coast, they did duty in the line, and very largely due to them the decisive battle of the Arakan campaign, the battle of Kangaw, was won. In that battle they landed on the beaches near Myebon village, took several small hills with tank support, seized a village, then crossed from the peninsular to the mainland, captured Hill 170, a key position in the advance on Kangaw, and held the hill in the face of fierce counter-attacks until the enemy finally withdrew.[1] Kangaw itself was taken by regular troops who had approached overland. In this, their last battle in the Far East, the Commandos had been engaged in a typical Commando role.

---

[1] For a description of this action, cf. Hilary St George Saunders, *op. cit.*, pp. 342 f.

CHAPTER 5

TASKS OF SPECIAL FORCES WITH
THE PARTISANS

Special Forces worked in the last war with partisans on a number of occasions. The following review takes its examples mainly from two theatres of war, Burma and France, which cover between them most forms of co-operation, and limits itself to British and American experience. The Soviets and Japanese did not have Special Forces with partisans, the Italians had no partisans on their side, and while the Germans tried to stimulate partisan support with the help of Special Forces—the Brandenburgers and Skorzeny's formation—their activities are of little interest; as we have seen, success was denied to them.

The British and Americans co-operated with partisans through various agencies. Prominent among them were the British Special Operations Executive (SOE) and the American Office of Strategic Services (OSS). It is, however, a matter of some doubt whether these agencies were Special Forces themselves. At first glance SOE at least looks like one; it was set up independently from the military hierarchy as a department of the Ministry of Economic Warfare. It can also be argued that in its paramilitary operations OSS—an Intelligence agency—had the character of a Special Force. One of the functions of both organizations was to raise and keep up the spirit of resistance. They supplied explosives, weapons and radios to the partisans, they built up radio communications, provided training facilities for resistance leaders and contact men,[1] and dispatched leaders and agents as well as military missions to partisan groups. But the officers sent to them can hardly be described as a Special Force; the force were not the individual officers but the guerrillas, and guerrillas are by definition not a Special Force either.

SOE and OSS also sent operational groups of four officers and

[1] Cf. 'Statement by UK Representatives', Brigadier-General Berry, in *European Resistance Movements 1939-45*, Oxford 1960, p. 350.

95

thirty men each into enemy occupied areas, and these groups had all the appearance of a Special Force. Yet since there were only eleven such groups in existence and all were employed in France, Special Force activities cannot be held to have been a prominent element in SOE and OSS work.

SOE and OSS co-operation with partisans in the field will nevertheless be reviewed in this chapter, if only because the British SAS and the new American Special Force will undoubtedly consider some of these activities as precepts for their own future operations. Furthermore, there is strong evidence that SOE and OSS themselves regarded their partisan activities as those of a Special Force; as will be seen, they directed some of them from a 'Special Force HQ', and SOE called certain of its liaison teams with the Army 'Special Force' detachments. We shall also discuss here some aspects of the work of Army teams with partisans. The Army regarded these teams as Special Forces;[1] their missions were, after all, outside the normal scope of regular warfare.

SOE operated in France, Norway, Denmark, Holland, Belgium, Greece, Yugoslavia, Albania, Italy, Poland, Czechoslovakia, Borneo, Malaya, Indo-China, Siam and Burma. It encouraged the peoples in the enemy-occupied countries to carry out economic and military sabotage, to raid on a small scale, to supply Intelligence and to form secret forces; the tasks of the latter were to destroy lines of communication, depots and repair shops at the opportune moment.[2] OSS was originally only represented in countries which were to become American theatres of war, but it subsequently extended its activities. Its aims were similar to those of SOE.

Political considerations had some influence on the direction of partisan warfare in the last war. There were divergencies between East and West, between Britain and America, and between communist and non-communist partisan movements.[3] In North Africa, where General de Gaulle's influence over the

---

[1] Cf., for instance, Geraldine Peacock, The Life of a Jungle Wallah, Ilfracombe, n.d., pp. 64 and 68.

[2] Cf. Major-General Sir Colin Gubbins, 'Resistance Movements in the War' (Lecture), Royal United Service Institution Journal 1948, vol. 93, pp. 210 f., and 'Statement by UK Representatives', loc. cit., pp. 350-1.

[3] Cf. for particulars Otto Heilbrunn, Partisan Warfare, op. cit., pp. 173 f. On the whole the Allies subordinated political considerations to military, but the same cannot be said for some of the partisan movements.

population was doubted by the Americans, political issues were considered predominant, and the OSS personnel who, prior to the Anglo-American landings, built up the local French underground groups, came under the direction of the State Department.[1] For paramilitary operations SOE was placed under the Chiefs of Staff, and when a Supreme Commander for a theatre had been appointed, both SOE and OSS came under his operational control. When operations in a theatre began, the SOE activities were co-ordinated with those of the troops by SOE Special Force detachments at Army Group and Army Headquarters.[2]

A tighter control was adopted before the invasion of France. SOE was placed under General Eisenhower in October 1943 and OSS in the following month. In March 1944 these two agencies were grouped together in Special Force Headquarters. This headquarters also took control of the SAS which co-operated with the Maquis, and so the three British and American organizations which worked with partisans in north Europe were brought together in one headquarters.[3]

In Burma, the table of organization presented a less tidy picture. The British Army, SOE, OSS and the Chindits recruited partisans there, and the competition led to grotesque situations. We have noted in Chapter 3 Field Marshal Slim's complaint about some of these organizations which on occasions acted in close proximity to the troops without the knowledge of the commander in the field. General Stilwell had equally good reasons for criticism; 'at that time', the historian of the Marauders' campaign remarks, 'the United States Army and the Office of Strategic Services were fighting independent wars in Burma'.[4]

In 1942 OSS set up in Assam and Burma a formation called Detachment 101. A number of Burmese and Kachins were trained by US officers in Intelligence and Counter-Intelligence work and in the handling of weapons and explosives, and officers and agents were then flown into north Burma behind the

[1] Cf. The Memoirs of Cordell Hull, vol ii, London 1948, p. 1185.
[2] Cf. Major-General Sir Colin Gubbins, loc. cit., p. 212.
[3] Cf. Forrest C. Pogue, The Supreme Command, United States Army in World War II, The European Theatre of Operations, Washington 1954, p. 152 f. The link with General de Gaulle's French Forces of the Interior was provided by the appointment of General Koenig to General Eisenhower's headquarters.
[4] Charlton Ogburn, The Marauders, op. cit., p. 139.

Japanese lines, where they organized, trained, equipped and led several hundred Kachin guerrillas; these operated in small parties against Japanese lines of communication and minor enemy forces; they also collected intelligence. It was hoped to expand these Kachin guerrillas into a force of 10,000.[1]

One of their parties operated in an area into which the Marauders had advanced. It fought against the same Japanese units as the Marauders. It had collected valuable intelligence. The Marauders were never shown this information; they had not even been notified of the presence of this party; they did not even know of its existence.[2]

The first attempts to start a guerrilla organization in Burma had been made by the British early in 1942 in the Shan States and then extended to the Karen country of north Tenasserim.[3] Recruiting for these and other forces was facilitated because when the 1st Burma Division retreated in the same year beyond the Chindwin, it sent home most of its Kachin, Chin and Karen elements with orders to join any organization the British would form to fight the Japanese, and these men provided the backbone for the resistance movement.[4] Contacts and men were therefore available among the loyal hill tribes when the call came later on.

Among the more important guerrilla forces in Burma were the following: on the northern front there operated in the Japanese rear the before-mentioned OSS-recruited Kachins, the northern (Kachin) Levies raised by the British Army, Dahforce which had come into the theatre with the Second Chindit Expedition and was partly composed of Kachins, and a force of Kachin and Chinese guerrillas organized by an SOE officer. Also behind the northern front was part of V Force, with Nagas, Kukis and other tribes raised by the British Army. V Force operated also behind the Japanese central and southern fronts, and Force 136, which

[1] Charles F. Romanus and Riley Sunderland, *Stilwell's Command Problems*, op. cit., pp. 36 f.
[2] The situation in other parts of the world was not always better. Lt.-General Sir John W. Hackett, 'The Employment of Special Forces' (Lecture), *Royal United Service Institution Journal* 1952, vol. 97, p. 40, states that in 1944-45 he knew of at least six organizations in Holland working in parallel without apparently any co-operation at the top.
[3] 'Report by Lt.-General T. J. Hutton on Operations in Burma from December 27, 1941, to March 5, 1942', *Supplement to The London Gazette* of March 5, 1948, p. 10.
[4] Field Marshal Viscount Slim, *op cit.*, p. 113.

had Burmese and other indigenous elements, fought by the Upper Chindwin and the Manipur-Burma border. There were the Patriotic Burma Forces which went over to the British in March 1945. Also west of the Chindwin were Chin Levies,[1] and in the south and raised by the British Army, especially P Force 136, there were Karen guerrillas. Finally, the Bush Warfare School in Maymyo, under Brigadier Calvert, carried out guerrilla raids in Burma until the middle of 1942. The forces operating in the north eventually came all under General Stilwell's control, while Field Marshal Slim took effective steps for the co-ordination or control of the forces in the other areas.[2]

The functions of these forces varied. They were:

1. Intelligence and small raids—carried out by V force.

2. Guide and scout duties—carried out mostly by Nagas and Kachins.

3. Guerrilla operations, including Intelligence, carried out by the other forces.

All except the Patriotic Burma Forces were raised, trained, led and equipped by British and American officers.

Varied methods were adopted for raising these forces. The Chin Levies, led by British officers, were stiffened from the start by the presence of the Chin Hills Battalion which was part of the Burma Army and had stayed behind when Burma was evacuated by the British. Before Dahforce set out with the Second Chindit Expedition in order to raise Kachin tribes, its leader, Captain Herring, had already ascertained the possibilities; he had gone with the First Chindit Expedition to the Kachin Hills on reconnaissance and came to the conclusion that a Kachin rising could be organized. In his own unit was a body of Kachins in support of his mission, and he also hoped to make contact with the SOE officer who was already working with Kachin and Chinese guerrillas in the Nahpaw area.[3] When Brigadier Felix-Williams was given

[1] Their story is told in the fascinating book, The Jungle in Arms, by Lt.-Colonel Balfour Oatts, London 1962.

[2] General Stilwell, in his capacity as Chief of Staff, HQ of the Supreme Command of the Allied Forces, China War Theatre, had also British-trained Chinese guerrilla units under his control. The British, Australian and Indian personnel, sent for this purpose as 204 Mission to China, had received its own training in the Bush Warfare School. Cf. Brigadier Michael Calvert, op. cit., p. 11; William Noonan, The Surprising Battalion, Sydney 1945; and Charles F. Romanus and Riley Sunderland, Stilwell's Mission to China, US Army in World War II, Washington 1953, p. 120.

[3] Cf. Major-General Kirby, op. cit., vol. iii, p. 205.

orders to organize V Force along the India-Burma border, he obtained Field Marshal Wavell's permission to commission his own officers, and he drew for this purpose on men who had worked in the various districts and were known to the population: planters, political officers and members of the Burma Forest Service.[1] Before the arrival of two officers, who were to raise the northern (Kachin) Levies, leaflets were dropped in the Kachin areas informing the people that the British would be coming soon. But no preparations had been made when ten British officers, a number of NCOs and eighty highly-trained veterans, most of them of P Force 136, were dropped blind into the Karen Hills in 1945. Yet, helped by the turn of the tide in Burma, they were successful: Colonel Peacock, who commanded P Force, won the immediate support of the local headmen and elders and rallied 600 Karens within a week.[2] The two officers who raised the northern (Kachin) Levies at a more difficult time were almost equally successful: within an hour of their arrival they had recruited twenty Kachins and there were 500 recruits within two months.[3] V Force, raised at the height of British misfortune in Burma, in April 1942, became operational in four weeks.

The Kachin and Karen guerrillas consisted of mobile and static levies. Training began at once with whatever arms were available; sooner or later more modern arms and equipment were supplied by air. Most forces seem to have been issued with wireless receivers and transmitters, V Force in particular for the transmission of intelligence and P Force for directing air strikes from the ground. Bases were selected in inaccessible areas. The guerrillas ambushed, skirmished, set up road blocks, mined and carried out demolitions. Especially the activities of the Karen guerrillas were closely co-ordinated with Army requirements. In the race for Toungoo they held up the Japanese forces for several days and as a result the British Army got there first.[4] In one area they killed almost 3,000 Japanese for the loss of thirty-four levies.[5]

[1] Cf. 'The Story of "V" Force'. *Indian Army Review*, vol. 2, No. 12, October 1946, pp. 14 f.
[2] Cf. Geraldine Peacock, *op. cit.*, pp. 20 and 77. Cf. also Captain Duncan Guthrie, *Jungle Diary*, London 1946.
[3] Major Ian Fellowes-Gordon, *Amiable Assassins*, London 1957, pp. 12 and 15.
[4] Field Marshal Slim, *op. cit.*, pp. 499 f.; Geraldine Peacock, *op. cit.*, p. 21.
[5] Report by Lieut.-Colonel Peacock, reprinted in Geraldine Peacock, *op. cit.*, p. 123.

Guerrillas also assisted some of the Special Forces. Kachin raiders were attached to the Marauders, and V Force guided the Chindits and members of the Special Boat Section, whom it also supplied with Intelligence. Altogether 16,000 guerrillas are supposed to have operated at one period in Burma.[1] But no figures are available on the number of Japanese troops which they tied down.

Two facts stand out: none of the guerrilla forces in Burma would have been raised had it not been for the British and American efforts,[2] and all guerrillas willingly accepted British and American officers as their commanders.

But where guerrilla forces are already in existence or foreign leadership is resented, different forms of co-operation may or must be adopted. Mihailovitch, Tito and others would never have handed over command, and many of their officers and men would not have followed foreign leaders. In such cases the foreign countries can:

1. Send a military mission to an already existing movement. The success of such missions depends on the skill of their commanders and the willingness of the indigenous guerrilla leaders to conform to the overall strategic plan. In the last war the partisans were often amenable to Allied requests in order to qualify for the supply of arms and equipment.

2. Try to raise a separate guerrilla movement under its own control.

3. Send Special Forces into partisan areas to bolster up partisan morale.

Britain adopted the first method towards Yugoslavia, Albania and Greece, and the second and third towards France.

In France, Britain built up her own partisan organization through SOE which, together with OSS, despatched agents to work with the partisans. SOE never managed to establish its leadership over all the partisan groups. Prior to the invasion of France, SOE and General de Gaulle operated separately and the General had by far the larger following. SOE restricted itself originally to providing the French Resistance with arms and ammunition. In the first six months of 1944 Britain and the US greatly increased their supplies to the Resistance and SOE intensi-

[1] 'Statement by UK Representatives', loc. cit., p. 354.
[2] With the exception of the Patriotic Burma Forces.

fied its efforts to establish direct leadership, drawing for this purpose on its agents in the centre and south of France and a small body of officers despatched from Britain. SOE tried to ensure in this way that the activities of the secret army in France would conform to the requirements of the Allies.[1]

The SAS functioned in France in a different role. Its teams were fighting formations. They did not as a rule build up partisan detachments but sometimes co-operated with existing ones. SAS missions would first make contact with the local Maquis and then prepare bases for one or more SAS parties to be dropped later. They stiffened the Resistance by their presence and activities. In return, the partisans would advise them about useful targets and the enemy's whereabouts. SAS teams and partisan detachments co-ordinated their ambush, sabotage and raiding activities, although the co-ordination was usually loose. They supported each other though not necessarily for all operations. If the partisan leadership was not good enough the SAS would some-times take general charge of an operation, but SAS and partisans always kept their separate identities. The period of co-operation was limited; the SAS moved on when its mission was accomplished or a change of base advisable. The SAS parties were strong enough to carry out operations without partisan support and they frequently worked independently from partisans.[2]

The French component of the SAS was charged with a specialized task in France. On D+1, SAS troops of the French 4th Parachute Battalion were dropped into Brittany, where they built up a resistance movement of 30,000 men; when the Allies advanced they ambushed the enemy, attacked isolated groups and guarded bridges against destruction; they also supplied Intelligence.[3]

---

[1] John Ehrman, Grand Strategy, vol. v, op. cit., p. 325; Forrest C. Pogue, The Supreme Command, op. cit., pp. 152 f. From D-day on, the previously-mentioned American Operational Groups (OG) were flown in and Intelligence and liaison teams (Jedburghs)—usually of three, including a wireless operator; one of the three was French, the others were British or American—were dropped. The OGs, after having performed some specified combat mission, and the Jedburgh teams were to co-operate with the higher echelons of the French Forces of the Interior.

[2] On SAS missions with the Maquis, cf. Roy Farran, Winged Dagger, London 1948, pp. 226 f., and D. I. Harrison, These Men Are Dangerous, op. cit., pp. 134 f., 195 f.

[3] Forrest C. Pogue, The Supreme Command, op. cit., p. 238.

The Special Force, formed in the United States after the war, has some characteristics in common with the SAS. Like the SAS it infiltrates deeply into enemy occupied country, and like the SAS it is trained to land from submarines and by parachute. Both are designed for long-term operations and both depend for this purpose on air supplies. Both carry out reconnaissance, and attack on special targets—launching sites, atomic installations and so on—is a primary mission of the SAS and a secondary one of Special Force. But there the similarity ends.

The SAS parties, up to fifty strong and provided with jeeps, can carry out independent missions and frequently did so, while the Special Force teams, composed as a rule of twelve members,[1] will usually work with other groups, viz. anti-partisans in a cold war and partisans in a hot war.

SAS parties can organize a partisan movement but they will do so only in exceptional circumstances, as in Brittany when the French component of the SAS was engaged on French soil; however, their more normal function is to work with existing partisan groups. The Special Force, on the other hand, is designed to form, organize and train guerrilla units. It is meant to provide the control of the partisan group. The SAS will do so only where the quality of the guerrilla command makes it necessary. The SAS might move on to another area and leave the partisans behind, the Special Force seems required to stay with the partisan detachment. Different from the SAS the Special Force is also trained in psychological operations and the study of languages is required.

The two officers and senior NCOs of each Special Force party will act as leaders and instructors of their partisan detachment and be in charge of Intelligence. The party is organized in five teams of two specialists in weapons, demolition, operations and Intelligence, communications and care of casualties. All team members receive cross-training.[2]

Special Force parties, designed to command and staff a partisan detachment, are precluded from acting as advisers, observers or

[1] In addition to these—normal—detachments Special Force has also two larger types of units which may take over a guerrilla area from a twelve-man detachment if the mission warrants it.

[2] Cf. Lt.-General Barksdale Hamlett, 'Special Forces: Training for Peace and War', *Army Information Digest*, June 1961, pp. 2 f., and Brigadier-General William P. Yarborough, loc. cit., pp. 42 f.

liaison officers or from merely providing an occasional stiffening to guerrilla forces, as the SAS did in France and Italy.[1] The activation of the Special Force, which intentionally renounces this flexibility, reflects the belief that the conduct of partisan warfare, at least in certain areas, is a full-time Army job and that the Army can provide the best leaders. Indeed, in some aspects the Special Force has more in common with the Army-inspired Special Forces in Burma than with the SAS.

Before a Special Force of this type can be dropped into enemy-occupied country, it must be established that:

(1) the selected area lends itself to guerrilla warfare. The last war provided a great number of examples in Europe and Asia;

(2) the population is friendly. No guerrilla force can operate for any length of time among a hostile population unless it can be kept in check by terror—a means of which the Special Force would not avail itself;

(3) the population is willing to fight as guerrillas under foreign leadership;

(4) capable and reliable indigenous leadership with a potentially greater appeal to the population is not available;

(5) existing guerrilla movements will not be roused into hostility because one movement is foreign led and equipped or consists of members of a faction disowned by the majority of its countrymen;

(6) the movement, once created, can be kept under control, particularly so that it is willing to fight the common enemy rather than rival movements,[2] as happened in the last war in Greece, Poland, Albania and Yugoslavia, and does not use partisan warfare as a means to gain control of the country.

Unless reliable contacts are available it therefore seems often warranted to investigate the situation in the field first before the Special Force party is despatched, and this investigation can as a rule be better carried out by agents than by—uniformed— members of the Special Force. The Special Force parties should start recruiting only when there is a prospect for an early and continuous employment of the detachment in the field; no guerrilla

[1] Cf. for Italy Major Roy Farran, *Operation Tombola*, London 1960, throughout.
[2] On the danger of the political type of guerrilla warfare cf. in particular Major J. G. Sloman, 'Guerrilla Warfare', *Military Review*, July 1956, p. 76, reprinted there from the article first published in the *Australian Army Journal* of September 1954.

movement can afford to remain inactive for long; by so doing it loses its morale. Recruits must be screened in order to avoid penetration of the movement by the enemy. Liaison with other partisan movements should be established at the earliest possible moment.

It is obvious that the Special Force is not meant to replace OSS, just as the SAS does not replace SOE. OSS and SOE will still be required to establish over-all control over the various guerrilla forces in a country, to guide movements outside the present or future theatre of operations, to train agents, to send military missions, agents and wireless operators to movements led by indigenous leaders, to supply arms and equipment, to receive Intelligence reports and, in the case of SOE, to provide permanent leadership to partisan detachments where required.

Special Forces with guerrilla detachments will, as a rule, increase the operational effectiveness of the guerrillas—although the Special Forces uniform may sometimes give the guerrillas away—and the guerrillas can count on priority for supplies and care of their wounded. The presence of Special Forces is not always an unmitigated blessing for the population which might easily find itself exposed to increased enemy reprisals. Special Forces, particularly those permanently assigned to guerrillas, must always weigh the consequences of their actions lest they lose the support of the population and even the allegiance of the guerrillas.

For the Special Forces parties, on the other hand, co-operation with the guerrillas is almost always advantageous. If there is a guerrilla force in existence, the Special Force need not drop blind and it will find either a prepared base or assistance in establishing one. The partisans will take care of guard duties, air drops and maintenance. They can more easily reconnoitre and they have contacts with agents and the population. They are familiar with the terrain and can act as scouts and guides. They supply manpower which would not otherwise be available to a Special Force, and they can either give direct support or mount a diversionary attack.

Furthermore Special Forces can enrol a guerrilla detachment for duties which they do not normally undertake themselves but which are familiar to guerrillas, such as monitoring enemy telephone conversations, preventing the destruction of important objectives by the enemy, providing bridging material for their own advancing troops or holding even extensive areas until their arrival. Sometimes only Special Forces' support will make it possible for the guerrillas to perform these services.

Where there are partisan detachments or where they can be formed, the decision to send or not to send a Special Force to the area will depend in the first place on whether the area is sensitive or not. It is sensitive if the presence of opposition there hurts the enemy so much that he must annihilate it. As a rule Special Forces should operate with partisans only in sensitive areas or in areas likely to become sensitive. Where a partisan detachment must first be formed, a Special Force may be sent for this purpose if partisan warfare is desirable there and the six conditions previously outlined are fulfilled. Special Forces may be sent to an existing partisan detachment if either the Special Forces need its services or facilities, or if it cannot or will not operate on the desired scale without outside leadership or support.

The final question: when should permanent Special Forces with guerrillas be recalled?

The effectiveness of guerrilla work can be measured by the intensity of the enemy's reaction. Well-led guerrillas employed in sensitive areas managed in the last war to tie down an equal number of the enemy. If well-led permanent Special Forces with partisans—who have not been assigned another mission—fail to achieve similar results, a change of battlefield is warranted.

If the higher commander watches, and acts upon, this performance figure, he will not only avoid unjustified criticism of the Special Force and the idea behind it but also and above all ensure its maximum contribution to the war effort.

CHAPTER 6

PARTISAN TASKS

Partisan movements can be classified by their motivation, structure or functions. There are movements which fight an independent war on their own—as they did in Malaya, Indo-China and Kenya—and others which operate in an international war, usually as auxiliaries to the Army—as most partisan movements did in World War II. We are here concerned only with this latter type.

The traditional duties of partisans are raiding, sabotaging and ambushing, and little need be said about them, but whether partisans should also engage in large-scale combat activities requires investigation; we shall deal with this question below in Chapter 11.

Wireless communications made it possible in the last war to co-ordinate partisan with Army activities to a hitherto unknown degree. Partisans could also be supplied by air. Thus while the partisans of the last war still adhered to their time-honoured tactics and techniques their efficacy was greatly improved: they had formerly to rely on their own initiative and resources; now the front line had ceased to be a barrier between the Army and its partisans, at least for the transmission of orders and the delivery of the material means for carrying them out.

It was therefore only natural that partisan detachments were in the last war handled at times as if they were Army units. 'Tremendous support was given by partisans to the Soviet Army in river crossings. The partisans procured in time the means for crossing, prepared the bridgeheads, seized them from the enemy and held them until the arrival of Soviet troops. This was the case in the crossings of the Desna, Dnjepr, Pripjet and other rivers.'[1] Soviet partisans were also ordered to hold large continuous areas,

---

[1] So B. S. Telpuchowski, *Die sowjetische Geschichte des Grossen Vaterländischen Krieges 1941-1945*, herausgegeben und kritisch erläutert von Andreas Hillgruber und Hans-Adolf Jacobsen, Frankfurt am Main 1961, p. 286.

a task normally assigned only to troops. In this way the partisans were meant to force the retreating Germans on to a limited number of roads and railways which were under partisan attack, to block or slow down the German withdrawals and give the Red Army a better chance for annihilating its opponent.[1] At the same time the Red Army could often advance unopposed through areas previously cleared by the partisans. Partisans there and elsewhere assisted the Army in other novel ways. They misled the enemy about the Army's intentions; before the Allied landing in Sicily, Greek guerrillas had to give the impression that the landing would take place in Greece, and the same role had been assigned to Mihailovitch in Yugoslavia. On the Soviet front the partisans allowed the German Army Group Centre, in the spring of 1944, to transfer its reserves without interference to a sector where it wrongly expected a Red Army attack and then played havoc with its communications when it wanted to shift its reserves back to the sector where the Red Army did attack and break through.[2]

But the most startling innovation was the systematic use of partisans for Army Intelligence and reconnaissance. Soon after the invasion of Russia Soviet partisans started to supply the Red Army with information, usually by contacting the Intelligence officer of the Army on the opposite side of the front. Initially the partisans suffered under two disadvantages: they had not been trained for the job and they had to rely on foot messengers, carrier pigeons and dogs for the transmission of their reports. By 1943 several improvements had been made: Army Intelligence officers had been seconded to the partisan staffs and the more important bands had been supplied with wireless receivers and senders; instructions to the partisans and their reports could now be speedily transmitted. In 1943 the French Secret Army was likewise charged with Intelligence tasks. There is no doubt that the value of partisan Intelligence was frequently very high.

Partisans did a number of other jobs: they carried out diversionary activities, they indicated targets to the Army and Air Force, they reported the results of bombing, they carried out propaganda, sometimes accompanied by terror, among the population, they eliminated traitors, they sabotaged the economic and

[1] Cf. Major Edgar M. Howell, op. cit., p. 196.
[2] Cf. below Chapter 10 for a fuller description of this incident.

military-economic programme of the occupier, but there was little in the way of psychological warfare.

What, then, are the aims of partisan warfare? They are different in the various areas of operation. Partisans in countries outside the future battle zones, such as Norway and Denmark in the last war, have as a rule very limited aims. Larger-scale military action on their part is undesirable because military assistance will not be forthcoming and the sacrifices of the population would not be commensurate with the contribution which guerrilla activities in such areas would make to the war effort. The task of those partisans is therefore to inconvenience the enemy by small sabotage actions directed against his property and his political and economic policy; they also carry out propaganda and Intelligence.

The partisan aims in future battle zones—such as France before the Allied invasion—are similarly restricted; the partisans must particularly avoid drawing large enemy forces to the area. Finally, in the theatres of operations—Soviet Russia in the last war—there are two distinct phases of partisan war. These phases were marked in Russia by the Soviet retreat on the one hand, by the stabilization of the front and the Soviet advance on the other. During the retreat the partisans in the near and far rear aim at slowing down the enemy's advance, by all means, in all places and at all times. Maximum general activity is required of the partisans and there is little in the way of specific action the guerrillas can execute in support of their retreating army. But when the enemy offensive peters out they have to facilitate their own army's advance. In the near rear they then carry out specific missions in specific locations at prearranged times. In Soviet Russia, 'wherever a break-through was intended, the guerrillas could be set to work: reconnoitring specified enemy positions, cutting certain strategic routes, occupying river crossings on which the retreating army had to fall back, and clearing those which their own army needed as a foothold, creating diversions in the forward area, and so on'.[1] They also attacked the enemy from the rear. In the far rear they cut communications and destroyed the means of transport and supply depots. The measure of their success in the near and far rear, as was stressed before, is found in the number of enemy troops which they contain because

[1] Cf. Dixon/Heilbrunn, *Communist Guerrilla Warfare*, op. cit., p. 84.

it indicates how much their activities hurt the enemy. Unless they operate effectively in a sensitive zone the enemy will not be greatly affected and will not divert many of his troops to static guard duties and anti-partisan operations.

It should be noted that partisans can contain the enemy in two ways: they can make life in his positions so uncomfortable for him that he does not move out or moves out only in day time, or they can draw him off towards their own positions and tie him down there.

The general objectives of partisan warfare are therefore three-fold: to deprive the enemy of reinforcements, arms, equipment and supplies; to drain his manpower; and to give direct combat support to the front. The type of contribution which the guerrillas make depends on the area in which they operate.

Partisans can operate only where the population is friendly—or kept in check by terror—and the terrain is favourable. If this is the case they spread out in a thin, frequently broken line behind the front and concentrate in thick clusters astride the main supply lines further in the rear. The reason for this deployment is not difficult to see.

The main targets of partisan attacks in the last war were the roads, railways, bridges, trains, vehicles and supply depots. Attacks on isolated enemy soldiers and small units were of secondary importance.[1] The very nature of their tasks in theatres of army operations requires partisan concentrations along the enemy supply routes, and situation maps usually show the main partisan areas stretching along the enemy lines of communication.

As far as the immediate rear is concerned, partisans cannot usually operate there because they would be at once overwhelmed by the enemy reserves. But small detachments are often found within a belt thirty or forty miles wide and parallel with the front, ready to move towards the front when their own army exercises strong pressure and the enemy has committed his reserves to the front. The partisans will then try to breach the enemy defences from the rear in co-ordination with a frontal attack by their army and block the enemy's retreat.

This basic partisan situation map—the thin belt parallel to the

[1] This statement is not applicable to Tito's partisans for the special reasons discussed in Chapter 11 below. Their disposition was also different.

front and the thick clusters along the communication lines to the front—changes, of course, when the front line moves, but to some extent the partisans keep moving too. Not all of them did in the last war and many considered their mission completed when their area was liberated, but others were transferred and fought on in areas where they were needed. Partisan detachments are in fact not quite as stationary as it is often assumed. Many of Tito's partisans kept moving for years throughout the length and breadth of Yugoslavia, in Soviet Russia Major-General Kovpak's detachment went in the summer of 1943 on a raid through the western Ukraine to the Carpathian Mountains, in the following year Shukajev's detachment moved along the same route into Czechoslovakia, and others were concentrated along the communication lines. While the advantages of such redeployments are obvious, the disadvantages must not be overlooked: the partisans are unfamiliar with the terrain in their new localities and they need time to establish Intelligence contacts.

A partisan movement must be mainly composed of nationals of the country in which it operates. It cannot be imported nor can large bodies of foreign partisans be stationed in places where partisan support is wanted but not available.

How many enemy troops should partisans contain by their activities in order to qualify as successful? There is no hard and fast rule; if the partisans draw too many of the enemy upon themselves they will be wiped out and if they draw too few the population's sacrifices are unjustified. While Special Forces of this type should draw more than their own numbers it seems fair to say that partisans are doing well if they contain about an equal number of the enemy and this was what Soviet partisans, operating in 1943 in the Army Group North and Army Group Centre areas, achieved: about 130,000 of them tied down roughly the same number of German and allied troops.[1]

This ratio may seem low if we keep the record of Colonel Mosby and the Spanish guerrillas in mind. It must be realized, though, that the anti-partisans have learnt a great deal in the past twenty years or so, and the figure for anti-partisans contained might become lower still in the future. But nobody can doubt that unless dramatic changes occur the value of partisan support is considerable.

[1] Cf. O. Heilbrunn, Partisan Warfare, op. cit., pp. 182 f.

CHAPTER 7

STRUCTURE OF SPECIAL FORCES AND
PARTISAN MOVEMENTS

It is obvious that even the most ardent supporter of Special Operations cannot but view with misgivings the plethora of war-time Special Forces, particularly of British ones. A reduction in the number of Special Forces is possible by an amalgamation of tasks, by reducing the number of tasks assigned to them, or by a combination of both.

The various Special Forces and their tasks in World War II are shown in the following table. It includes the Special Forces of all the main belligerents of the last war but mostly only British and American Special Forces will subsequently be discussed. Between them they cover almost every situation in which Special Forces can be employed and every task in which they can be employed but we shall instance other countries' Special Forces to fill remaining gaps.

The table refers to Royal Marine Commandos and to Army Commandos. It understands by the first the Commandos as at present established and earmarked for coastal warfare,[1] and by the latter Commandos or, as we have suggested, airborne forces,[1] in their land warfare role, that is seizure of key points in the enemy rear.

The tasks of the Special Forces are divided in the table into Reconnaissance and Intelligence Tasks on the one hand and Offensive Tasks on the other. Major-General Laycock has subdivided the latter in a lecture into (i) Raids in direct or indirect support of larger operations (including diversions and deceptions) by attacks on isolated targets, flanks or rear, (ii) Harassing Raids, and (iii) Sabotage Raids; but as the title of the General's lecture on the subject indicates, he was concerned only with the raiding and not the other activities of Special Forces.[2]

[1] Cf. above Chapter 3.
[2] Major-General Sir Robert Laycock, 'Raids in the Last War and their Lessons' (Lecture), Royal United Service Institution Journal, 1947, vol. 92, pp. 528 f.

SPECIAL FORCES TASKS IN WORLD WAR II

RECONNAISSANCE AND INTELLIGENCE TASKS

1. PRIMARY MISSION OF:

a. Amphibious Forces

  (i) Shallow Infiltration

    Combined Ops. Pilotage
    Parties (UK) ⎫
    Amphibious Scouts (US) ⎬ Beach Reconnaissance
    Alaska Scouts (US) ⎭

  (ii) Deep Infiltration

    Special Boat Section (in ⎫ Strategic Reconnaissance
      Burma) (UK) ⎭

b. Land Forces

  (i) Shallow Infiltration = Near Rear

    Phantom (UK) ⎫
    Brandenburg Intelligence ⎬ Battle Information
      Units (German) ⎭

  (ii) Deep Infiltration = Far Rear

    Long Range Desert Group ⎫
      (UK) ⎬ Strategic Reconnaissance
    Small Operational Group ⎪
      (UK) ⎭

2. OCCASIONAL MISSIONS OF:

a. Amphibious Forces

    Royal Marine Commandos ⎫ General and Technical
      (UK) ⎬ Intelligence; Recce for
    Special Boat Service (UK) ⎭ Navy and RAF

b. Land Forces

    SAS (UK) ⎫
    Popski's Private Army (UK) ⎪
    Commando Fiji Guerrillas ⎪ Reconnaissance for Army
      (NZ) ⎬ and Air Force
    F. Squadron (Italy) ⎪
    Special Forces with ⎭
      guerrillas

OFFENSIVE TASKS

1. COASTAL WARFARE:

a. *Independent Operations*

Royal Marine Commandos (UK)	Assault Landings
Small Scale Raiding Force (UK)	Sabotage Raids
Underwater Swimming Unit (UK)	
Royal Marine Boom Patrol (UK)	
Special Boat Section (UK)	
Underwater Demolition Team (US)	Underwater Demolition
K Men (Germany)	
Special Underwater Raiding Forces (Italy)	
Special Boat Units (Japan)	

b. *Operations in Conjunction with Army*

Royal Marine Commandos (UK)	
Rangers (US)	Special Tasks in Major Assaults
Special Service Force (US/Canada)	
Coastal Hunter Company (Germany)	

2. LAND WARFARE:

a. *Shallow (tactical) Infiltration=Near Rear*

(i) *Independent Operations*

SAS (UK)	Spreading rumours, creating despondency, kidnapping individuals
Skorzeny's Special Formation (Germany)	

(ii) *Operations in Conjunction with Army*

Army Commandos (UK)	Seizing key points, reducing enemy defences (Offensive Operations on ground to be gained)
Rangers (US)	
Brandenburg Division (Germany)	

Raiding Units (Japan)	Sabotage Raids
Brandenburg Division (Germany) Skorzeny's Special Formation (Germany)	Slowing down or halting enemy advance (Guerrilla Ops. on ground lost)

b. *Deep (strategic) Infiltration = Far Rear*
  (i) *Independent Operations*

SAS (UK) Special Boat Service (UK) Raiding Forces (UK) Popski's Private Army (UK) Skorzeny's Special Formation (Germany)	Sabotage Raids and Ambushes. Short stay behind the enemy lines. Small parties.
First Chindit Exp. (UK) Independent Companies (Australia)	Full-scale Guerrilla Ops. Long stay behind enemy lines. Larger parties.
SAS (UK) Special Operations Executive (UK) Special Force (US) Office of Strat. Services (US) Brandenburg Division (Germany) Skorzeny's Special Formation (Germany)	Operations with Guerrillas and/or Political Warfare. For SOE, OSS and Skorzeny's Special Formation also Economic Warfare.

  (ii) *Operations in Conjunction with Army*

Second Chindit Exp. (UK) Marauders (US) All Special Forces with Guerrillas	All types of operations

Colonel Tobin has reduced the Special Forces' actual and possible offensive tasks to eight.[1] He lists them as follows:

(i) Operations in the enemy rear, strategical or tactical, in conjunction with the main forces.

(ii) Raids upon enemy installations, including coast defences, docks, submarine pens, airfields, radar installations and secret weapon sites.

[1] Colonel P. A. Tobin, The Bertrand Stewart Prize, *Army Quarterly*, vol lxv, January 1953, pp. 161 f., on p. 174.

(iii) Attacks on enemy headquarters or leaders.

(iv) Operations on the flank of the main army.

(v) Raids upon sources of material strength, such as power stations and oil storage depots.

(vi) Offensive operations with guerrillas.

(vii) Attacks upon enemy shipping in port.

(viii) Demolition of enemy lines of communication.

Since (i) comprises operations carried out in conjunction with the main forces, the missions under (ii) to (viii) are obviously all independent operations. Any classification of this type is bound to show some overlapping, and the present one is no exception: when the Marauders were first employed, they operated in conjunction with the main army (above (i)) on its flank (above (iv)) and demolished lines of communication (above (viii)) in co-operation with guerrillas (above (vi)); and offensive operations with guerrillas will almost always include demolition of enemy lines of communication (above (viii)) and frequently also raids upon enemy installations and sources of material strength (above (ii) and (v)). The list ought also to include as Special Forces tasks the formation of guerrilla movements, fighting like guerrillas on lost ground—as the Independent Companies did and the Brandenburgers and Skorzeny's Force were meant to do, and spreading of rumours and political warfare might also be added.

Keeping these observations in mind, the offensive tasks might be classified as follows:

OFFENSIVE TASKS

Coastal Warfare Operations:
> Assault landings; Sabotage raids on enemy shipping and installations; Underwater demolition; Flank attacks. Special tasks in major assaults.

Land Warfare Operations:
> Army Commando/Ranger-type Operations
>> Seizing key points (including reduction of enemy defences)
>
> Guerrilla-type Operations (by Special Forces only)
>> Harassing and Sabotage raids; Ambushes; Kidnapping; Spreading rumours and despondency.
>> Full-scale guerrilla operations.
>> Economic and political warfare.

116

Operations with Guerrillas (Special Forces with Guerrillas)
Formation of guerrilla detachments. Guerrilla operations.

The guerrilla-type and guerrilla forces also provide Intelligence for the Armed Forces. The following are the Special Forces'

RECONNAISSANCE AND INTELLIGENCE TASKS

Amphibious Missions:

Beach and coastal reconnaissance. Strategic reconnaissance under special circumstances (Special Boat Section in Burma). General and technical Intelligence, especially also reconnaissance for Navy and Air Force.

Inland Missions:

Battle information. Strategic reconnaissance, especially for Army and Air Force.

Great Britain had during the last war more than a dozen different Special Forces. The above grouping indicates that very much fewer than that are really required; their numbers must therefore be reduced because too many Special Forces are undesirable since they cannot easily be controlled, and uneconomic since they cannot easily be employed if they become too specialized.[1] If Special Forces for land warfare operations are trained to approach their target areas by land, air and sea, as they mostly are, one and the same Special Force can be employed in its particular task for shallow as well as deep infiltration, and it goes without saying that every Special Force can fulfil its task in coordination with or independently of the Army. Furthermore, there is no reason why special reconnaissance forces should not be incorporated as a reconnaissance squadron into the Special Force which operates offensively in the same area; there was no need in the desert for the separate existence of SAS and LRDG. Lastly, the various amphibious and coastal warfare tasks—assault landings, reconnaissance and underwater demolition—can be performed by one Special Force. This Force would be in Great Britain the Royal Marine Commandos, while in the United States reconnaissance and underwater demolition parties could be incorporated into one Force.

[1] Cf. Lieut.-Colonel J. P. O'Brien Twohig, 'Are Commandos Really Necessary?', *Army Quarterly*, October 1948, vol. lvii, p. 88, Major-General Sir Robert Laycock, *loc. cit.*, p. 529, and Colonel P. A. Tobin, *loc. cit.*, p. 175.

The number of Special Forces would thus be reduced to four, viz:

1. *Coastal Warfare Force*, with tasks taken care of in the last war by the Royal Marine Commandos, Royal Marine Boom Patrol, Small Scale Raiding Force, Underwater Swimming Unit, Special Boat Section, Combined Operation Pilotage Parties for the UK and Rangers, Special Service Force, Underwater Demolition Teams, Amphibious Scouts and Alaska Scouts for the US.

2. *Army Commandos/Rangers*.

3. *Guerrilla-type Force*, with tasks taken care of in the last war by SAS, Special Boat Service, Raiding Forces, Popski's Private Army, and Chindits on the British side, Independent Companies on the Australian side, and Marauders—as originally designed—on the American side.[1]

4. *Force with Guerrillas*, consisting in the last war of Army and SOE-inspired forces on the British side and of OSS-inspired forces and now also the Special Force on the American side.

It may be tempting to extend the streamlining process still further and think of amalgamating the Guerrilla-type Force and the Force with the Guerrillas, but the two tasks are too different for such a fusion to be practical. This becomes at once evident when one compares the performance of Popski's Private Army with the role of the new American Special Force. Furthermore, the Guerrilla-type Force is self-contained, it is a military unit and it can be employed anywhere while the Force with the Guerrillas consists only of commanders and staff, the formations are irregular detachments, and the Special Force can be deployed only where partisan detachments are or can be formed.[2]

One may, however, reduce the number of Special Forces further by reducing the number of their tasks. Field-Marshal Lord Slim is of the opinion that Special Forces must operate only in small parties. This means that Army Commandos' and Rangers' tasks would no longer be performed by Special Forces and that Chindits and probably even Independent Companies would not be required in the future. Field-Marshal Slim lists five Special Forces' tasks, namely:

[1] This Force can, of course, still co-operate with guerrillas in the way the SAS and others did in the last war.
[2] The German Special Forces acted as Army Commando-type Forces and as Forces with Guerrillas; this combination is explained by the fact that the Germans had practically only one Special Force for land warfare at a time.

1. to sabotage vital installations;
2. to spread rumours and misdirect the enemy;
3. to transmit intelligence;
4. to kill or kidnap individuals; and
5. to inspire partisan movements.[1]

Since the Field-Marshal speaks as a soldier he probably does not wish to eliminate the Royal Marine Commandos as a Special Force. He therefore approves of three types of Special Forces, that is to say a Coastal Warfare Force, a Guerrilla-type Force operating in small parties, and a Force with Guerrillas.

Colonel Tobin suggests that only two types of Special Forces should in future be maintained, namely:

1. 'Royal Marine Commandos: These will undertake all amphibious, shallow penetration tasks up to brigade strength', and

2. 'SAS Regiments: These will undertake all deep penetration operations up to approximately battalion strength. Above this the task is likely to devolve upon regular airborne units.'[2]

This scheme would exclude the Army Commandos/Rangers, the Chindits/Marauders, Independent Companies and the Force with Guerrillas. Field-Marshal Slim and Colonel Tobin are thus agreed on eliminating the Army Commandos, Chindits and Independent Companies;[3] they disagree in as much as Field-Marshal Slim envisages only small parties of Special Forces while Colonel Tobin proposes to employ them in up to battalion strength; finally the Field-Marshal makes provision for a Force with Guerrillas, the Colonel does not.

General Laycock, on the other hand, wants to have the Commandos retained and advocates that they should do the business of all Special Forces raiders.[4]

The discussion, at least in Britain, on the future design of Special Forces therefore revolves around the following questions:

1. Are Army Commandos/Rangers, Chindits/Marauders, Independent Companies and Special Forces with Guerrillas desirable?

2. What size should the Special Forces be?

---

[1] Field-Marshal Lord Slim, op. cit., p. 548.
[2] Colonel P. A. Tobin, loc. cit., p. 175.
[3] Also against Army Commandos is Lieut.-Colonel J. P. O'Brien Twohig, loc. cit., p. 88.
[4] Loc. cit., p. 530.

There must obviously be added

3. Does the experience of other countries suggest that still other Special Forces are wanted or that existing ones should perform further tasks?

As far as the first question is concerned, official thinking in Great Britain and the United States differs if we can take the respective orders of battle as a guide. At the present time the British have a Coastal Warfare Special Force, viz, the Royal Marine Commandos, but the Americans have not. The British have no Army Commandos, but the Americans have Rangers. The British have a Guerrilla-type Force, the SAS, but the Americans have none. The British have no Force with Guerrillas, but the Americans have the new Special Force for this purpose.

These variances are due to the difference in numbers of the British and American regular forces. The British 'War Office believe that the needs of small regular forces are best served by the "One Army" concept—by giving the whole Army a common basic training upon which training for special operations is later superimposed. The special problems of the British Army make it impossible for them to follow the American practice of forming and training a number of special units designed for operations in special circumstances and in specific geographical areas."[1]

The point of divergence—and this applies to all these discussions—is therefore not whether a specific task in the rear should be done but by whom—regulars or specials—it should be done, and the practical results are not as different as the respective approaches seem to suggest.

In the first place neither country has at present a Special Chindit/Marauder Force or Independent Companies. Those who recognize the value of well-directed partisan operations will not deny the usefulness of soldiers on such missions in sensitive areas where partisans are not available. We have stressed before that regular troops should be trained to do the job because it teaches them the art of survival against odds if they are overrun by the enemy. That regular troops can be so trained is evidenced by the Chindits themselves; they were more regular than it is commonly supposed. They consisted of ordinary units, not volun-

[1] Article by the Defence Correspondent in the London *Times*, June 13, 1962, p. 10.

teers or picked men; only the unsuitable men were taken off. A number of officers were volunteers but 99 per cent of the officers and men were detailed in the normal way.[1]

As for the Special Force with guerrillas, it does not really need a British counterpart in peace-time. Britain has had several occasions—in Malaya, Kenya and Cyprus—to gain practical experience in anti-partisan warfare and as a result the knowledge so gained can be transmitted on a broader basis to conventionally organized formations. Again, in guerrilla warfare the SAS is adaptable enough to concentrate more on Special Force work if necessary. Anything required above this, especially officers as leaders of, or liaison officers with, partisans will be found, as in the 1939-45 war, at the outbreak or in the course of hostilities when the requirements and possibilities can be assessed.

The real difference in British and American official thinking revolves about the need for Army Commandos/Rangers. We have stressed in Chapter 3 that a specialist unit is required for this purpose so that it will be available, and available in the necessary strength, at the right time and in the right place. If the airborne forces take over this task, the difference in the Anglo-American approach would to some extent be bridged: in the United States there are now Airborne Rangers who will be airlifted behind the enemy lines. The tasks of airborne troops and Rangers—even if they are not airborne—are so similar that their amalgamation would appear only logical.

Under such an arrangement the number of Special Forces would be considerably reduced. The Royal Marine Commandos and the US Marine Corps would provide all the forces for coastal warfare. Army Commandos and Rangers would lose the 'Special' attribute, and so would Chindits, Marauders and Independent Companies. Apart from one or two Reconnaissance and Intelligence Forces only the SAS, the Special Force and agencies for inspiring, leading and guiding partisan movements would constitute the Special Forces; they are all engaged in partisan work.

The size of these special and regular forces cannot be determined dogmatically and no elaborate set of rules can be worked out. The forces must be strong enough to do the job and survive, but this safety is not always found in numbers. Broadly speaking, we must distinguish between the fighting forces (Commandos/

[1] Cf. Brigadier Sir Bernard Fergusson, *The Wild Green Earth*, op. cit., p. 260.

Rangers), harassing forces of the roving kind (SAS), and the stationary harassing forces (Chindits, etc.). The fighting forces must have the chance to hold out against the enemy until they are relieved and they must be numerically strong enough to do so. They operated in the last war in up to brigade strength and must be prepared to do so again or in even greater numbers. The roving harassing forces do not make a stand; they evade the enemy, and the smaller they are the better they can succeed. SAS parties, as already stated, are now designed to operate in a strength of from three to fifty men and this should enable them to carry out their missions. They can do so if the front is fluid, the population friendly, air superiority secured,[1] air supply arranged,[2] and a base can be set up. If the theatre of operations is in a less developed country, the parties might even operate in battalion strength, as Colonel Tobin has suggested.[3] Stationary harassing forces should contain more of the enemy than their own numbers. They must not be numerically stronger than the enemy, but how much weaker they can be greatly depends on the type of terrain in which they operate.

Finally, what can we learn from the Special Forces of the other belligerents of the last war?

There is no counterpart in the British and American order of battle to the Japanese Raiding Units which infiltrated at night a large number of very small parties and carried out sabotage on tanks, artillery and headquarters in the enemy's immediate rear. Since the number of men required is not great, British and American divisions could train their own personnel for these jobs if and when required.

No land warfare unit is at present available for the immediate rear to spread rumours and undermine enemy morale among his troops in the way Skorzeny's formation did during the Ardennes offensive. SAS is assigned this job for the far rear and the civilian population. The work will be effective in the immediate rear only if the force has some foreign language speakers and dons foreign uniform, and the same holds true for the Brandenburg way of

[1] Lt.-General Sir John W. Hackett, 'The Employment of Special Forces' (Lecture), *Royal United Service Institution Journal* 1952, vol. 97, p. 31, and Colonel P. A. Tobin, loc. cit., p. 170.
[2] Cf. Major Roy Farran, *Winged Dagger*, op. cit., p. 226, and Colonel P. A. Tobin, loc. cit., p. 170.
[3] Loc. cit., p. 175.

infiltrating by deceiving the enemy. There may be a feeling of repugnance against adopting such devices although it was not always evident in the last war. There were Chindits in Japanese uniform,[1] Japanese in Burma Rifles uniform[2] and Indian National Army men in British uniform,[3] British and SIG on a few occasions in German uniform[4] and Germans on a number of occasions in a collection of enemy uniforms. It must be remembered that in naval warfare it is permissible to deceive the enemy by all kinds of ruses including the wearing of his uniform until fire is opened[5] and the rules for land warfare are no different.[6] The problem should be studied.

Lastly, apart from the Independent Companies and some instances in the Burma theatre, Allied Special Forces were not employed to slow down the enemy's advance. Brandenburg and Skorzeny's formation were designed to do this job.

The structures of the various partisan movements of the last war, with which we deal now, varied almost from country to country. Again, as in Chapter 6, we are concerned only with movements which operate in an international war in support of one of the belligerents or a group of belligerents, and these movements can be divided for our purpose here into three categories:

1. Partisans supporting their own Army in the field—for instance the Soviet partisans in the last war;

2. Partisans whose Army is no longer in the field and who fight in preparation for and support of the liberation of their country by their allies or their own Army—as the French partisans did; and

3. Partisans whose Army is no longer in the field and who fight to liberate the country themselves, possibly with allied support—as Tito's forces did in the last war.

The first two groups usually restrict themselves to harassing, raiding, ambushing and sabotaging; the third group also engages in large-scale combat activities.

[1] Cf. J. H. Denny, Chindit Indiscretion, London 1956, p. 56.
[2] Field-Marshal Viscount Slim, op. cit., p. 64.
[3] J. H. Denny, op. cit., pp. 182 and 229.
[4] Cf. Gordon Landsborough, Tobruk Commando, London 1956, p. 28, and John Lodwick, The Filibusters, op. cit., p. 30.
[5] Cf. Hilary St George Saunders, The Green Beret, op. cit., p. 87, for the Campbeltown's approach to St Nazaire when such ruses were applied.
[6] For legal sources cf. Die Geschichte des Panzerkorps Grossdeutschland, op. cit., vol. iii, pp. 40f.

The first group takes orders from the established authorities of the country. Its structure is laid down by the Government or the Army. The second group often maintains a measure of autonomy. Especially if a number of partisan movements have sprung up and are to be unified, its structure is rather a matter of agreement between the government in exile and the various partisan leaders. Both structures are designed to ensure maximum co-operation with the Army in the field or the expected Army in the field. The third group aspires to the status of an ally and determines its structure itself. This movement operates independently. It needs its own semi-regular formations to fight the invader and partisans proper to support them, and its structure therefore provides for both elements.

The structure of the French partisan movement was complicated because a number of detachments were under British and others under French control, and that of the Soviet partisan movement was intricate because it was a Party formation and had to serve two masters, the Party and the Army. Any attempt at streamlining the partisan structure by prescribing a basic scheme for general adoption would be futile because the special circumstances of each movement defy such rigidity.

A belligerent who wants to employ partisans in a foreign country can try to form a movement or influence and unify existing movements, but by and large he will have to take the movement, including its structure, as it is.[1]

---

[1] On the importance of the structure for the efficient functioning of the partisan movement cf. Otto Heilbrunn, Partisan Warfare, op. cit., pp. 19 f. The basic structures are set out there on pp. 26 f.

II. CONVENTIONAL FORCES AND THEIR TASKS

CHAPTER 8

AIRBORNE TROOPS' OPERATIONS

Soviet pre-war experiments and German successes with their air-borne troops early in the war induced the other belligerents to form and expand their own airborne formations, viz. paratroops and air landing troops. But the various nations used them in greatly differing ways. The British, American and Japanese employed them in a tactical role, the Germans assigned operational functions to them on two occasions, and British, Americans and Germans sometimes also deployed them in a *coup de main* or, as it is loosely called, in a 'Commando' role. The Russians made little use of large airborne formations; only on one occasion were they given a tactical assignment; on another they were deployed as airborne reinforcements of their ground troops.

Airborne formations were usually dropped and landed in a sector occupied by the enemy but the Russians also infiltrated them by air into areas in the enemy rear which their own forces controlled. The near rear was the usual battlefield of the airborne forces. They expected as a rule to be relieved by their advancing front troops within a short time but the infiltrated Russians fought on for months.

The airborne forces' operations of the last war can therefore be fitted into the following scheme:
    I. Operations in areas under their own control—as reinforcements.
    II. Operations in areas under enemy control:
        (a) 'Commando' assignments
        (b) Tactical assignments
        (c) Operational assignments,
and we propose to survey some typical operations in this sequence.

    I. Operations in areas under their own control. At the end of 1941 the German advance in Soviet Russia had come to a halt. A strong Soviet counter-offensive compelled the Germans to withdraw and large gaps appeared in their lines in the process. Two Soviet cavalry corps, two armies and parts of another army poured through the gaps in the Vyazma-Smolensk-Roslawl area and fought for the possession of the supply lines of four German armies.

There were also Soviet partisans operating in this area and from January to March 1942 six or more brigades of paratroops and airlanding forces were flown in small parties by the Russians into the sectors controlled by their troops and partisans. The paratroopers usually jumped on to ground held by their own forces and partisans often prepared the landing zones. The function of the airborne troops was apparently to stiffen the morale of the partisans and reinforce the ground troops. Only on one occasion do the airborne forces seem to have carried out a larger independent attack when three brigades tried to break through to the major German supply road. They then joined up with the other forces in the area. All troops were supplied by air until they were finally eliminated by the Germans in June 1942.[1] The experiment was not repeated by the Russians in the subsequent campaign.[2]

II. Operations in areas under enemy control. There is no rigid division between 'Commando', tactical and operational assignments but the distinction has a certain usefulness. In a 'Commando' operation the airborne forces carry out a *coup de main*. In a tactical assignment, usually on a larger scale, the airborne troops facilitate the landing or the advance of their own ground troops or block the enemy's retreat, usually by seizing a key point; the effort of the airborne troops is subsidiary and the major effort is made by the ground troops. In an operational assignment the airborne effort is the decisive one, at least in the opening stage, and if it fails the battle is lost.

(a) Typical 'Commando' operations were the German *coup de main* against Fort Eben Emael where, in May 1940, an assault force landed in gliders inside the fortifications, and the airlanding in December 1942 on a French-held airfield at Gabes in Tunisia, followed by the capture of the railway station on the

[1] Cf. for a description of this operation General-Major Hellmuth Reinhardt in *Russian Airborne Operations*, Office of the Chief of Military History, MS P-116, Washington 1952, pp. 5 f.
[2] Reinforcement missions by airborne troops for their own front are outside the scope of this discussion.

supply route of the Africa Corps. The best-known British operation of this type was 'the adventure of Bruneval' where German radar equipment was dismantled and removed.[1] Japanese paratroops were employed to capture important installations intact, such as refineries, airfields, and so on. Airborne troops of the other belligerents also undertook similar operations.

(b) In the Allied landing operations in Africa and Europe airborne forces were assigned the tactical task of protecting the troops which landed on the beaches, by delaying an enemy counter-offensive. In the landing in Algeria paratroops were ordered to neutralize airfields near Oran, and in the Sicily landings the airborne troops had to take and hold high ground, establish road blocks and hold bridges and crossings; they also had to keep a road clear for their own quick advance.[2] In the Normandy invasion British and American forces were employed on the eastern and western flanks respectively. The American forces landing from the sea on the Utah beach would be pinned down unless the exits through the inundation behind the German defences could be kept open. Two US airborne divisions were therefore allotted this task; they were also to assist the advance of their own ground troops by destroying coastal batteries and bridges and engaging the enemy retreating from the beaches. The task of the British airborne forces, a portion of one division, was to protect the eastern flank against a German armoured attack.

In this type of mission airborne troops and Commandos are often interchangeable. At Dieppe and Anzio it had been decided that parachute troops were to seize batteries and high ground, but when it turned out that paratroops were not available for the tasks they were carried out by Commandos instead. Likewise for the invasion of Southern France in 1944 it was at first planned to drop paratroops near Cape Bénat but it was then decided to land French Commandos at Cape Nègre and block the coastal road there. Sometimes airborne troops and Commandos were

---

[1] Cf. Hilary St George Saunders, The Red Beret, London 1950, pp. 55 f.
[2] For a detailed description of the planning and execution of American and British airborne operations cf. the excellent accounts by Dr John C. Warren in Airborne Missions in the Mediterranean 1942-45, September 1955, and in Airborne Operations in World War II, European Theater, September 1956, USAF Historical Studies, USAF Historical Division, Studies Nos. 74 and 97, Research Studies Institute, Air University, Alabama. For British paratroop operations cf. Hilary St George Saunders, The Red Beret, op. cit.

employed in identical tasks on the same battlefield, as was the case in the Sicily landing. 'In the immediate path of the advance were three all-important bridges, the nearest, Ponte Grande, at the entering-in of Syracuse. This, it was eventually decided, should be captured by a glider-borne attack; the next, north-east of dusty Lentini . . . was assigned to No. 3 Commando, and the third and farthest off . . . was to be taken by the 1st Parachute Brigade.'[1] Airborne troops, like Commandos and Rangers, frequently seized key points in the rear on the line of advance.

Airborne troops, though, cannot always operate where Commandos can. The weather, the terrain, availability of aircraft and gliders, enemy air strength and anti-aircraft defences must all be taken into consideration in an airborne operation and if any of these factors are adverse it may be too risky or impossible. Commandos landing from the sea have to take other circumstances into account, such as availability of ships and landing craft, the nature of the coast and the tide; in river crossings the availability of assault boats, artillery support, the nature of the opposite bank and so on must be considered, while for land infiltration missions bad weather, darkness, and a difficult terrain are helpful factors. Airborne troops and Commandos on this type of mission did not exclude but supplemented each other.

Of all the inland airborne missions undertaken by the Allies in World War II the Eindhoven-Nijmegen-Arnhem operation in September 1944 was by far the largest. Two American divisions, one British division and a Polish brigade were to capture the bridges across the canals, the Maas, Waal and Rhine more than fifty miles behind the front in order to accelerate the British advance and establish a bridgehead across the Rhine. The operation was only a partial success; the ground forces did not link up in time with the most distant airborne troops at Arnhem.

The Japanese never allowed their airborne troops to be deployed more than 12 miles behind the enemy front.[2] Nor did the Russians when they drove the Germans back across the Dnjepr in the Cherkassy-Kiev area in September 1943 and dropped three brigades into seven dropping zones across the river, in advance of the crossing by ground forces, in order to establish bridge-

[1] So Hilary St George Saunders, The Red Beret, op. cit., p. 125.
[2] Cf. Japanese Parachute Troops, Military Intelligence Division, War Department, Special Series No. 32, Washington, July 1, 1945.

heads. The drops were not made this time into partisan areas and the airborne forces did not link up with each other. One brigade jumped right into the middle of a Panzer division and suffered heavily; most of the other troops were rounded up by the Germans before Soviet ground forces could come to their relief.[1]

When the Allies crossed the Rhine in March 1945, they sent a British and an American airborne division to the other side in order to smash the enemy's defences from the rear and deepen the bridgehead. It was not only by the weight of the airborne assault that the Rhine operation differed from the Dnjepr crossing. At the Rhine ground troops crossed in advance of the airborne divisions; the ground troops started during the night, the airborne troops were dropped and landed the next morning. Ground and airborne troops, only a few miles away from each other, could thus make contact within a short time; the airborne elements, dropped closely together in a concentrated lift, could also quickly link up with each other. Furthermore, Allied air forces flew several interdiction missions in support of the airborne forces. They also enjoyed close air support after landing and, in addition, they had artillery support from the other side of the river.

The German operation in April 1941 at the Isthmus of Corinth achieved success without most of these benefits. The task of these troops, a paratroop regiment, was to keep the entrance from the Greek mainland to the Peloponnesus open for their ground forces and block the escape of British troops to Crete and Egypt. The drop was preceded by intense air attacks and the paratroops overwhelmed the defence which had been haphazardly assembled and was ill-equipped. The Rhine crossing, by contrast, will serve as a model operation against a prepared enemy.

(c) The Germans were the only ones to carry out airborne missions of an operational character. In the invasion of Holland in May 1940 three paratroop task forces were employed, one near Amsterdam to paralyse the city, another one at Rotterdam in order to capture the airport and, assisted by troops landed

---

[1] The operation is described by General Walter K. Nehring in *Russian Airborne Operations, op. cit.,* pp. 35 f, and also by J. M. Mackintosh, 'Soviet Airborne Troops', in *The Soviet Air and Rocket Forces,* ed. by Asher Lee, London 1959, p. 165.

there, take the town, and the third one had to secure the bridges which the German armour must cross. The second and last operation of this kind was the invasion of Crete. An airborne corps was to drop and land in three waves, the first in the morning of May 20, 1941, in the west of the island and the second in the afternoon of that day in the centre and east. Their task was to secure airfields, the most important towns and a harbour and thus open the way for the third wave consisting mostly of ground troops brought in by air and heavy weapons delivered by sea. The success of the whole operation therefore depended on the success of the airborne assault. The initial attacks miscarried and no seaborne transport got through during the battle but with the help of paratroop reinforcements the Germans eventually gained possession of Maleme airfield, and although it was still under fire they landed there the advance elements of a mountain division in the afternoon of May 21st. The next day the airfield was secure in their possession, they brought in further portions of the mountain division, they spread their hold on the island, linked up with their other forces and finally gained the island. But their losses had been such that from then on German paratroops were usually employed as ground troops only.

(d) The Allies had planned an airborne operation on the strategic level. In March 1945 First Allied Airborne Army envisaged the invasion of the Kassel-Fritzlar-Hofgeismar area in Central Germany. A fortress would be established there from which a decisive offensive against the eastern end of the Ruhr could be launched; an airhead would be provided to which the Southern Group of Armies could advance and then cut off the northern from the southern half of Germany. The order of battle for the airborne force called for the use of three corps and ten divisions. Because of the difficulty of finding the men and the speed of the ground advance the operation was cancelled.[1]

On occasions the belligerents used paratroops for sabotage actions. However, the main function of airborne units is to fight.

Unless great risks were accepted, the area of activity in *tactical* missions was limited in the last war to the immediate

[1] Cf. Lieutenant-General Lewis H. Brereton, *The Brereton Diaries*, New York 1946, pp. 399 f. For the strategic employment of airborne forces at the beginning of a war for the seizure of strategic positions on a global basis cf. 'Romulus', 'Future Employment of Airborne Forces', *Royal United Service Institution Journal*, vol. 100, No. 598, May 1955, p. 239.

rear. Improved logistic capabilities since the war and the possibility of providing airborne forces with heavier arms seem to suggest that they can now operate far deeper in the enemy rear than hitherto but improved air defences may invalidate such a conclusion. However this may be, the principle still holds good that the front troops must be able quickly to reach them or the enemy, by drawing on his reserves in neighbouring areas, will overpower them.

In *operational* assignments the distance between the battle-field of the airborne troops and the position of the ground forces was usually much greater, although the battle of Crete has shown that reinforcements could be quickly brought in by air once an airfield had been secured. The success of such an operation greatly depended on the application of the proper tactics.[1] But it also needs emphasizing that the Germans chose for these operational assignments closed battlefields—Holland and Crete—where no reinforcements from outside would be brought in by the enemy. They therefore could from the outset adapt their own strength to the expected strength of the enemy in the area of operation. Under such conditions the use of airborne troops deeper in the enemy rear must still be considered worthwhile if the importance of the operation justifies the risks.

Because airborne troops on tactical missions must be quickly relieved they can fight in the enemy rear only to support the advance of their own troops and they must therefore not be used there to slow down the advance of the enemy when their own troops retreat.[2]

Airborne troops on tactical and operational assignments and on most of the 'Commando' missions must be deployed on the

[1] The German tactics are set out by Professor Dr Freiherr v.d. Heydte, 'Die Fallschirmtruppe im Zweiten Weltkrieg', in *Bilanz des Zweiten Weltkrieges*, Oldenburg/Hamburg 1953, p. 192. The attack starts in several places and several perimeters are formed. From there the enemy defences are disrupted, his lines of communication are cut, and he will be impeded in forming a rally-ing point for the defence. One of the perimeters is then strongly built up by continual reinforcement and spreads like an 'ink-blot' until it reaches the other perimeters and absorbs them.

Soviet tactics are described by Raymond L. Garthoff, *Soviet Military Doctrine*, Glencoe 1953, p. 353.

[2] The Germans used paratroops differently for this purpose. In August 1943 they inserted a portion of a paratroop division in the Etna sector in Sicily between the retreating Italians and the advancing Allies in order to gain time for the evacuation of Sicily.

axis of advance of the ground forces. Otherwise the ground forces reap no benefit from their effort and are only deflected into an area which they would otherwise by-pass.[1]

Just as ground forces can infiltrate the enemy lines by filtering through in small numbers or penetrate by massed action, so can airborne forces infiltrate and penetrate. Airborne infiltration serves a purpose only in small-scale actions, such as sabotage. For all combat missions—*coup de main,* tactical and operational assignments—a more compact effort is necessary.

There will certainly be modifications in a future war, conventional or nuclear. Huge air convoys are no longer feasible, landing and dropping zones may have to be dispersed and missions be scaled down; paratroops may be replaced by air landing troops in ground-hugging aircraft, but it does not appear that airborne forces while dropping, landing or on the ground, will be more vulnerable than hitherto because an enemy will be reluctant to use nuclear weapons in his own hinterland.

In airborne missions co-operation is required between air force and troops. The solution adopted by SHAEF in the last war may well serve as a model: Combined Airborne Headquarters, later renamed First Allied Airborne Army, was in command of all Allied airborne troops and in operational control of British and American troop carriers. The Army was directly under SHAEF and was in control of the operation until the airborne elements joined the ground forces.[2] They then came under control of the ground commander of the front whose action they supported, and they fought on with the ground troops, sometimes for weeks, until they were relieved.

---

[1] After SHAEF had approved a paratroop attack on Boulogne, 21 Army Group turned down the plan because the port was off the main line of advance. Cf. Dr John G. Warren, *Airborne Operations in World War II, op. cit.,* p. 87.
[2] *Ibid.,* p. 82.

CHAPTER 9

THE AIR EFFORT IN THE REAR

The Air Force makes a double contribution to the fight in the rear. In the first place it gives support to the ground forces of the rear: it assists them by transporting men and material, it carries out reconnaissance for them, it may give fighter cover and establish air superiority over a rear theatre, and it can give close battle support; we have mentioned some such instances in the foregoing chapters. In return the ground forces assist the air by target indication, observation of bombing results, preparation of landing strips, and rescue operations for stranded air personnel. The Air Force has a second role: it wages the air offensive.

It is the purpose of this chapter to find out how the offensive air activities in the rear fit in with those of the ground forces and what measure of joint control or consultation appears indicated to avoid omissions or, alternatively, duplications of effort in the rear war as it developed in World War II.

It is obvious, though, that much of that experience will be of little value in the future. Air defences have in the meanwhile been greatly improved. In a nuclear war, even before nuclear weapons are used, air forces will hardly embark again on conventional 1,000 bomber raids or on area attacks because the bombers can hardly be expected to get through, and after nuclear weapons have been fired there is even less room for a conventional air offensive but it must not be ruled out entirely; if the enemy has occupied friendly territory, the Air Force might prefer to stage a conventional raid in order not to alienate the population, that is, until missiles take the place of Air Forces. The air offensive of the last war has also little relevancy in a future antipartisan operation since partisans are not dependent on factories, rail transport, etc., which then formed a main target for the air forces. There remains the limited, Korea-type war. But even such a limited war might escalate into a nuclear war and the same restrictions therefore apply. The epoch of air warfare which started in 1940 has almost ended with the Korean war and this chapter surveys to some extent history which is unlikely to repeat itself.

The strategic air offensive had two main objectives in the last war: they were, as the Combined Chiefs of Staff laid down at the Casablanca Conference of January 1943, 'the progressive destruction and dislocation of the German military, industrial and economic system and the undermining of the morale of the German people to a point where their capacity for armed resistance is fatally weakened'. The priority targets, earmarked then and later, included submarine yards and bases, the aircraft industry, ball-bearings and oil, and V-weapon sites, while a secondary objective was military motor transport. At the Quebec Conference of August 1943 another objective was added: the disruption of vital elements of lines of communication which was considered a prerequisite to the Normandy landings.

As far as German territory was concerned, only the Air Forces could achieve these objectives; no ground forces of the rear operated in Germany before the Allied front lines approached the frontier. There were no pro-Allied partisans in Germany, and the other ground forces of the rear did not venture into Germany ahead of the front. After the Allies had crossed the frontier SAS parties roamed far into the rear, but apart from supply drops, SAS attacks on aircraft on the ground and target indication there was little that ground and air could have done in mutual support or in co-ordination of their tasks.

Of the western theatres it was only in France that some integration of effort seemed at all feasible. Before the Allied landings partisans, SOE parties and Commandos operated there; on and after D-Day Rangers, airborne troops, OGs and SAS parties sprang into action, and the Allied Air Forces operated all the time over France. The Washington Conference of December 1941 to January 1942 outlined two phases of the war against Germany and assigned their functions to the Air Forces and some of the forces of the rear.

The first phase had as its aim to wear down Germany's resistance and only after this aim had been achieved could the second phase start, viz. the attack by land armies. The 'main methods of wearing down Germany's resistance' were defined as:

(a) Ever-increasing air bombardments by British and American Forces;

136

(b) Assistance to Russia's offensive by all available means;

(c) The blockade;

(d) The maintenance of the spirit of revolt in the occupied countries, and the organization of subversive movements.[1]

The Special Forces came into this scheme under the heading 'Assistance to Russia's offensive' and the 1942 Dieppe raid in which a thousand Commandos took part was carried out with this purpose, among others, in mind, while the partisans represented the 'spirit of revolt' and of organized subversion. But although these forces, bracketed together with the Air Force, were to be deployed in pursuance of a common purpose, viz. the wearing-down process, no attempts were made at integrating the agencies concerned or co-ordinating their plans for the execution of this policy, and little indeed would have been gained by so doing. In Britain the strategic air offensive was under Bomber Command, the Commandos came under Combined Operations Command, the blockade was entrusted to the Ministry of Economic Warfare, the Royal Navy and the RAF, and revolt and subversion were organized and supervised by SOE under the Ministry of Economic Warfare. Integration was only sought and carried out for inter-Service raids and landings on the enemy coast, through Combined Operations Command, and on the Intelligence level in as much as the bombing policy of the British and American Air Forces was influenced by the Ministry of Economic Warfare's Intelligence reports which were made available to both the RAF and the US Board of Economic Warfare.

It is difficult to see what more could have profitably been done at this stage. Morale operations were nicely split up: USAAF and RAF had to undermine morale in Germany, the Commandos, SOE and OSS had to raise it in France. In coastal operations the Air Forces on the one hand and Commandos and Rangers on the other did not usually compete, and the same applied to operations inland. Prior to the Allied landings only the Air Force and partisans had to some extent common tasks; both worked on the progressive destruction and dislocation of the German military, industrial and economic system. But the Resistance's share was then necessarily a modest one and in theory, though not always in practice, the Air Force and Resistance had different sets of targets.

[1] Cf. Robert E. Sherwood, *The White House Papers of Harry L. Hopkins*, vol. i, September 1939 to January 1942, London 1948, p. 472.

The Resistance, it will be recalled, was then only building up, and any subsequent exuberance of its members was—almost always—effectively restrained by the Allies who did not want them to engage prematurely on large-scale sabotage which would result in retribution and do more harm to the population than good to the war effort. The Air Force would carry out destruction on a big scale while the Resistance would at this stage supply Intelligence and do minor sabotage work. 'Ambushes on the roads used by German supply convoys, sabotage of the trains transporting enemy personnel or equipment, attacks on careless patrols or badly-guarded posts, the destruction of vehicles in depots, of petrol in tanks, of munitions in store—these were the Maquis' objectives until the landing of the Allied armies offered them a larger field of action.'[1]

There were other reasons too which made this division of labour necessary. The Air Force had a definite bombing policy and had worked out lists of priority and secondary targets. On the other hand specific missions could only exceptionally be assigned to the Maquis while they lacked a hierarchy and organization, which took time to establish. Finally, most of the Air Force targets were out of partisan reach: the factories situated in cities which partisans find a difficult theatre of operation and the submarine bases which were almost inaccessible; as for marshalling yards they could, at any rate, be more effectively hit by air than by ground operations, especially since the bands were usually small.

There were of course exceptions: through partisan action the Hispano-Suiza works were severely damaged and the Le Peugeot factory and others were put out of action by the workers themselves in return for the promise that the town would not be bombed. Yet for all practical purposes air and ground forces operated against different targets.[2]

But with the Allied invasion of France some sort of co-operation became necessary. The Air Force did not compete with the newly-arriving paratroops and air landing troops and only to a minor extent with the SAS parties. But the Resistance went now over to large-scale destruction. A redesignation of targets as be-

[1] General de Gaulle, *War Memoirs, Unity, 1942-1944*, London 1959, p. 254.
[2] It should be noted, though, that air as well as ground forces attacked railway trains.

tween Air Force and Resistance was thus called for, all important targets had to be allocated and the attacks in the rear had to be co-ordinated with the frontal attack.

By this time the Resistance in France had become organized and it was therefore now possible to assign specific tasks to the various partisan detachments. Four sets of plans had been worked out, the Green Plan for railway sabotage, the Violet Plan for sabotage to telephonic and telegraphic communications, the Blue Plan for sabotage to electric power stations, and the Tortoise Plan for blocking roads. Each of the detachments knew where and when to strike after their plan had been brought into operation.

The Air Force, on the other hand, no longer bombed industrial targets in France. As the British Assistant Chief of Air Staff (Ops.) put it in his directive to Bomber Command of March 4, 1944, 'there are now outstanding no industrial targets of primary importance in Occupied Countries, the destruction of which can be regarded as paying big dividends in the general weakening of the German war effort'.[1] The air offensive in France was directed instead against marshalling yards, airfields and ammunition dumps.

The enemy rail transportation system had thus become a common target for the Air Force and the Resistance. The delineation was now made on a geographical basis: the Air Force was to attack the targets near the front, the Resistance was to take care of those in the more remote regions of Lyons, Dijon, Doubs, the east, the centre, and the south-west.[2] The Air Force kept these partisan detachments supplied and it was laid down in Air Force directives that all SOE and OSS operations undertaken by Air Force units 'will be in accordance with the requirements of the Supreme Allied Commander'.[3]

Another Resistance task, insurrection near the front, had to be concerted with front line requirements and this, as we have seen, was done by sending the French SAS component to Brittany where it took charge of the rising. We have also mentioned before that SAS, SOE and OSS established a common headquarters

[1] Cf. Sir Charles Webster and Dr Noble Frankland, *The Strategic Air Offensive Against Germany*, History of the Second World War, vol. iv, London 1961, p. 166.
[2] General de Gaulle, *op. cit.*, p. 282.
[3] Cf. Sir Charles Webster and Dr Noble Frankland, *op cit.*, p. 170 and seq.

under the Supreme Commander. The—French—Commander of the French Forces of the Interior to which most of the Resistance belonged also served in the Supreme Commander's headquarters. Since the Commandos, Rangers and paratroops came under the control of the unit to which they were assigned, the Supreme Commander was thus in effective control of all the forces of the rear. This arrangement made it possible, within the limits of forces available, to assign each target to one force of the rear and to avoid duplication of effort where it could otherwise have occurred, that is between SAS, partisans and the Air Force on the one hand and between paratroops, Commandos and Rangers on the other.

There is no doubt that this arrangement was working well and no better one could have been found in the circumstances of the last war where Special Forces kept a large measure of independence and part of the Resistance took orders from General de Gaulle and part from Britain and the United States. But there cannot be any doubt either that every commander in the field would prefer a structure with fewer chains of command and fewer links.

It has been suggested that the Special Forces should come under the control of the Air Force because both are responsible for deep penetration and the Air Force looks after their requirements.[1] But such an arrangement would hardly be welcome. In the first place, it must be remembered that the SAS sometimes works with partisans and the US Special Force will control some partisan detachments. These partisans would necessarily also come under Air Force control under this scheme with the result that there would be in future not only Army partisans, SOE/OSS partisans and 'free' partisans but Air Force partisans as well. Furthermore, basic training for Special Forces is army training[2] which the Air Force could not provide. Next, and this conclusion is reinforced by the battle of France, the ground operations in the rear are closely tied up with the frontal ground operations; this was true of the Maquis whose various sabotage missions against the railways, power stations and so on as well as the Brittany rising were concerted with Army requirements, and it equally

[1] Cf. Discussion after the Lecture by Lt.-General Sir John W. Hackett, loc. cit., Royal United Service Institution Journal 1952, vol. 97, p. 38.
[2] Major L. E. O. T. Hart, ibid., p. 40.

applied to the SAS parties who operated on the Army's axis of advance. On the other hand, there was little contact, except for air cover and supply drops, between the air and ground forces of the rear, once their respective spheres of operation had been demarcated. The air is in fact almost as much involved in the activities of the ground forces on the front as in those of the ground forces in the rear. There is therefore no reason why the air should take charge of the latter, and this applies also under nuclear conditions.

Another conclusion can be drawn from the preceding discussion. If the system of control over the forces of the rear in theatres of operations is improved, as it ought to be, the Air Force should not be drawn into the scheme or lose in any way its present status and independence. There is no difficulty in dividing up the rear missions between air and ground, be it by targets, as it was done in France before the landings, or by areas, as it was done afterwards, and the present system of having the Air Force represented in the theatre commander's headquarters fully safeguards the requirements of both Army and Air Force.[1]

We have so far discussed the air effort in a conventional war. If in a future war destruction of a target is required on a nuclear scale, the ground forces of the rear are ineligible for the task because they have no nuclear weapons. The delineation and demarcation system evolved in the last war can serve as a guide only if the destruction of the target can be carried out with conventional weapons.

---

[1] In March 1944 General Eisenhower took command of the US Strategic Air Forces in Europe, RAF Bomber Command and Allied Expeditionary Air Forces. He lost control in September but the change in command structure made little difference in practice. Cf. *The Army Air Forces in World War II*, vol. iii, *Europe—Argument to V-E Day (January 1944 to May 1945)*, ed. by W. F. Craven and J. L. Cate, Chicago 1951, p. xiv.

The interdiction force of medium bombers, which is to isolate the European battlefield by attacking enemy lines of communication with nuclear weapons, is at the disposal of the Supreme Allied Commander.

III. THE REAR THEATRE OF WAR

CHAPTER 10

THE SCOPE FOR WARFARE
IN THE NEAR REAR

There is no exact demarcation between the near and far rear, the zones of shallow and deep infiltration, and little is gained by explaining that one understands by near rear a zone which can be reached by front troops in a comparatively short time. The immediate rear is that part of the near rear which adjoins the front line, but again its depth cannot be accurately defined and may vary, just as the depth of army areas varies. The topography, the fluidity of the fighting, the rate of advance or retreat determine what is near or far and any dogmatism would be misplaced.

The offensive land warfare forces, with which the discussion is from now on m..inly concerned, are principally composed in the near rear of Commandos/Rangers, airborne troops on 'Commando' and tactical missions, SAS and guerrillas, and in the far rear of airborne forces on operational and strategic missions, Chindit-type forces, SAS and guerrillas. SAS, Chindit-type forces and guerrillas are formations which operate in the rear for an extensive period, while airborne troops and Commandos/Rangers usually fight a short engagement and are then withdrawn.

The forces of the near rear have two functions: they fight[1] and they harass. Commandos/Rangers and airborne troops are combat forces, the SAS is a harassing force. The guerrillas in the near rear fight and harass; in the immediate rear they are more often than not involved in fighting since they usually give direct combat support to the front. While guerrillas should as a rule harass and not fight, as will be seen in Chapter 11, no objection can be taken to their combat activity in the immediate rear since they are meant to be quickly relieved by the advancing front troops and to fight for only a short period, and their co-operation

[1] They may avoid fighting by deceiving the enemy and then often wear enemy uniform or civilian dress.

is sometimes indispensable especially if no troops are available for the task.

These forces of the near rear are of course not necessarily the only friendly forces in that area. There may also be troops which have infiltrated or penetrated from the front into the enemy rear. It is therefore opportune to inquire what the relation of the forces of the rear is to those formations and, in particular, whether they can replace or at least supplement them.

In the last war forces from the front, mainly tank formations, surprisingly often found their way into the enemy rear, either by a break-through or by an outflanking movement. Especially in the German advance in Poland and France and in the Allied and German operations in North Africa and Soviet Russia armoured forces played an often decisive part; they cut off enemy communications, blocked his retreat and closed the ring of encirclement.

Where the front is a continuous strongly defended line or natural obstacles favour the defence, a break-through may be impossible or possible only at great cost. Most of the tank incursions into the rear were in the last war effecte' through gaps in the front or by way of an open flank. Where such inlets cannot be found, the advantage of having forces of the rear is obvious. Where there are forces of the rear, and tank or other formations are also available for breaking into the rear, the following distinctions must be made:

1. There are tasks which only a force of the rear can perform, such as raiding, sabotaging and kidnapping.

2. There are other tasks which either a force dispatched from the front to the rear or forces of the rear can perform. The enemy's route of retreat and his communications can for instance be blocked by armoured formations or a force of the rear (partisans, Commandos, paratroops).

3. There are tasks which both forces can jointly perform. Brandenburgers kept the route open for panzer formations, Soviet partisans prepared river crossings for the Red Army, and so on.

4. The foregoing tasks of the forces of the rear are mainly tactical. Can the forces of the rear also achieve the commander's strategic aims as forces dispatched from the front to the rear do?

It must be recognized that the effort of the forces of the rear is different in a number of aspects from that of forces dispatched from the front.

(a) Forces dispatched from the front start fighting in the rear at or after the beginning of the battle. The SAS, the Special Force (Chindits), the Special Force with partisans, and partisans can commence action long before. They can hit the enemy's command posts and centres of administration, they can paralyse or impede his build-up and weaken him long before battle is joined.

(b) Forces from the front come into the rear for a short mission, while some of the forces of the rear are stationed and active there for a long period.

(c) The forces dispatched from the front are combat forces, the forces of the rear also harass.

(d) Both forces can contain the enemy but usually only forces of the rear can contain him in areas away from the front line.

(e) Forces from the front are usually sent to the rear for a decisive effort. The forces of the rear, apart from airborne troops on operational and strategic missions, made in the last war only a subsidiary contribution. The first have heavy weapons, the latter are lightly armed.

The efforts of the two forces therefore differ in four respects: by their timing, duration, type, and scope. These differences seem so great that it appears at first glance unlikely that the forces of the rear could take over some of the tasks hitherto performed by forces from the front. Yet it appears that such a transfer is to some extent possible. What, then, can the forces of the rear do to achieve the aims of strategy?

The battlefield does not begin and end where front line troops meet. It extends from the rear of our own troops—an enemy will see to that—to the remotest corner of his rear, and the forces of the rear contribute in their way to the outcome of a battle or campaign just as front line troops do in their fashion on the other side of the front. But regardless of the side of the front on which they are deployed, both forces are meant to contribute to the achievement of one and the same strategic aim.

In every campaign or battle the intention of the commander is to spoil the enemy's strategy and tactics and to advance his own. 'While we strive for superiority and initiative,' says Mao Tse-tung, 'the enemy strives for them too; thus, war is in truth a contest in ability between the commanders of opposing armies in their struggle for superiority and initiative.'[1] But while Mao sees the basic principle of war in one's own preservation and the annihilation of the enemy[2] and describes attack as the chief means of annihilation,[3] his compatriot Sun Tzu had found almost 2,500 years earlier that 'to fight and conquer in all your battles is not supreme excellence. Supreme excellence consists in breaking the enemy's resistance without fighting.'[4]

In his superb *Strategy: The Indirect Approach*, Captain Liddell Hart has developed this theory and shown the ways and means for achieving 'supreme excellence'. The true aim of the strategist, Captain Liddell Hart explains, 'is not so much to seek battle as to seek a strategic situation so advantageous that if it does not of itself produce the decision, its continuation by a battle is sure to achieve this'. 'In other words, dislocation is the aim of strategy; its sequel may be either the enemy's dissolution or his easier disruption in battle.'[5]

Captain Liddell Hart shows that this dissolution can be attained in the physical and the psychological sphere, the first producing the disorganization and the second the demoralization of the enemy.

The enemy's disorganization can be brought about, as Captain Liddell Hart explains, by one or more of the following moves:

1. by upsetting his dispositions and, by compelling a sudden change of front, dislocating the distribution and organization of his forces;
2. by separating his forces;
3. by endangering his supplies;
4. by menacing his routes of retreat.

Demoralization of the enemy is 'the result of the impression on the commander's mind of the physical effects listed', especially if he suddenly realizes his disadvantage and feels trapped. 'This is the reason why it has most frequently followed a physical move on to the enemy's rear.'[6]

[1] Mao Tse-tung, *On the Protracted War*, in *Selected Works of Mao Tse-tung*, vol. ii, London 1954, p. 214.
[2] *Strategic Problems in Guerrilla War*, ibid., p. 121.
[3] *On the Protracted War*, op. cit., p. 205.
[4] *Sun Tzu on the Art of War, The Oldest Military Treatise in the World*, translated by Lionel Giles, London 1910, p. 17.
[5] B. H. Liddell Hart, *Strategy: The Indirect Approach*, London 1954, p. 339.
[6] Ibid., pp. 339-40.

It is striking that the enemy's disorganization is mostly also engineered from the rear: the change of front of the enemy, the threat to his supplies, the cutting of his retreat route. In fact only two of these aims—the change of front and the separation of forces—can also be realized by operations from the flank and the latter can also be achieved by frontal operations. By those moves the forces dispatched from the front to the rear intend to disorganize and demoralize the enemy.

How can the forces of the rear, by their own efforts, disorganize and demoralize the enemy? In order to answer this question we try to find out firstly which of the moves aimed at the disorganization and demoralization of the enemy can be made by the forces of the rear, and secondly on what conditions they can achieve the desired strategic result.

1. (a) It is probably true to say that the forces of the rear never compelled the enemy in the last war suddenly to change his front. Only combat troops could do so, and neither the Allies nor the Axis Powers used their airborne troops and Commandos for this purpose. But the Allied airborne operation planned in March 1945 for the invasion of Central Germany would have had this effect,[1] and so would have had the operation envisaged by General Wingate for the airborne advance into Indo-China.[2] Operations of this type in the far rear—where both were meant to take place—can only hope to succeed if the enemy is already dislocated or demoralized—the troops have otherwise little chance of holding out indefinitely—but in the near rear strong forces of the rear can produce that effect in exceptional circumstances, and the French underground army, led and stiffened by paratroops, almost proved the point in Brittany in its operations from June to August 1944.

As a rule, however, the forces of the rear will proceed by other means in order to upset the enemy's dispositions and dislocate the distribution and organization of his forces. Their working methods were demonstrated by Soviet partisans in 1944. The German Army Group Centre was entirely dependent for its transport on one solitary railway line which ran through partisan territory. The partisans had for months strongly attacked this line. Suddenly, at the orders of the Soviet High Command,

[1] Cf. above Chapter 8.
[2] Cf. below Chapter 11.

these attacks stopped completely, and at this moment the Red Army made a feint attack against the southern part of Army Group Centre's front line. Army Group Centre sent at once all available reserves by rail to the southern front, and the partisans allowed the trains to pass without any interference. 'Hardly had the German reinforcements arrived in the south, when, surprisingly, the Red Army attacked with full force in the north, and when the Germans wanted to send the badly-needed reinforcements back by rail to the north in order to prop up the tottering northern front, the partisans, again on Red Army orders, in an unprecedented demonstration of mass destruction, brought the rail traffic to an almost complete standstill. Army Group Centre, denuded of troops and cut off from reinforcements, collapsed.'[1]

(b) Again, the forces of the rear do not as a rule attempt to separate the enemy force; they are not strong enough to drive a wedge into it. They cannot therefore open a gap in the front line. What they do instead is to thin out and contain the enemy's troops, preferably troops drawn from the front. As the reader will remember, the Second Chindit Expedition was expected to draw off and disorganize the enemy troops opposing General Stilwell's forces but this aim could not be realized on the chosen battlefield. The possibilities for success are limited. The battlefield, as we have seen, must be sensitive. The chance to draw off front line troops is greatest if the forces of the rear operate near the front; but the combat forces of the rear are too lightly armed to fight out a lengthy engagement and the harassing forces usually too thinly spread in that area to attract many of the enemy. It is only when the enemy has denuded his rear of troops and committed practically all his forces to the front that he will call front line units back to deal with the menace in his rear. The forces of the rear are, however, well equipped to delay the arrival of reinforcements for the front, as the French Maquis have shown.

(c) The forces of the rear are obviously also in an excellent position to endanger the enemy's supplies, in many places and over a lengthy period. The Chindits, French, Yugoslav and

[1] Cf. Dixon/Heilbrunn, *Communist Guerrilla Warfare*, op. cit., p. 91, and Oberst Hermann Teske, *Die silbernen Spiegel*, Heidelberg 1952, pp. 192 f., 210 f.

Soviet partisans have given outstanding examples.

(d) Finally, Commandos and Rangers, airborne troops and partisans have often and successfully menaced the enemy routes of retreat.

It is therefore obvious that the forces of the rear can make any or all of the four moves within the limits discussed. It must be realized, though, that if they start their operations in advance of battle, the commander's aim may become obvious and the enemy can then alter his dispositions in time to meet the expected thrust; but the commander will as a rule be able to mislead his opponent by diversionary activities elsewhere in the rear.

Can the forces of the rear also execute moves aimed at demoralizing the enemy? They can do a lot to this effect, by kidnapping, raiding, ambushing, sabotaging, spreading rumours, and so on, but the effort is lengthy and any effect will be produced only as the cumulative result of many actions. Psychological dislocation, as Captain Liddell Hart has shown,[1] is brought about especially if the enemy commander becomes *suddenly* aware that his troops have become disorganized by one or more of the above four moves. Yet since the forces of the rear can carry them out, they can also produce the shock effect.

2. It is therefore not always correct to regard the effort of the forces of the rear as a merely subsidiary one. It frequently is but need not always be so. Yet there are definite limits to a major effort of theirs. They could not have matched in speed and effect the German panzer break-through at Sedan and the subsequent advance to the coast in 1940. They cannot cause the Blitzkrieg type of disorganization on a continuous front. They have their place rather:

(a) behind a defence system consisting of a series of pillboxes and posts. This system was adopted by the French Union Forces in Indo-China, especially in the Red River delta. The forces of the rear can dislocate an enemy so deployed by tying down the garrisons and thus preventing him from establishing a front. By completely immobilizing the Union Forces in their positions and infiltrating some of the southern delta regions, the Viet minh had by 1954 succeeded in making the entire southern zone of the delta untenable for the French Union Forces and forcing

[1] *Op. cit.,* p. 340.

151

them to evacuate it without battle.[1] This episode ranks as a classic in 'supreme excellence'—breaking the enemy's resistance without fighting.

(b) behind a short front with open flanks. This type is represented by the northern front in Burma where one Japanese division opposed General Stilwell's forces. In such a situation the forces of the rear can disorganize the enemy's force. The Japanese had committed practically all their troops in Burma to the three fronts and they would have had to withdraw from the northern front more than the one battalion which they actually withdrew to fight the Chindits, had the battlefield been sensitive.[2] By containing a considerable number of front troops and cutting the supply lines, the Chindits would have disorganized the enemy's front especially since their appearance was unexpected.

(c) behind a continuous front. A surprise attack—such as the Soviet partisan knock-out blow against the railway line in the Army Group Centre area—can be successfully directed against the enemy if he has first been isolated. The German panzers in France (1940) delivered the blow and achieved the isolation simultaneously in one quick move by cutting through the opposing front and the supply lines. Where there is a continuous front, any part of it can be isolated—apart from penetration— only if the adjoining parts are fully engaged on their own front and unable to lend assistance. It usually requires time to achieve this kind of isolation. It was in Soviet Russia the result of the preceding drawn-out operations to which the Soviet rear made the minor contribution, and even in the battle itself the partisans produced only the advantageous strategic situation while the Red Army had to produce the decision.

The strength of the forces of the rear lies as a rule in their capacity to assist in disorganizing the enemy rather than in disorganizing him by their own efforts. This assistance can be given to the forces dispatched from the front to the rear as well as to the front troops. The tasks of the forces of the rear in this connection are the tasks for which they have been designed. How much the rear can contribute to the enemy's disorganization

[1] The infiltrating forces were regulars and guerrillas but there is no reason why the part of the former could not also be played by forces of the rear when the enemy's forces are so split up as they were in the delta.
[2] The reference to Chindits is by way of an example; they operated in the far rear.

anl demoralization becomes evident when one applies to the forces of the rear Captain Liddell Hart's exposition of the indirect approach by forces from the front. He emphasizes that the strategic indirect approach requires that the enemy is prevented from changing his dispositions and forming a new front. He insists that the enemy must be drawn asunder in order to deprive him of his freedom of action, both in the physical and the psychological sphere. In the former the strategic indirect approach should cause a distension of his forces or their diversion to unprofitable ends, so that they are too committed elsewhere, and in the latter it should play on his fears and deceive the command.[1]

Mao Tse-tung and Ho Chi-minh have provided object lessons on how forces of the rear can assist in depriving the enemy of his freedom of action and preventing him from forming a new front. 'The extensive development of our guerrilla warfare in his rear,' says Mao of his former Japanese enemy, 'has driven his garrisons in the occupied territories into a completely passive position,'[2] and the same applied to his opponent in the 1946-49 Civil War. Ho developed this concept further, his regulars and guerrillas drew the French Union Forces from one corner of Indo-China to the other, he kept them occupied by guerrillas wherever he could and so made it impossible for the French to build up a strong defence line anywhere. Nor was the psychological impact of his strategy lost on his adversary.

[1] Loc. cit., p. 341.
[2] In On the Protracted War, loc. cit., p. 218.

CHAPTER 11

THE SCOPE FOR WARFARE IN
THE FAR REAR

We have seen in Chapter 8 under what conditions airborne troops could be used operationally for combat action in the far rear. We have particularly noticed that the Germans chose for their employment in Holland and Crete a closed battlefield to which the enemy was unable to bring reinforcements and they could match his strength almost from the outset.

Such operations are by their nature short and the strain on supplies and transport is therefore also short. Likewise, the enemy's opportunities for interfering with lines of communication are considerably reduced if the airborne attack is unexpected. Airborne troops of this type, deployed for one short engagement, have therefore a chance to fight successfully and to hold their ground.

But the problem is a different one for the more permanent formations in the enemy rear, especially the Special Force, the Special Force with Partisans, the Independent Companies and the partisans. They are stationed in the rear for an extended period. The enemy can usually bring up reinforcements. To a greater or lesser extent these forces depend on their lines of communication for a considerable time. It is a matter of doubt whether they should fight the enemy or restrict themselves to harassing him.

This subject has attracted little attention so far. In the last war the more permanent units in the far rear usually regarded it as their main function to harass, ambush and raid rather than fight the enemy. However, there were two notable exceptions, the Army of National Liberation in Yugoslavia and the Special Force (Second Chindit Expedition) in Burma, both of which fought and harassed. In the case of the first, it appears, it is tacitly assumed that Tito's decision to fight was right because he contained so many enemy troops while in the case of the

154

latter it is held that Wingate's decision to fight was wrong because he needed a fairly large force for this purpose yet contained relatively few of the enemy.

Units in the enemy rear cannot avoid combat altogether because the enemy will attack them whenever he can, and they must attack on occasions, but as a rule the more permanent forces will not seek battle. Especially the partisan leaders of the last war usually restricted themselves to harassing actions but Marshal Tito as well as General Wingate regarded fighting as the main function of their respective forces.

It might be held that it does not matter much whether the more permanent forces in the far rear fight or harass the enemy as long as they seriously inconvenience him by their activities. But this is not so. In the first place, it is obvious that rear forces which fight need heavier arms and more ammunition and supplies than those which only harass, and to a greater or lesser extent those arms and supplies have not only to be found but they must also be constantly transported to them by the regular forces on the other side of the front. If these demands have to be met out of resources needed by the regular forces, they may well lose more by denuding themselves of matériel and transport services than gain by the activities of the rear, especially if a sizeable part of the Air Force is required for transport and possibly also direct combat support in the rear. Whether the Air Force could in future stand the strain, in view of the improved defences, is not beyond doubt. But this is not all. The heavier arms of fighting rear forces might well impede their mobility on which they rely for gaining the initiative, achieving surprise and vanishing after a strike, and the better they are equipped with heavier weapons the lower may be their effectiveness. Their own losses will be higher if they are involved in pitched battles. Finally, if the rear forces lose towns and liberated areas they have held, the population, exposed to the ravages of war and the retaliation of the enemy, might well turn against them and they might have to give up, either because they consider the sacrifices of the population no longer commensurate with their own achievements or because they cannot continue the fight any longer without popular support. Harassing forces have to some extent to face the same problem, but it is magnified if they fight.

The question whether the more permanent forces of the rear

should fight or harass therefore needs closer investigation, both for soldiers and partisans.

As far as Tito's formations are concerned, they are generally referred to as partisans but this description obscures the fact that they really had two different components, viz. semi-regular units and partisans proper. The Tito forces did not differ much in their structure from Mao's forces against Chiang Kai-shek (after 1945) and Ho's Viet-minh forces against the French Union troops; all three revolutionaries had formed semi-regular as well as irregular units, and the semi-regulars engaged the enemy in combat.

There is, however, one difference between the three in the conception of their roles: Mao and Ho had necessarily to engage in large-scale fighting in order to achieve victory since their units were the only forces confronting the enemy; they were without a national army or allies to join them in the field. Yet Tito had a choice: he too could liberate his country by his own efforts and seek battles with the Axis forces, but he could also wait for the Allies to liberate the country for him and restrict himself to harassing the enemy in the meanwhile. Tito chose the first course because it gave him a better, if not the only, chance to establish communist rule over the country. He therefore needed a semi-regular army, in addition to his partisans, and he appropriately called his forces 'National Liberation Army and Partisan detachments of Yugoslavia'.

On June 22, 1941, the day of the German invasion of Soviet Russia, the Central Committee of the Communist Party of Yugoslavia called the people to arms. Tito started to form his semi-regular forces soon afterwards. His first Order of the Day referred to the National Liberation Detachments as 'fighting' formations, and by December of that year he had activated the First Proletarian Brigade, 'the nucleus of the future People's Army', as another Order of the Day made clear. More Proletarian Brigades soon came into existence. 'They formed the nucleus of an armed and disciplined force which would fight, not just in defence of its own village or strip of country, but in any part of Yugoslavia whatsoever.'[1]

Apart from the various brigades and later divisions and corps there existed the partisan detachments and battalions which had not yet been formed into brigades. They were attached to the

[1] Sir Fitzroy Maclean, *Disputed Barricade*, London 1957, p. 160.

fighting forces. They took part in the defence of liberated areas, they recruited volunteers,[1] and they harassed the enemy in his rear, particularly by destroying his lines of communication, when he attacked the fighting forces.[2] They were full-timers and went with the brigades wherever they were needed. By contrast yet another element, which the Germans called *Hauspartisanen* or Home Partisans, stayed in its own locality; they lived as civilians among the population, followed their normal occupations and worked as part-time partisans. They collected intelligence and acted as scouts and guides to the fighting units, but above all, they were harassing elements and therefore partisans proper. They killed sentries, threw hand-grenades into German barracks, burned down garages, mined village streets and house entrances, destroyed railway lines—in one night they blew up the rails of the Agram-Belgrade railway in eighty places[3]—and did all the other jobs which partisans usually perform. So much so that Colonel-General Rendulic, who commanded a German Panzer Army in this theatre, has stated that 'the life and tasks of the German troops would have been much easier if the opponent had had only closed formations. The Home Partisans were a much more dangerous enemy because it was from them that all the hostile acts emanated against which the troops could protect themselves only with the greatest difficulty and which caused them large losses. They could seldom, if ever, be caught.'[4]

In view of this German appreciation one might have thought that Tito would have greatly accelerated the expansion of the Home Partisan force, even at the expense of other formations, but this was not so. A German contemporary estimate puts the number of local, that is Home, Partisans in Slovenia, Croatia, Serbia and Macedonia in June 1944 at 8,000.[5] They therefore seem to have amounted to less than two per cent of Tito's total strength. Indeed, Tito intentionally kept the number of Home Partisans small, and he described it as one of his principles 'to

[1] Cf. Lt.-Col. Brajus Kovic-Dimitrye, 'La Guerre de Libération en Yougoslavie (1941-45)', in *European Resistance Movements 1939-45*, Oxford 1960, p. 322.
[2] Sir Fitzroy Maclean, *op. cit.*, p. 236. On the numbers of these partisan units cf. Lt.-Col. Brajus Kovic-Dimitrye, *op. cit.*, pp. 321, 327, 334 and 336.
[3] General-Oberst Dr Lothar Rendulic, 'Der Partisanenkrieg', in *Bilanz des Zweiten Weltkrieges*, Oldenburg 1953, p. 106.
[4] *Ibid.*, p. 106.
[5] Cf. Gerhard Hümmelchen, 'Balkanräumung 1944', *Wehrwissenschaftliche Rundschau*, 1959, 9. Jahrgang, p. 566.

overcome the tendency of villagers to stay in or near their villages and gradually to accustom them to the idea of fighting wherever they were needed'.[1]

Tito's preference for semi-regulars and mobile partisans is understandable: the Home Partisans could contribute nothing to his fight against Mihailovitch and little to the conquest of areas where he could establish his régime. But he also considered the semi-regulars as the more important element in the war against the occupying powers. All the three aims of Tito found their final fulfilment in Serbia: there was the old hunting ground of Mihailovitch whom he must defeat to establish his own claim to rule the country, there was Yugoslavia's capital Belgrade which he must conquer to exercise his rule over the country, and there he could establish his first contacts with the Red Army whom he wanted to assist and whose support he needed to defeat the Germans in battle. Without large formations or Shock Divisions, as Tito called them, none of these aims could be attained.

With the help of his Shock Divisions Tito was able to liberate most of the country. If he lost one area he conquered another one. Three times he tried to gain Serbia whose undisturbed possession was vital to the Germans, not only because they had to prevent the eventual junction of Tito's forces with the Red Army but particularly also because the interruption of the Belgrade-Saloniki railway traffic by Tito's forces would have completely undermined the German position in South-East Europe. Twice, at the end of 1943 and in March 1944, he was effectively stopped by the Germans, but the third time, during July to September 1944, they had hardly any troops available to oppose him; they used their operational reserves, they drew on units in less important sectors, even the coast, but there were still too few of them and Tito could finally occupy most of Serbia without large-scale fighting and often without opposition.[2] The German troops had been depleted by a number of events: Italy had left the war the year before and German troops had to take over the Italian occupation zones, and in August 1944 Rumania and in Septem-

[1] Sir Fitzroy Maclean, op. cit., p. 236.
[2] Kriegstagebuch des Oberkommandos der Wehrmacht, eingeleitet und erläutert by Percy Ernst Schramm, Band iv, 1. Halbband, Frankfurt am Main 1961, pp. 685 and 699.

ber Bulgaria had changed sides and compelled the Germans to man a new front against them and the Russians. All that Germany could do from then on was to secure the railway lines and some of the centres of raw material.

Tito's success against the occupying forces seems to confirm the correctness of his policy to fight. He also held that large fighting formations would contain even larger numbers of the enemy by forcing him to increase the numerical strength of his garrisons in order to withstand attack. The enemy would need at least one reinforced battalion for each garrison or a division for nine garrisons.[1] But this calculation assumes that the semi-regulars have always the initiative, that they are not equally vulnerable, that outside assistance cannot reach the garrison in time, or that the enemy cannot retake a lost position. None of these conditions prevailed in Yugoslavia until the middle of 1944.

Yet this much is certain that the Germans and Italians could try to encircle Tito's forces only if they had large formations available, and in their Fifth Offensive, in Montenegro (May to June 1943), no less than 50,000 German troops, 40,000 Italians and well over 10,000 Bulgarians and others took part against less than 20,000 partisans.[2] Tito lost over 10,300 men killed or missing,[3] but his enemies' success was even less complete than this figure suggests because only a part of Tito's forces had been engaged in the battle.[4] Since Tito distributed his Shock Divisions after this battle over various parts of the country, the occupying forces were from then on unable to attack all his forces simultaneously, they did not succeed in annihilating those they

[1] Lt.-General Dusan Kvedar, 'Territorial Warfare', Journal of the United Service Institution of India, vol. lxxxix, April-June 1959, No. 375, p. 131.
[2] Cf. Sir Fitzroy Maclean, op. cit., p. 220. But also against the Axis forces fought an unknown number of Chetniks as will be seen later.
[3] Les Efforts de Guerre de la Yougoslavie, 1941-1945, Institut Historique de l'Armée de la République Fédérative Populaire de Yougoslavie. N.d., p. 32.
[4] While figures for partisan strength are always difficult to ascertain, the estimates for Tito's forces show particularly great discrepancies. Vladimir Dedijer, Tito Speaks, London 1953, p. 186, gives the strength of Tito's forces in the autumn of 1942 at 150,000 fighting men or nine divisions, yet the Germans estimated the strength of a division before 1944 at 3-5,000 or a total of 45,000 at the utmost. Even Yugoslav sources differ; cf. for instance Dusan Plenca. Le Mouvement de Libération Nationale en Yougoslavie, Paper read at the Second International Congress on the History of the Resistance, Milan, March 26/29, 1961, against the figures in the Chart below in the text.

attacked, they were unable to prevent the expansion of his movement, and could only dislodge him from sensitive points.

It therefore seems that it was due to the fighting element of Tito's forces that so many enemy troops were tied down in Yugoslavia, especially after the former had spread out over the country. Yet the Germans viewed things differently. They calculated that they would have to use even more troops if Tito dissolved his closed formations and assigned the men to harassing work. The War Diary of the High Command of the Armed Forces makes this clear. After the Sixth Offensive had not had the desired results for the Germans, they decided quickly to mount another large-scale attack; 'among other reasons this was necessary,' the War Diary observes, 'because Tito, after his unsuccessful invasion of Serbia, apparently intended to revert to small-war tactics which would impose considerable handicaps on the German conduct of the war.'[1]

It is therefore evident that harassing partisans had a greater impact on German strategy and dispositions than the same number of men in fighting formations. The reasons are not far to seek: If the partisans fight like regular formations, they are no more formidable an enemy than any other regular troops. The attacking forces, it is true, need large numbers if they want to encircle them, just as large numbers are required for the encirclement of other regular forces, but they can contain them, compel them to give battle and attack them frontally even without sizeable numerical superiority especially as they have as a rule superior weapons available. But where widespread small partisan detachments harass the occupation forces they constantly need a very large superiority in numbers, for static guard duties as well as for locating and hunting down their elusive opponents, and their superiority in weapons is often of no consequence. Hence the harassing partisans are more feared since they are as a rule more effective. The menace from small-war tactics in Yugoslavia would have been all the greater because its repercussions would not have been confined to the country itself but would also have been felt in Greece, Albania, Rumania, Bulgaria and on the southern front against Russia since the German communication lines ran through Yugoslavia.

[1] *Kriegstagebuch des Oberkommandos der Wehrmacht* (subsequently quoted as 'Kriegstagebuch'), *op. cit.*, p. 645.

The occupying forces had in fact a much better chance to overcome the resistance of large formations than of the Home Partisans. As the reader will remember, over 10,300 fighting partisans were killed or missing as the result of one single engagement, the Fifth Offensive, carried out by 100,000 enemy troops. In Malaya it took 70,000 troops, 75,000 police and 250,000 Home Guards twelve years to kill 6,710 harassing guerrillas. While conditions in both countries are not strictly comparable, the striking contrast in effort, time and result remains. The Yugoslav National Liberation Army lost 305,000 killed[1] while the total German losses in killed and missing in the entire Balkan theatre, including the casualties in the initial conquest and final retreat, amounted to just over 34,000.[2] The total losses of the occupation forces in Yugoslavia, including those killed by the Red Army, Rumanians and Bulgarians and possibly Mihailovitch's forces, were 447,000 killed.[3] The Liberation Army's losses seem disproportionate. Harassing guerrillas have often, though not always, managed to inflict very much higher losses on their enemy than they sustained themselves.

The fact remains, of course, that the occupation forces did not manage to defeat Tito's formations and an important factor was that Yugoslav generalship, fighting qualities and morale were all excellent. But it must not be overlooked that the strength of the occupation forces was most of the time inadequate to suppress the rebellion.

It would have needed over one-third of the occupation troops to deal effectively with the Home Partisans alone; the French forces in Algeria had a seventeen-fold superiority and could not overcome the partisan menace, and in Malaya the successful fight against some 7,000 rebels required a twenty-fold superiority, even if the Home Guard is excluded. But apart from the fight against

---

[1] Nikola Kapetanovic, *Tito and the Partisans*, Belgrade, n.d., p. 46. The figure may include those killed by Mihailovitch's forces.
[2] *Kriegstagebuch, op. cit.*, 2. Halbband, Appendix by Professor P. E. Schramm, Frankfurt am Main 1961, p. 1510.
[3] Cf. *Les Efforts de Guerre de la Yougoslavie, op. cit.*, p. 7. The figure includes 150,000 killed in 1945, *ibid.*, p. 30. That those killed by the Red Army, etc., are included in the figure of 447,000 follows from the text of 'Les Efforts' etc.: 'Pour toute la durée de la guerre les pertes de l'occupant se chiffrent par 447,000 morts. . . .' This source also gives the figure for Axis prisoners at 559,434; most of them were Italians who surrendered in 1943, and Germans and others who surrendered in 1945 when the war had ended.

Tito, the occupation forces in Yugoslavia had other commitments as well which drained their manpower: they also fought against Mihailovitch's forces, they manned the coast against an Allied invasion, and in the last year of the war most of their troops were required at the front against the East.

No precise assessment can be made as to how many troops were needed for these purposes; the requirements constantly varied. Sometimes coastal defence reserves took part in partisan warfare and sometimes the same occupation troops fought simultaneously against Tito's and Mihailovitch's forces, as in the First and Fifth Offensives. The latter is commonly regarded as having solely been directed against Tito, but the Germans conceived it as primarily aimed at Mihailovitch,[1] and they took at least 2,000 of his men prisoner.[2] There were, however, periods when more peaceful relations prevailed between Mihailovitch's and the occupation forces. A number of subordinate commanders of Mihailovitch had made accommodations with the Italians; in May 1943, just before the start of the Fifth Offensive, Mihailovitch is said to have concluded a general armistice with a German commander but it was annulled by the German High Command;[3] in the autumn of that year local agreements between a number of Mihailovitch's subordinate commanders and the Germans were actually reached and kept until they were renounced by some of the former in the beginning of 1944. In March Mihailovitch sought again accommodation with the Germans but the latter refused to oblige.[4]

Up to February 1943, the Germans were more worried about the Mihailovitch than the Tito movement. Indeed, as a German Intelligence report put it at that time, 'among the various insurgent movements which increasingly cause trouble in the area of the former Yugoslav State, the movement of Draja Mihailovitch stands in first place with regard to leadership, armament, organization and activity'.[5] In 1942 and 1943, as in 1941, the

[1] Kriegstagebuch, 1. Halbband, p. 634.
[2] Ibid., p. 638.
[3] Cf. Major Herbert Kriegsheim, Getarnt, Getäuscht und doch Getreu, Die geheimnisvollen 'Brandenburger', Berlin 1958, Part II, p. 312, and Paul Leverkuehn, Der geheime Nachrichtendienst der deutschen Wehrmacht im Kriege, Frankfurt am Main 1957, pp. 124 f.
[4] Kriegstagebuch, 1. Halbband, p. 640.
[5] Trials of the War Criminals before the Nuremberg Military Tribunals, vol. xi. The Hostages Case, Washington 1950, p. 1015.

Germans fought a number of engagements against Mihailovitch's forces; thanks to their Intelligence, the latter usually succeeded in extricating themselves from encirclements.[1] Again, in
January 1944, the Germans considered it necessary to mount a
major offensive against Mihailovitch, but finding their forces insufficient for the task, they decided instead on a number of minor
actions.[2] There cannot be any doubt that until then Mihailovitch's forces constituted a drain on the occupation troops.

Coastal defence tied down an even greater number of occupation troops yet the studies on the subject hardly ever make any
allowance for this requirement when the respective strength of
the opposing forces is calculated. More than once was an Allied
invasion on the coast expected, first at the end of 1942 after the
Anglo-American landing in North Africa and the occupation
of Tunisia, then in the autumn of 1943 when Italy defected, and
again early in 1944 when the Allied advance in Italy had come
to a halt and much of Yugoslavia was in revolt. On January 1,
1944, no less than ten divisions were assigned to coastal defence:[3]
In North Croatia the 264 (territorial) Division, 114 Jäger Division, 373 and 392 Croat Infantry Divisions, 367 Infantry Division, 1 Kossack Division (minus one brigade), 42 Jäger Division
and 173 Reserve Division, and in Bosnia-Montenegro the 118
Jäger Division and 181 Infantry Division. These divisions repre-
sent about one-third of the total occupation strength and even
more if the coastal reserves temporarily assigned to partisan warfare are included. Altogether there were at this time 360,000
occupation troops in Yugoslavia[4] against 300,000 men of the
National Liberation Army,[5] 108 Tito partisan units,[5] and perhaps
50,000 or more Mihailovitch guerrillas. In the spring of 1944
more than six German divisions were withdrawn to other fronts
and only two legionary divisions were then available for fighting
Tito's forces; all the remaining troops under German command
in Yugoslavia were required to man the coast.[6] For a short spell
the occupying powers could assemble forces for the Seventh

[1] *Kriegstagebuch*, 1. Halbband, p. 730.
[2] *Ibid.*, p. 640. The Germans estimated the strength of the Mihailovitch Movement in August 1944 at 60-70,000 men.
[3] *Kriegstagebuch*, pp. 610 f.
[4] According to a German appreciation. Cf. Sir Fitzroy Maclean, *op. cit.*, p. 248.
[5] Cf. Dusan Plenca, *op. cit.*, p. 27.
[6] *Kriegstagebuch*, 1. Halbband, p. 647.

Offensive. Soon afterwards they were sent to the new eastern front.

Yugoslav sources give this picture of the comparative strength:[1]

	Nat. Liberation Army	Occupation Troops
1941	91,000	360,000—510,000
1942	137,000	660,000
1943	306,000	700,000—480,000[2]
1944	488,000	500,000
1945	793,000	

Tito as well had another commitment, apart from fighting the occupation troops. His first clashes with Mihailovitch occurred in 1941 in Serbia, in 1942 there were a number of engagements in Montenegro and Bosnia, Dalmatia and Hercegovina, in 1943 there was heavy fighting in Bosnia, Hercegovina, Montenegro and elsewhere. How many of Tito's forces took part in these encounters it is impossible to say; sometimes, as in the Fourth Offensive, Tito's Shock Divisions fought at the same time against Mihailovitch and the occupation troops. Tito probably employed larger numbers against Mihailovitch than the occupying powers did, but very many of their troops were often needed elsewhere, as we have seen. Their numerical superiority over Tito's forces, after due allowance is made for the other commitments of both, was problematic in 1943; it depended on the Italian contribution —the Italians had about twice as many troops as the Germans in Yugoslavia—but action against Tito 'was hampered by the officially promised but actually non-existent or inadequate co-operation of the Italians',[3] and in 1944 the superiority in numbers had vanished.

In 1941 and probably most of 1942 the occupying powers

[1] Les Efforts de Guerre de la Yougoslavie, op. cit., pp. 5 and 34.
[2] The second figure, relating to the time after Italy's surrender, should read 360,000 according to German sources.
[3] Kriegstagebuch, 1. Halbband, p. 602. According to Vladimir Dedijer, op. cit., pp.186 and 202, the strength of the National Liberation Army increased from over 150,000 men in the autumn of 1942 to 300,000 men in the autumn of 1943. Nikola Kapetanovic, op. cit., p. 45, estimates the strength of the occupation forces for the period ended 1942 and first half 1943 at 400,000 Italians, 150,000 Germans and 110,000 other troops.

could have marshalled between them the superior forces necessary to defeat Tito. Yet it was only from the autumn of 1942 on
that Tito's movement was regarded by the Germans as a 'factor
which had to be taken seriously'.[1] They underestimated Tito and
this was understandable since he then operated mainly in
Italian-occupied territory. But even if they had recognized the
threat earlier it seems unlikely that they would have succeeded
in suppressing it. The occupation troops, like any anti-partisan
force, had to learn the hard way—in the beginning they were
satisfied with dispersing Tito's formations—and no partisan
movement of any consequence has ever been defeated in this
century within the period of eighteen months or less in which the
occupying forces in Yugoslavia were really superior in numbers
to their adversary.

The following assessment seems therefore warranted:

Harassing partisans are a greater threat to the occupation
force than fighting partisans. The activities of the former are
more feared, they bind larger enemy forces and they have a
better chance of survival. Added to this, their requirements in
arms and equipment are lower, and their activities are as a rule
less harmful to the population than those of fighting partisans.

It may be said against this that without fighting all the time
Tito would not have gained sufficient popular support and fewer
recruits would have joined his forces.[2] But it must be remembered that the Soviet Russian partisans also attracted large numbers of recruits, yet these partisans restricted themselves mainly
to harassing.

Partisans in the far rear should therefore not fight but harass.

Do similar considerations apply to the Special Force?

It would not be justified to proceed with this part of the inquiry on the same lines as hitherto and draw conclusions by
comparing the strength of Special Force with the strength of
the enemy it contained. We have noted in Chapter 4 that Special
Force was employed on the wrong battlefield and no inference
in regard to its effectiveness can therefore be drawn from statisti-
cal evidence on the mutual strength, success and losses.

When General Wingate outlined his plans for the Second

[1] *Kriegstagebuch*, 1. Halbband, p. 633.
[2] The Germans maintain that Tito introduced conscription in 1943 for all
persons in the liberated areas between the age of eighteen and fifty.

Chindit Expedition, he conceived Special Force as a harassing formation whose task it was to support the main operation on the front. The role of Special Force was clearly subsidiary. The weight of the attack was to be borne by the front. But he changed this *Schwerpunkt* conception by stages: first he held that if the front could not attack the rear should do so, and then he envisaged the rear as the main operational area while the forces at the front were relegated to a subsidiary role.

General Wingate's original views are set out in his Memorandum of August 10, 1943, for the British Joint Planning Staff: The operations of the Long Range Penetration Groups (LRPGs) should aim at disrupting the enemy communications and installations. These activities would throw the enemy into a state of confusion, progressively weaken him and cause him to squander his forces. The LRPGs would also indicate suitable targets for the tactical air force. As a result of their activities favourable conditions for an offensive would occur; they would have to be exploited at once by the front.[1]

When the Commander-in-Chief in India, Sir Claude Auchinleck, was informed of this plan which had been endorsed by the British Chiefs of Staff, he took the view that the timings and areas of employment of LRPGs must be governed by the activities of the main forces. He stressed that without exploitation by the main forces operations by LRPGs were unjustifiably costly against a first-class enemy and not capable of achieving decisive results against organized forces of all arms; unless the main forces could take advantage of the situation created by LRPGs, the latter's efforts were wasted. Their role, the Field-Marshal emphasized, was not to fight but to evade the enemy and by guerrilla tactics to harass him.[2]

General Wingate replied that 'as regards the necessity of a follow-up this is most certainly vital' but he strongly contested the statement that LRPGs should not fight. 'The whole object of the LRPGs,' he said, 'is to fight.'[3]

Both generals agreed, however, that if the Japanese attacked

[1] Major-General S. Woodburn Kirby, *The War Against Japan, op. cit.*, vol. ii, pp. 399 f.
[2] Cf. Despatch by Field-Marshal Sir Claude Auchinleck, 'Operations in the Indo-Burma Theatre from 21st June, 1943, to 15th November, 1943'. *Second Supplement to The London Gazette*, April 27, 1948, p. 2665.
[3] Christopher Sykes, *op. cit.*, pp. 460 f.

first before the British were ready to do so, the LRPGs would also have to play a part. The Field-Marshal was in principle against the expansion of the Special Force proposed by its commander because the resulting demands would disorganize the Army in India but he readily admitted that an enlarged Special Force might be of benefit to counter a Japanese offensive.[1] In the event the Japanese did attack immediately after the Special Force had been flown into its allotted area.

It does not appear that higher authority ever ruled on the question of whether or not Special Force should fight. General Wingate did not at that time envisage that it should launch an all-out offensive against the Japanese. But he objected to having to evade the enemy, possibly because he thought that this type of warfare would make little impression on the enemy. He may also have believed that evasionary tactics had a recognized function only in protracted wars and that quicker results were necessary in preparation of the follow-up. The most likely explanation is that 'the defensive irked him: he thought always in terms of the offensive'.[2] His orders, at any rate, left him with a considerable measure of discretion.

They were, as the reader will recall, to draw off and disorganize the enemy troops opposing General Stilwell, to create a favourable situation for the advance of the Chinese Expeditionary Force, and to inflict the maximum confusion, damage and loss on the enemy forces in Northern Burma. By the time the orders had percolated to battalion level, Special Force was to inflict as much damage as possible on the enemy and his material and thus to gain such moral and material ascendancy over him that 'he will be forced to withdraw his remnants south of parallel 24 degrees in defeat and rout'.[3] Only by fighting could the enemy be routed.

With this conception of its role Wingate had to some extent stripped the Special Force of its guerrilla character and vested it with the functions of a regular formation. Unlike supporting guerrillas, but like regular troops, it intended to gain and hold ground. 'We wanted reinforcements,' Brigadier Calvert has

[1] Ibid., p. 459.
[2] So Brigadier Sir Bernard Fergusson, The Wild Green Earth, op. cit., p. 145.
[3] So Brigadier Calvert's order to his battalions, reproduced in his Prisoners of Hope, op. cit., p. 27.

stated, 'to hold what we had taken and then we would go on and conquer more'.[1]

General Wingate had envisaged 'that the enemy will be in superior force in our neighbourhood',[2] and if that was so it was obvious that Special Force could fight him only under favourable conditions. General Wingate created them in the form of Strongholds. They assured, as much as possible, local superiority to a numerically inferior Special Force. They had other functions as well. In General Wingate's words:

'The Stronghold is a machan overlooking a kid tied up to entice the Japanese tiger.

'The Stronghold is an asylum for LRPG wounded.

'The Stronghold is a magazine for stores.

'The Stronghold is a defended airstrip.

'The Stronghold is an administrative centre for local inhabitants.

'The Stronghold is an orbit round which the columns of the brigade circulate. It is suitably placed with reference to the main objective of the brigade.

'The Stronghold is a base for light planes operating with columns on the main objective.

'The motto of the Stronghold is "No Surrender".'[3]

It would be foolish, General Wingate explained in his Training Note, 'to direct attacks against defended enemy positions if by any means he can be met in the open' or in the Chindits' defended positions. 'We wish, therefore,' the Note emphasized, 'firstly to encounter the enemy in the open and preferably in ambushes laid by us, and secondly to induce him to attack us only in our defended Strongholds.'[3] A Stronghold is 'in the heart of enemy-held territory, an impregnable fortress from which to dominate the countryside in the manner of a Norman baron'.[4]

For the Strongholds a location had to be selected which was in or near the area of operations but inaccessible to wheeled

---

[1] Ibid., p. 100. After Broadway and Aberdeen Strongholds had been constructed, the area under Special Force control was eighty miles by at least thirty miles; cf. Brigadier Calvert, ibid., p. 67.
[2] In his 'Special Force Commander's Training Note No. 8—The Stronghold', issued February 27, 1944. Reprinted in Brigadier Michael Calvert, op. cit., pp. 274 f.
[3] Ibid.
[4] Quoted by Brigadier Sir Bernard Fergusson, op. cit., p. 74. Cf. ibid., for a sketch and description of a Stronghold, pp. 80 and 85 f.

transport, enemy artillery and tanks. The Stronghold should cover, but not include, an airstrip and a separate supply-dropping area. 'The Stronghold relies upon earthworks and mine-fields for immediate defence from the enemy's weapons, with a well-co-ordinated and thoroughly tested fire-plan for the employment of its own weapons.' A floater company outside the perimeter would harass and attack the enemy if he advanced against the Stronghold, and if necessary, floater columns would attack the enemy in his rear. Air defence would be provided either from the airstrip or from the airbase behind the front.

In some aspects the Stronghold takes the place of the rear of the brigade: it provides the means for the brigade to preserve itself, to care for the wounded, to receive and maintain stores, and to protect the inhabitants. It is also the front because the enemy is meant to attack there.

The Stronghold has a garrison of a battalion plus two troops of artillery. It is a fitting tribute to General Wingate's ingenuity that Aberdeen Stronghold was never molested by Japanese ground troops, and to the bravery of the Chindits that White City Stronghold withstood three ground attacks—even though it was accessible to enemy artillery.[1] It is evident that a Special Force must fight for its Stronghold.

It is also obvious that a Special Force is bound to meet and fight the enemy in the course of its sabotage work. But can it be the task of a Special Force to defeat the enemy in a series of combat actions and liberate large areas?

General Wingate stated in his Training Note that LRP columns will have an unrivalled chance of meeting the enemy in the open. But contrary to his expectations the enemy force was not superior in numbers. In the event, as noted before, Special Force did not bind more than two-fifths of its own strength. Its experience cannot therefore be adduced as proof that it can successfully fight an equally strong or stronger enemy and liberate territory.

One of the maxims of guerrilla war is that guerrillas must concentrate absolutely superior forces for every battle. A second is that in battle the harassing element must strongly support the

---

[1] As Brigadier Michael Calvert, op. cit., p. 159, states: 'We had been fortunate in that the Japs attacked White City with too few and too early.' On the lessons of the loss of Blackpool Stronghold, also accessible to enemy artillery, cf. ibid., pp. 161 f.

fighting component by guerrilla activities in the enemy rear. A Special Force which is numerically inferior to the enemy cannot weaken its fighting strength further by sending some of its troops as guerrillas to the rear. Other things being equal, it fights at a disadvantage.

If it tries to hold large areas its fighting strength decreases still further because it must detail part of its forces to static defence and guard duties. Guerrillas, it is true, also establish liberated areas and indeed require them in order to carry on and win their war. But to them the liberated areas are a source of new strength; it is there that they educate the population, levy taxes and gain recruits. These base areas provide the means for a guerrilla movement to transform its inferior forces into superior ones. Unless a Special Force wants to recruit guerrillas on a large scale and succeeds in doing so, it finds its strength sapped by holding large areas.

There is another aspect: It normally requires less manpower to hold a line of the front than an area in the enemy rear. The latter operation is therefore wasteful and undesirable unless there are compensating advantages. In theory there could be two: rear areas might be easier to conquer and the fight might lead to a quicker destruction of the enemy. But neither is true in practice.

The enemy is vulnerable in his rear because his lines of communication run through there. He can be harassed by guerrillas but he cannot harass them in turn since they usually have no rear. But Special Force had a rear and depended on its line of communication; it was comparatively safe because ammunition and supplies came in by air and the Allied Air Forces had superiority in the theatre. Special Force would have been just as affected by an interruption of its air supply line as the enemy was by the interruption of his land supply lines. In view of the greatly improved defences the air supply line is no longer immune; it is, in fact, as vulnerable as any land line, and a Stronghold, ringed by enemy anti-aircraft guns, can quickly be starved out.

A formation of the Special Force type cannot therefore count any longer on harassing without suffering retaliation in kind, and it is thus deprived of the one great advantage over the opposing forces which it has hitherto enjoyed. In a future war a

Special Force and the enemy will meet in his rear at least as equals: *both* can harass, ambush, raid and fight. In all probability the advantage will regularly lie with the enemy: he has troops of all arms, especially artillery, available, while the Special Force has not. Under such conditions it requires more effort and probably more time as well to rout the enemy in his rear instead of at the front.

The difficulties facing a Chindit force which tries to defend an area against enemy attack are strikingly set out by one of its commanders, Brigadier Fergusson. He was ordered to take Indaw with his 16th Infantry Brigade but the first attack failed. 'We would have had a sticky time holding the objective after its capture, and we might have had difficulties over getting supply drops. Indaw had AA guns which could have interfered with them, and the open space over the Lake and in the paddy areas would have made the enemy's task of interrupting them fairly easy. The airfield would have been tricky to defend against attack from the south and south-east; but if the Japs could do it, we could also.'[1] But the Japanese could employ troops of all arms while the Chindits could not.

A Special Force should therefore not fight if it needs a constant flow of ammunition and supplies but harass and as much as possible try to provide the means itself in the way guerrillas can. The last war would probably have taught this lesson already, had the Japanese had equality in the air and put stronger forces into the Chindit area.

But if this is so, General Wingate's last concept in which he envisaged to shift the entire weight of attack from the front to the enemy rear and to conquer Hanoi and Bangkok with the Special Force is only of historical interest. Under this plan twenty to twenty-five airborne LRP brigades of altogether 100,000 men would be needed. They would build up behind them in the enemy rear a chain of defended airports which could be manned by normal garrison troops. The operations of the LRP columns would force the enemy progressively to withdraw, and the areas thus liberated would be controlled by strong garrisons stationed in fortifications.[2] In this way, by constant leap-

[1] Brigadier Sir Bernard Fergusson, *op. cit.*, p. 121.
[2] 'Appreciation of Exploiting Operation Thursday' by Major-General O. C. Wingate for the Supreme Commander South-East Asia, February 10, 1944, and

frogging, the LRP brigades would liberate the whole of South-East Asia. The rear was thus to become the main theatre of operations.

The plan was conditional; it was to be carried out only if the Second Chindit Expedition achieved success. For the reasons already indicated there is little chance for this kind of warfare to succeed in the future. General Wingate himself had once warned against attacking defended enemy positions in which he is capable of putting up 'a most obstinate and prolonged defence against greatly superior forces'[1] and especially against lightly armed Special Forces. The scheme found no supporters in the last war and it could only have succeeded if the enemy had been completely demoralized.

A Special Force in the far rear, like partisans, should therefore primarily harass and not fight, and the same applies to regular forces which might possibly replace it in the future. It also applies to small forces because they are only equipped to harass.

The far rear is therefore a harassing zone for the more permanent forces stationed there.

These forces—including also the SAS, Independent Companies, Special Force with Partisans and Brandenburg-type formations —all therefore make their contribution to the defeat of the enemy by containing his troops, knocking out centres of production, interfering with transport and supply routes, ambushing and raiding, undermining enemy morale, kidnapping enemy leaders, disseminating propaganda, waging political and economic warfare, indicating targets and supplying intelligence. We have seen in Chapter 10 that these activities can lead to the disorganization of the enemy, and this General Wingate had expressly been ordered to achieve.[2]

The far rear thus offers no novel strategic possibilities.

Nor does it appear that tactics stand in need of revision. The last thirty years have seen such a widespread application of harassing tactics in the enemy rear, and successful ones at that, that any tactical advances are likely to be made only in reply to tactical advances by the opponent. The main threat to opera-

'Note by Major-General O. C. Wingate on LRP Operations against Siam and Indochina', both reprinted in Major-General S. Woodburn Kirby, op. cit., vol. iii, pp. 486 f. and 491 f.
[1] 'Training Note No. 8.'
[2] Cf. above Chapter 4 for the order of February 4, 1944.

tions in the far rear comes from improved air defences and the use of helicopters by the other side.[1] The appearance of these weapons may severely curb activities in the far rear but is not likely at this stage to lead to a reappraisal, especially of partisan tactics.

This, then, is the type of war which a commander will wage in the far rear of the enemy and which he will expect the enemy to wage against him in the far rear of his forces.

[1] Cf. O. Heilbrunn, *Partisan Warfare*, op. cit., pp. 128-37 and pp. 166-7.

IV. THE FRONT AND THE REAR

IV. THE FRONT AND THE REAR

CHAPTER 12

THE INTERRELATION BETWEEN
FRONT AND REAR EFFORT

(a) The forces of the rear usually make a subsidiary, not a main effort.

There are three exceptions to this rule:

1. Forces of the rear can make a main effort if and when they have a chance to disorganize and demoralize the enemy.

2. Airborne forces on operational and strategic missions always make a main effort.

3. If partisans make a main effort, as Tito's forces did by fighting a revolutionary war within an international war, they do so often for their own ends and to this extent not necessarily in furtherance of their allies' military effort.

(b) Where the forces of the rear make a subsidiary effort, they support the army's aims in three ways:

1. In an advance they act as accelerator.

2. In a retreat they act as brake.

3. At all times they isolate and weaken the enemy.

They accelerate the advance by securing road crossings, bridges, hills, aerodromes and harbours, by removing obstacles on the way such as coastal batteries and strongholds, or by seizing a key position, by eliminating opposition, and so on. They slow down the retreat by harassing the enemy, destroying anything of use to him and, sometimes, by holding on to key positions.[1] They isolate and weaken the enemy by cutting his lines of communication and destroying his war industry, thus preventing men and material from reaching the front, by immobilizing troops in their positions and, by drawing others upon themselves, containing them elsewhere; they block the retreat, they raid, ambush, sabotage, kill and kidnap, and they under-

---

[1] General Wingate thought that they could also supply the answer to the enemy's penetration by deeper counter-penetration. But the counter-penetrating force would soon be involved in large-scale combat, without much chance of holding out for long.

mine the enemy's morale by their activities in general, including air attack, and by propaganda, spreading false information and by their Intelligence activities in particular.

They achieve these results by fighting, deceiving, and harassing. The harassing forces are either the roving type (SAS) or the more stationary guerrillas and guerrilla-type forces.

(c) The dispositions of the forces of the rear are affected by their functions, the terrain, and the attitude of the population.

1. The functions. The fighting forces are deployed along the axis of advance of their own front troops, and the harassing forces in operational theatres along the enemy lines of communication. The SAS operates along both and also where a special target —a secret weapon site or a headquarters—is located. Partisans are also found in the immediate rear all along the front line. The partisan clusters astride the enemy communications get thicker the farther they are from the front.

2. The terrain. The last war has shown in which parts of the world partisan movements can carry out their activities. There must be plenty of space and of natural cover so that partisan detachments can form up and develop unobserved and, after they have started operations, can evade the enemy, escape and vanish after an engagement.[1] But since partisans do not wear uniform and can melt into the countryside, speak the local language and can justify their presence in the district when questioned by the enemy, they can sometimes operate in small groups where the terrain is less favourable.

Different conditions apply to the uniformed formations. Troops which will be quickly relieved—airborne forces on tactical missions, Commandos/Rangers—can operate almost anywhere, and airborne troops on operational and strategic assignments can be deployed where the battlefield is closed or the enemy demoralized. Finally, Special Forces on longer-term assignments can be deployed in sparsely populated areas, such as the Middle East. In Western Europe, as Colonel Tobin points out, the uniformed forces of the rear will find their most profitable targets for raiding far from the battle area. Deep penetration on land by uniformed parties is impossible there unless the front is fluid and the enemy disorganized. They can otherwise be inserted only

[1] Cf. Hellmuth Rentsch, *Partisanenkampf, Erfahrungen und Lehren,* Frankfurt am Main 1961, p. 50.

E.G.M.

Lines of communication

Axis of advance

FRONT LINE

Lines of communication

A — Airborne Forces
C — Chindit-type Forces
P — Partisans
R — Rangers
S — S.A.S.

Near Rear
Fighting and Harassing Forces

Far Rear
Harassing Forces

HQ

AIR FIELD

THE DISPOSITIONS OF THE FORCES OF THE REAR

by sea, for operations against coastal objectives, or by air for a strike against any objective in the near or far rear, provided their evacuation is assured.[1] In other parts of the world Special Forces can, as General Hackett puts it, operate 'in difficult country, wherever cover is offered by jungle, or desert, or tundra, or marsh, or mountain, or forest, near something worth watching, or taking, or blowing up, or near people we have to help'.[2]

The more permanent forces of the rear must have a base where their parties can find food, fuel, ammunition, rest and replacements and where their equipment can be repaired. As General Hackett makes clear, a base can easily be maintained if the force is employed on an open flank but the problem is rather difficult if the base must be entirely air supplied.[2] The security of the base lies in the depth of the surrounding warning belt measured in time required to traverse it.[3] If the base is seriously threatened by the enemy, the force must move to a reserve camp. But, in the words of General Hackett, 'we have not yet reached the stage of continuous operations on an extended scale, in which considerable numbers of parties are operating from moving bases which are entirely air-lifted and air-maintained'.

3. The attitude of the population. It has often been pointed out that partisans can operate only where the population is friendly. While this is true in principle, they have also managed in some instances to maintain themselves in the midst of a neutral or even hostile population by using terror methods against it. Allied uniformed forces to which such methods are alien depend on the support of the population for defeating enemy Intelligence and strengthening their own, that is to say, to a greater or lesser extent, for their safety and the success of their operations.

The attitude of the population can in certain circumstances not only influence the dispositions of the forces of the rear but also determine the nationality and type of force which should operate in a given area. The popularity rating of British and of Americans is not everywhere the same, and partisan forces made up of minority groups might enjoy less local goodwill than an Allied force.

[1] Loc. cit., pp. 179 f.
[2] Loc. cit., p. 36.
[3] Loc. cit., p. 35.

(d) The choice of force for the task. Apart from this consideration, which force should be chosen for a particular task? The question arises when Commandos/Rangers and airborne forces can be deployed, and it has been discussed before in Chapter 3. It is also pertinent where a Chindit/Independent Company type force and a partisan movement are available or can be formed. In such a case the commander will keep in mind that Chindit-type forces should only be employed to promote the offensive of their own front or to counter that of the enemy,[1] and also that even the more permanent Special Forces will have to be relieved after a time while partisan detachments can continue to operate throughout the war. Since partisans are also, as a rule, more numerous than Special Forces, they may well contain larger forces than the Special Forces can do, and will tie down the enemy for a much longer period.

On the whole Special Forces are better equipped to do the precision work while partisans are better qualified for mass output. When both are equally qualified for the execution of a particular mission, the partisans have usually a number of advantages on their side: they are stationed behind the front and need not be transported there and back, they know the terrain better, they are not recognizable by their dress as enemy and have a better chance to vanish. Furthermore, they live on the country, frequently provide themselves to a great extent with arms and equipment and their supply requirements can be more easily satisfied. Finally, while Special Forces are recruited from the army's ranks, partisans are an addition to its manpower. But one must not overlook that partisans are irregulars, and their control may present the army commander with problems which do not arise with Special Forces.

There is another factor that must be taken into consideration. Most partisan movements fought surprisingly well during the last war but it must not be overlooked that they reached this stage of efficiency only in the course of the fighting. They had time on their side and could profit from their experience. A commander will be safe in his calculations if he assesses the operational efficiency of partisans at about 40 to 50 per cent of that of soldiers and at the beginning of partisan operations at rather less than that.

[1] Cf. above Chapter 4.

Two points emerge from the discussion in the preceding paragraphs: the commander of the forces of the rear cannot determine their dispositions at will to suit the strategic aims of the Commander-in-Chief in the Field, and partisan control and performance require special attention. These factors are liable to restrict the support which the rear can give to the front.

(e) The interrelation of rear and front forces. Front and rear must act in co-ordination wherever possible, that is where their efforts are interrelated, or should be so. They are not interrelated when forces of the rear carry out independent missions outside the theatre of operations, as airborne forces can do when seizing strategic positions at the beginning of a war.

If their own army retreats, the efforts of the forces of the rear operating in this theatre and those of the front are also as a rule not interrelated. The fighting forces of the rear may on occasions be required to hold on to a key position but they will not usually operate in the rear because they would have to fight for a longer period and could not be quickly relieved. During a retreat only Chindit/Independent Company type forces, partisans and possibly the SAS will as a rule be operating in the rear. Each force will harass and each will do so in its own area in order to slow down the enemy's advance. The commander will deploy his forces of the rear, if feasible, in the most sensitive areas but there is little possibility for co-ordinating the various efforts because each force of the rear is required, as we stressed for partisans before, to impede the enemy with all means, in all suitable places, and at all times. But the picture changes when the commander plans to attack.

Where the necessary forces of the rear are available, where they are capable of making a decisive effort and such an effort is required of them, their activities can and must be co-ordinated. The commander who follows Captain Liddell Hart's precepts will try to achieve one or more of the following aims: dislocation of the distribution and organization of the enemy forces, their separation, the interruption of the enemy's supplies and his routes of retreat, and his demoralization. The commander will have to decide on what he wants, and by whom, how, where and when he wants it done.

If he decides on all five moves outlined by Captain Liddell Hart, he may try to make the enemy transfer his *Schwerpunkt* (centre of gravity) of defence to a part of the front which he will not attack, say the southern part, and then attack the denuded part of the front in the north while making sure that the enemy's reserves cannot be shifted back. He may therefore send airborne forces to an area behind the southern part of the front, make a frontal feint attack there and order partisans not to interfere with the enemy's north/south communications as long as he reinforces the south, but cut his communications and keep them cut when he tries to move forces back to the north. The commander will seek to draw enemy forces, preferably from the front, through strong efforts by the harassing forces; partisans or Chindit-type forces will interrupt the enemy supply lines to the front, and Commando-type forces will cut the enemy's route of retreat. SAS or Skorzeny-type forces will demoralize the enemy. In making his decisions the commander will be mindful of the previously discussed factors governing the dispositions and choice of forces.

Having decided on the what, by whom and how, he must determine the where. Two points require mentioning here. Firstly, should the harassing formations meant to draw enemy forces be as widely spread or as concentrated as possible? It seems unlikely that the enemy would withdraw front line troops in order to deal with numerous relatively small forces dispersed over a wide area since he could not quickly recall his troops in case of need, and line of communication troops, reinforced by security forces, would probably be considered sufficient to fight the harassing forces. Concentrated harassing activities, as near to the front as possible, therefore seem to offer a better bait for front line troops. However, as we have noted before, harassing forces are not as a rule very numerous in this area. Secondly, should enemy communications be cut near the front, further back or just anywhere? Captain Liddell Hart has considered this question for a force which moves to the rear from the front either by manoeuvre round the enemy flank or by a rapid penetration of a breach in his front, and he comes to the conclusion that 'in general the nearer to the force that the cut is made, the more immediate the effect; the nearer to the base, the greater the effect'.[1] The same considerations apply to a force of the rear. Frequently, it may be added, a line can be kept cut more easily

[1] Op. cit., p. 344.

further back than near the front, and the commander will have to decide whether he prefers a short, immediate effect or an extended, greater effect—unless he can arrange for both.

The commander must time the operations. The rear activities should start with harassing, aimed at drawing enemy forces, before the enemy commander realizes that this is the prelude to battle since he would not otherwise send front line troops to deal with the menace. Next the feint attack should go in and only afterwards should airborne forces be dispatched to the rear of this part of the battlefield so that their stay there is as short as possible. Then the attack in the north will be launched and Commando-type forces dispatched to cut the enemy's retreat. Immediately afterwards morale operations will begin. They always succeed best when the enemy already feels the pinch, and Skorzeny-type activities should therefore not start before the enemy commander can be assumed to realize his mistake in having reinforced the southern front.

Similar considerations for the co-ordination of rear activities apply if the effort of the forces of the rear is only a subsidiary one, in support of a frontal or flank attack. These activities of the forces of the rear will probably be smaller in scale and scope than those just illustrated.

(f) If the commander has the choice whether the main effort should be made from the front or the rear, he will appreciate that the former may require a concentration of his forces which may be undesirable under nuclear warfare conditions. On the other hand the forces of the rear are usually smaller formations and for that reason less exposed to the risk of a nuclear attack. Furthermore they are stationed in the rear of the enemy and he will be reluctant to endanger his own rear by using nuclear weapons against them. Likewise, if the forces of the rear can only make a subsidiary effort in a nuclear war, the commander will delegate to them, as far as possible, all tasks which only larger concentrations of forces could carry out from the front. Otherwise the commander will choose for a mission the force which can more easily be spared and has a higher chance to succeed, and he will in this context consider the accessibility and distance of the objective, the time factor, the expected strength of the opposition on the way and at the objective, and whether the force must and can quickly be relieved.

(g) Finally, what can the front do to assist the forces of the rear? It can give air support and come quickly to their relief but there will seldom be an opportunity for diversionary activities or any other form of direct or indirect support. The forces of the rear must mainly rely on themselves.

CHAPTER 13

THE CONTROL STRUCTURE

The war-time arrangements for control of the forces of the rear have been briefly touched upon in previous chapters. Field Marshal Slim instituted in his Burma Army area a system of co-ordination and sometimes control under a staff officer of the commander in the area.[1] Special Force (Chindits) was first under his and then under General Stilwell's control, and the latter also controlled the Marauders. Before the invasion of France General Eisenhower set up under him Special Force Headquarters which took control of SOE, OSS and SAS;[2] the American and British airborne forces and troop carriers were commanded or controlled by First Allied Airborne Army which was directly under SHAEF,[3] and Commandos and Rangers were under control of the units to which they were attached.

It has been widely felt that these *ad hoc* arrangements were not entirely satisfactory, and we have previously mentioned the suggestion to subordinate the Special Forces to the Air Force, but the disadvantages of such a scheme seem to outweigh its advantages.[4] Most of the senior officers who have since the war discussed the possible control systems for the forces of the rear have come to the conclusion that the Army or supreme commander should control and direct them. However, Field Marshal Lord Wilson of Libya has proposed that SOE should come under the Ministry of Defence since Army and Air Force are involved in its operations.[5] General Sir Reginald Denning believes that 'control and direction of guerrillas by a Governmental Ministry would be going back to the days of "private armies" which, however gallant and determined they may have been, did not make the contribution which they might have made, had they been

[1] Cf. above Chapter 3.
[2] Cf. above Chapter 5.
[3] Cf. above Chapter 8.
[4] Cf. above Chapter 9.
[5] Cf. Major-General Sir Colin Gubbins, loc. cit., p. 212.

under the Commander-in-Chief in the Field',[1] and he insists that guerrillas must operate under the orders of the C-in-C in the Field because only he can decide the guerrilla action which will help him to attain his object.

Colonel Tobin, who has discussed the command structure for Special Forces, comes to a similar result. He too wants control to be with the highest headquarters in the theatre because the majority of Special Forces operations are on a strategic level, independent action in the same theatre must be avoided, and the RAF with whom co-operation is necessary is also represented at the highest headquarters. 'Only where a force is operating specifically in the tactical zone of an Army or lower ground forces headquarters, should the control of Special Forces be delegated below the highest level.'[2]

General Hackett agrees that Special Forces should only exceptionally come under Corps or Division. He suggests that if the target is in the enemy Army area, control should rest with the Army commander, if it is deeper it should be with Army Group, and if deeper still it ought perhaps to come under still higher authority.[3] Finally, Field-Marshal Slim wants Special Forces put under direct control of the higher command.[4]

The first question to decide in this context is whether each of the forces of the rear should be controlled separately or whether there should be a system of unified control over all forces of the rear.

There are, of course, great differences between the forces of the rear: some come by land and others by sea and air, some wear uniform and others do not, some fight and others harass, some are deployed in the near rear and others in the far rear, some are on long missions and others on short ones. But regardless of what they do and how and where they do it, they have one thing in common, and that is their strategic and tactical aims.

We have tried to show in the foregoing chapters what they are. On the strategic level the forces of the rear prepare, assist in, and achieve by their own efforts the disorganization and demoralization of the enemy, and on the tactical level they act as

[1] General Denning's Foreword to Dixon/Heilbrunn, *Communist Guerrilla Warfare, op. cit.,* p. vii.
[2] *Loc cit.,* p. 176.
[3] *Loc. cit.,* p. 34.
[4] *Op. cit.,* p. 548.

accelerator in an advance, as brake in a retreat, and they weaken and isolate the enemy. Not all forces of the rear participate in each of these operations and only one force may be concerned in some of these operations, but three facts stand out:

1. In some operations one of two possible forces must be selected for a task.

2. In a number of operations two or more forces of the rear and possibly all of them operate and co-operate.

3. In all operations the forces of the rear try to achieve a common, specific tactical or strategic aim.

It therefore seems opportune to bring all offensive land-warfare forces together in a single integrated control system and thus assure the most imaginative and effective handling of these forces.[1]

The argument in favour of a single control system is reinforced by war-time experience. Field Marshal Slim's system of area co-ordination and control took in guerrillas, Special Forces and Intelligence, and General Eisenhower's the guerrillas and SAS. Let us recall Field Marshal Slim's verdict: as a result of co-ordination and control 'confusion, ineffectiveness, and lost opportunities were avoided'.

The second question: How should unified control work? It must work on three levels:

1. Outside the present or future theatres of operations.

2. In future theatres of operations.

3. In active theatres of operations.

Every area of rear land operations concerns the Army. The area outside present or future military operations may be of minor interest to them and earmarked for Intelligence and sabotage acts—such as Denmark in the last war—but it may also be of considerable importance. Yugoslavia was outside the British and American theatres of operations, yet it was there that Rommel's supply lines to North Africa and the principal German communication line in the Balkans could be cut, German troops be contained in large numbers and their retreat route from Greece be blocked. The Supreme Allied Commander in the Mediterranean had control over assistance measures to the Balkans and, when Tito asked for help, the Supreme Commander could dispatch the necessary forces to Yugoslavia. They

[1] Cf. The reasons for excluding the Air Force are given above in Chapter 9.

consisted of Commandos and American Special Operations Force, infantry, engineers and artillery, units of the Royal Navy, and the Balkan Air Force based on Italy. Elsewhere again, for Norway, only small, isolated operations were decided on, such as coastal raids or raids by airborne parties.

In future theatres of operations activities were often on a small scale and this is the rule, if only in order not to warn the enemy of an impending invasion. A number of attacks will be staged in order to mislead the enemy and probably only air and coastal operations will be carried out on any significant scale. However, planning of land operations, including rear operations, will increasingly gain in importance, especially when the Supreme Commander has been appointed.

Finally, the rear will come into its own once operations have started.

In addition to the Army, the Air Force is frequently and the Navy sometimes concerned with planning and operations, but this survey seems to indicate that unified planning is required only from the time when a Supreme Commander or his planning Staff have been appointed, and unified control before battle commences. Unified planning and control are also desirable when a zone outside the actual theatre of operations, that is to say an ally's theatre of operations, requires and is given considerable assistance, as was the case with Yugoslavia.

The Supreme Commander should be given control of the rear forces as soon as he has been appointed. A Supreme Commander might also profitably be given control over assistance measures to an ally's area if it adjoins his own theatre, again as in the case of Yugoslavia. If the area is not adjoining, a task commander should be appointed instead.

The reason for vesting control into the Supreme Commander is that all three Services are represented at his headquarters. As to the choice of the task commander it seems appropriate to quote from Sir Winston Churchill's Memorandum to General Ismay, for COS Committee, dated March 2, 1944: 'The Task Commander should be the new feature, who might sometimes be an admiral, a general or an airman. This would also be true of the staff work and joint planning. When any plan is to be studied an officer of one or other of the three Services should be told to make a plan and the others to help him. Which Service is selected depends upon (a) the nature of the operation and which Service is predominant, and (b) the personality concerned."[1]

There is little point in outlining a control scheme in detail. The Supreme Commander should decide whether control should be delegated to lower ground forces headquarters for all or some of the forces of the rear, be it for the duration of the campaign or for shorter periods. He might well use General Hackett's outlines as guide but the Supreme Commander must avoid too frequent changes in the exercise of control which happen when the front moves quickly and the enemy army and army group areas change as a result quickly too.

Finally, if SOE-type organizations should be set up again they ought to come under a Service Ministry.

---

[1] Sir Winston Churchill, The Second World War, vol. iv, p. 755.

CHAPTER 14

THE WAR IN THE REAR OF
ONE'S OWN TROOPS

In the Franco-Prussian War the Germans set the pattern for securing their rear against enemy interference by establishing communication commands, one with each army. These communication commands followed their armies in the advance and secured the lines of communication by installing station commands alongside, at intervals of about fifteen miles. The size of the garrisons of the station commands varied; the large garrisons consisted of up to five infantry companies and a squadron of cavalry.

This system, similar to that adopted by the British in the Boer War, is interesting for two reasons: the security of the entire communication lines of each army was under a unified command, and the introduction of the cavalry element provided the mobility, necessary for security troops.

In the First World War rear security was of little importance because the rear was never disturbed by forces of the rear in the main theatres of operations, and the same holds largely true for World War II as far as the Allies were concerned. The Germans, however, found their rear threatened by forces of the rear on an unprecedented scale, and they complicated their problems in Soviet Russia, where the threat was the most serious, by artificially dividing responsibility for rear security between military and civil authorities. In the occupied Russian hinterland, which came under the civilian administration of the German Reichcommissars, security and particularly the fight against partisans was a matter for the Reichsführer SS and his subordinates, the military area commanders and the Higher SS and Police Leaders who had police units, security divisions, some Security Service (SD) formations and allied security units at their disposal, while in each of the three Army Group rear areas a Rear Area Commander was charged with the maintenance of security and military administration.[1] This division of authority made it necessary for the Wehrmacht and the Reichsführer SS to work out delineation agreements in general, and for larger engagements a specific agreement on the subordination of units of the Wehrmacht and of the Reichsführer SS under one commander had to be reached in advance of each operation.

Another and in the circumstances extraordinary feature of the German rear security system was abolished in 1943. Until then the rear area commanders were members of the Quartermaster-General organization from whom they received their operational directives. From 1943 on they were subordinated to the Operations Staffs of the Army Groups, and the Operations Section of the General Staff set up a special sub-section for anti-partisan warfare. There was also a Commissioner for Anti-Partisan Warfare with the Reichsführer SS.

The rear area commanders had Security Divisions at their disposal. In each Army Group rear area there were three divisions of three infantry regiments each; attached were artillery and signal units and usually a motorized police battalion, SS brigades, as well as allied, mainly Hungarian, formations and indigenous units; some battalions were equipped with bicycles. Other divisions including front troops were assigned to anti-partisan warfare for a number of larger operations.

During the German advance in Russia one division closely followed its Army Group, secured the communications, occupied important towns nearby, and furnished protection for operational headquarters. The other divisions spread out on both sides, occupied the larger towns and protected communications to the flanks and the lateral communications between units. Alert regiments provided the mobile reserves for any larger engagement.[2]

The Germans, after a period of trial and error, based their security arrangements on the following principles:

1. Railways, roads, and a number of installations must be protected against rear attack.

2. The menace in the rear must be eliminated by constant

[1] It should be noted that the three German Army Groups did not operate under a theatre commander or supreme commander to whom the rear area commanders, or a rear area commander for the entire rear, could have been subordinated.

[2] Cf. for the above Major Edgar Howell, *The Soviet Partisan Movement, 1941-44*, Department of the Army Pamphlet No. 20-244, August 1956, p. 52.

offensive actions of all suitable types from the smallest to the largest scale.

3. The population must be won over.

The techniques have since become familiar, and the principles have been refined and elaborated in post-war anti-partisan campaigns. These principles are not only applicable in anti-partisan warfare but also in any kind of rear warfare, be it against Special Forces, Chindit-type and other airborne or guerrilla-type formations. Hostile guerrillas, it should be noted, may even form up in allied countries where the foreign ideology has gained the allegiance of certain sections of the population.

The need for security commands arises where widespread enemy activities in the rear are expected or take place. There should be one commander for the entire rear of each theatre and he should be in charge of the area extending from the combat zone—security in the combat zone itself is a front-line troops' responsibility—to the farthest point back where trouble may arise. In this way security troops can be used more flexibly than if each army group or army had its own security command, and territorial border problems are avoided. The rear area commander should be subordinate to the theatre commander.

It is the rear area commander's responsibility to discover and eliminate any threat to the security of his area. His main problem is how to achieve maximum security with a minimum of forces and weapons. By its nature, rear security is wasteful in manpower since so many objects must be guarded and large forces are required for locating and rounding up the elusive enemy in the rear. The size and level of efficiency of the security troops is not usually fixed in accordance with requirements but with availability, and relatively few units can be spared since the front needs them more. The same goes for weapons: the desirable numbers of fixed wing aircraft, helicopters, tanks and so on will seldom be available for the rear because the front has priority in their allocation. The security forces cannot therefore always be expected to fight larger engagements on their own, for instance against Chindit-type forces or large partisan concentrations. If their own forces are insufficient, reinforcements must be sent to them, composed either of reserves or, if necessary, even of front-line troops.

Excellent Intelligence, constant initiative, superior mobility and the mobilization of the population are the four main requirements for the maintenance or restoration of rear security.

1. Intelligence. The first concern of the rear area commander in any newly-occupied area will be to set up Intelligence. Its sources of information are its own observations, the contacts with the population in general and indigenous agents in particular, monitoring and interrogations. The local Intelligence reports must at once be evaluated on the spot, so that action can immediately be taken either by the men in the locality if the necessary forces are available, or by their superiors if outside forces are required. In addition to this local evaluation there must also be a constant evaluation by the central rear area Intelligence agency for patterns and trends, short and long-term implications, expected actions or counter-actions, and so on. The lower Intelligence agencies must be appraised of the results.

These rules apply regardless of whether the army is fighting in its own country or in allied or enemy territory.

2. Initiative. The initiative must always lie with the security forces, and constant patrolling, followed if necessary by action, coupled with a good Intelligence system, are the means to seize and keep the initiative. Each garrison, down to the smallest post, must always find men to move out on patrols. In this way three purposes are served: the patrols locate the enemy, fight him or call on reserves to fight, the men detailed for static guard duties are also made available for fighting the enemy, and they defy by their activity the enemy's attempts to immobilize the garrisons in their posts.

Security cannot be achieved if the security forces always keep to the roads and consider the protection of the communications and installations as their only job. They must prevent the enemy from building up his forces in the rear, and he will often attempt to do this in remote parts of the country, far away from the towns, main roads and railways.

The main purpose of all security actions, once the enemy has taken the field, is to eliminate him. To keep the enemy merely on the move brings some temporary relief to the security forces: the enemy may be unable to carry out his specific mission, he may run into supply difficulties, and he is cut off from his normal Intelligence channels. But he may still achieve his mission at a later date and he contains security forces all the time.

The tactical and operational aspects of the fight against enemy forces in the rear, especially partisans, are now clearly understood, and there is no point in going over the subject again.[1]

3. Superior mobility is required to bring the enemy forces of the rear to battle and defeat them. Mobility does not depend only on physical fitness of the security forces and availability of transport, but also on intimate knowledge of the terrain and excellent wireless communications. Again, these points are now well appreciated and do not require elaboration. Only one aspect ought to be stressed, and that is the need of the security forces for a strong air component of fixed wing aircraft and helicopters.

The Air Force has a number of functions in rear security. It should:

(a) prevent the arrival of enemy troops, agents and supplies in the rear;

(b) carry out reconnaissance before and during an engagement;

(c) bomb enemy camps and spray his plantations;

(d) carry ground patrols part of the way and take care of the wounded;

(e) give direct battle support by acting as airborne artillery and transporting troops, particularly for surprise attack, closing the encirclement ring, and blocking escape routes;

(f) keep the troops supplied and carry heavy weapons to the battlefield;

(g) act as air escort to ground convoys.

In anti-guerrilla operations in Malaya, Indo-China, Algeria, Cyprus and Vietnam the Air Force has acted in one or more of the above roles and done so with sometimes outstandingly good results.[2]

The rear, especially if it has not enough ground forces, can never have enough aircraft; at best, fixed wing aircraft will have to do duty where helicopters would be more suitable, and *vice versa*. If the Air Force is ever reduced in strength because missile developments have made it obsolescent, it must not be cut back to a level which prevents it playing a major part in the defence of the Army rear.

[1] For a discussion of these aspects cf. Otto Heilbrunn, *Partisan Warfare*, op. cit., pp. 53 f.
[2] Cf Otto Heilbrunn, *Partisan Warfare*, pp. 128 f, for particulars.

4. The mobilization of the population. Recent literature abounds with advice on how to gain the support of the population, which is especially needed where there are widespread guerrilla activities. The points to be stressed are these: Normally the population of an alien non-allied country will not give its support unless protection can be provided. The occupying forces can only ensure such protection if the people assist by self-help, that is by self-defence. And this might not be forthcoming unless they believe in the victory of the occupying power and expect a better future as a result of it.

The function of the rear area commander is to provide the military administration and deal with military and paramilitary intruders in the rear, and while his headquarters should be in charge of psychological warfare against those forces, the moulding of public opinion and winning over of the populace should be entrusted to a separate agency, the Directorate of Information Service, working in close contact with the former. This was the system adopted by the British in Malaya during the emergency and it worked.

The war in the rear will be supplemented, or must be expected to be supplemented, by the war without battlefield, that is enemy espionage by infiltration, subversion and political warfare.

Espionage by infiltration is carried out in the rear mostly through the partisan movement. The Viet-minh guerrillas had little difficulty in finding 'intermediaries' and creating cells among the enemy, and Grivas managed to penetrate the civil service in Cyprus.[1] Soviet partisans had in the last war their own personnel in the German administration at all levels and managed to infiltrate even the Gestapo.[2] As a result, Soviet partisans often knew beforehand not only of impending actions against themselves but also of troop movements to the front. Since the Germans needed large numbers of the indigenous population to supply them with so-called voluntary helpers, form anti-partisan units and run the local administration, they could do little to purge those organizations of the well-camouflaged partisan supporters. The remedy

[1] Cf. Dudley Barker, *Grivas, Portrait of a Terrorist*, London 1959, p. 138.
[2] Cf. Oleg Anisimov, *The German Occupation in Northern Russia during World War II: Political and Administrative Aspects*. Research Programme on the USSR, New York City 1954, p. 20, Mimeographed Series No. 56.

lies in security consciousness, which the German Army did not always display.

A case history of subversion was furnished in France, during the phoney war period. The campaign, waged by the French Communist Party, aimed at demoralizing the mass of the people and especially the Army; leaflets, chain-letters to the soldiers and broadcasts were the media used. The technique is familiar: the agitators sought to sow the seeds of disunity and exploit alleged or actual grievances, and they called on the French to fight against the imperialist war and for immediate peace. While it is difficult to assess the impact of this campaign it appears that the morale of the French Army, 'gnawed by Soviet-inspired Communism',[1] did not remain unaffected by this subversive propaganda.[2]

A classic in political warfare in the enemy rear was provided by Tito's overthrow of the Royal Yugoslav Government in exile and the assumption of power by himself. This campaign was waged by military means against Mihailovitch, but it was fought just as hard on the psychological and political front. By denouncing Mihailovitch as a traitor and collaborator with the Germans at a time when neither he nor his subordinates had any such contact but actively fought the Germans, Tito intended to isolate his adversary and deprive him of Allied recognition and aid. At the same time Tito laid the foundations for the Communist State. Just before Soviet Russia was invaded, the military commission of the Central Committee of the Yugoslav Communist Party decided to prepare organizationally and politically for the fight. When Tito moved into the field he aimed at setting up as many liberated areas as possible in which communist-controlled National Liberation Committees would take over the administration and maintain order. In November 1942, the Anti-Fascist National Liberation Committee of Yugoslavia met for the first time and a year later it decided to transfer power from the Royal Government to the newly-created National Committee of Liberation; Tito was unanimously appointed Prime Minister, Minister of Defence and Marshal of Yugoslavia. With the fall of Belgrade the National Committee moved into the capital and governed

---

[1] Sir Winston Churchill, *The Second World War*, vol. ii, London 1949, p. 26.
[2] Otto Heilbrunn, *The Soviet Secret Services, op. cit.*, pp. 56 f, where the campaign is described in detail. For the German share in it, cf. Paul Leverkuehn, *op. cit.*, p. 81.

the country. All these happenings took place right in Axis-occupied territory; the Germans and Italians were powerless to destroy the political structure of the movement or stop the rise to power of its leaders.

The rear commander will not normally be called upon to deal with these dimensions of warfare in the rear. He will, of course, have to take measures against any infiltration of his organization and, by defeating the revolutionary guerrillas, smash the political infrastructure of their movement from the top. He will also reduce the impact of subversive and political propaganda on the population by treating it correctly and protecting it. But it is up to the Directorate of Information Service to counter subversionary and political warfare activities. The security forces may have to give assistance to the Information Service on occasion, and both may have common agents in the field, especially in Intelligence work.

If the population can be won over, the maintenance of security in the rear does not pose insoluble problems. The intervention of the helicopter has reduced the importance of popular support, as the British campaign in Cyprus has shown, provided that plenty of helicopters and security forces are available. In a war, as distinct from an emergency, the rear will have neither in plenty. Hence the importance of thinking of the rear not only in military but especially also in political terms. This was the lesson of many post-war anti-guerrilla campaigns. It is equally applicable to the occupied areas in an international war.

However, the significance of the political element must not be overrated, especially not at the expense of the military one, yet we are in danger of doing just that. A short discussion of the underlying problems therefore seems called for.

It is, of course, well known that in Soviet Russia the Germans were unable to pacify the rear because their occupation policies were shortsighted and seemed almost designed to alienate and antagonize the population. There were many Germans who at the time raised a warning voice but did so in vain. Some of the contemporary German documents make curious reading today. 'The necessary trust (of the Soviet population) into German leadership must be gained by severe but just treatment of the population. The bands can be exterminated only if the minimum means of subsistence are available to the population. If they are not, and especially if the available goods are not fairly distributed, the bands are bound to expand. The co-operation of the population is indispensable in anti-partisan warfare.' Nobody contributed more to defeating these modest policies than the man who signed this document, Hitler himself. The sentences, strangely enough, are taken from the Führer Directive of August 18, 1942.[1]

Others were slow after World War II to learn from German experience. The French did not indulge in Nazi excesses in Indo-China but they never gave the people a cause to fight for and hardly knew themselves what they were fighting for. French officers promptly blamed the military defeat in Indo-China on political shortcomings and others developed a new concept for anti-revolutionary warfare or, as the Americans call it, counterinsurgency. This French concept culminates in the doctrine that the army plays an important role in overcoming the partisans but that its action is not decisive; the opponent cannot be annihilated by military means but only by the destruction of his infrastructure, his politico-military network, and the army's measures must therefore be guided perhaps more by political and psychological considerations than by military ones. This theory has found qualified acceptance outside France.

Yet when the French tried to fight their next war, in Algeria, on the political front as well, success was again denied to them. It has rightly been pointed out that it was the legacy of broken promises in the past which deprived French political assurances on the future of any element of conviction and success.[2]

But, surely, this was not all. In the first place, the French made a serious mistake in their timing. They announced their political aims only after they had failed to make any progress in the war. Their proclamations thus bore the imprint of reluctant concessions rather than of ardent aspirations. Political, economic and social aims should be announced immediately after the area has been occupied in an international war or hostilities have started in an emergency, and work on the implementation of the programme should begin at once.

[1] *Hitlers Weisungen für die Kriegführung 1939-1945*, edited by Walther Hubatsch, Frankfurt am Main 1962, p. 202. The underscoring is in the original.
[2] Cf. London *Times*, March 4, 1958.

Furthermore, even if the Algerians had believed in French sincerity, public opinion would hardly have swung over unless, as we indicated before, the people had also believed in a French victory. Without that victory even the most high-minded political promise would not only have remained unfulfilled; what is more, those who sided with the French would have had to fear bitter consequences for themselves in case of a French defeat.

If we restrict our discussion to conditions in an international war, we must take World War II experience in Soviet Russia and Yugoslavia as a guide. After their initial successes over the Red Army, the Germans enjoyed wide popularity and Ukrainians, White Ruthenians and others 'placed themselves at our disposal willingly and freely with body and life', as a contemporaneous German report put it. In Yugoslavia, Mihailovitch's Cetniks and Tito's partisans took up the fight against the occupation troops before the British and Soviets had won a single important victory but 'the population, by nature conservative and loyal to the monarchy, were inclined to prefer the passive attitude of the Cetniks or even the open collaboration of General Nedic to the all-out resistance and revolutionary policies of the partisans', and the popular attitude changed only when 'they realized, too, that the Germans, who had for so long seemed invincible, were at last beginning to weaken and that, when in the end they withdrew or were driven out, power would almost certainly pass to the partisans'.[1]

The conclusion seems inevitable that while there will always be men willing to fight for their ideals under any conditions, the mass of the population will usually give its support only after the troops have been successful in the field. Political work is of the greatest importance in achieving or maintaining rear security in non-allied country but as a rule it will be effective only if the Army is successful. Without military success the political effort is almost bound to fail.

It is therefore important to get the order of priorities right: first there must be military success, then progress can be made on the political front with what the Americans call nation-building tasks. If as a result the population is being won over, the guerrillas will be deprived of informers, recruits and food supplies, while the anti-guerrillas will gain sources of information

[1] Brigadier Sir Fitzroy Maclean, op. cit., pp. 267 and 268.

and volunteers for the Home Guard and self-defence corps. Then the last stage begins and by a combined military-political effort victory can be achieved.

The French Marshal Bugeaud, a veteran of the Peninsular War, was not the first nation-builder but he certainly understood his mission when he defeated Abd-el-Kader's guerrillas over a century ago and took possession of Algeria. He knew how to fight and how to pacify. As to the first, he 'organized his forces in small, compact columns—a few battalions of infantry, a couple of squadrons of cavalry, two mountain howitzers, a small transport train on mule and camel-back; as speed was the first consideration, he employed only picked men, those inured to the climate and fatigue. . . . By these admirable methods of celerity, the Marshal won success after success over the wild followers of the Emir.'[1]

His pacification measures—which he introduced after a period of punitive raids on rebels' homes and crops—were no less impressive. 'When one re-reads the history of the conquest one is struck by the constructive zeal which animated Bugeaud's soldiers. How much they managed to build! Here the small stone and earth walls in order to prevent flooding, there a eucalyptus grove to improve the soil, and elsewhere gardens and orchards.'[2] By his pacification measures the Marshal achieved final victory.

His formula was simple:

Military success, political-economic advance, combined victory. This formula still holds good today.

---

[1] Percy Cross Standing, *Guerrilla Leaders of the World*, London 1912, p. 114.
[2] George R. Manue, 'Le Rôle de l'Armée en Algérie', *Revue Militaire d'Information*, July 1956, p. 13.

CHAPTER 15

CONCLUSIONS

Joint operations by forces of the rear were comparatively rare in the last war, and the performance of the individual forces was not always in line with expectations: some did distinctly better and others less well than anticipated. The Soviet Russians had every reason to feel disappointment with their airborne troops, but if so, it was not due to their performance but to the unimaginative planning of their missions. The Germans, whose planning of airborne operations could hardly be faulted, considered the price paid for victory in Crete too high and hardly used their airborne forces again in their original role, except in December 1944 in the Ardennes offensive, and there on a modest scale only. The Anglo-American airborne forces were the only ones who made a continuous contribution in the war, from the Anglo-American landing in North Africa to the crossing of the Rhine. They were used very much less frequently and less ambitiously than their own command had desired and planned. Indeed, the airborne forces of all countries were underemployed in the role for which they had been designed.

Many had thought that the SAS could not operate in Western Europe but their activities, once fighting had become fluid, confounded the pessimists. While it was thus shown that a small number of small parties with moving bases could be air-maintained, the Chindit Expedition proved that larger formations on the move could be kept air supplied if they had fixed bases to which their main requirements could be delivered. The next step would be to airlift and air-maintain considerable numbers of parties with moving bases; as the reader will recall, this problem has, in the words of General Hackett, not yet been solved.

The main surprise of the last war, as far as the forces of the rear were concerned, was no doubt caused by the partisan performance, from the Philippines to France and from Norway to Ethiopia. The Germans did not expect such activities on a large scale, and certainly not that they could 'threaten seriously to menace the supplies to the front and the exploitation of the country', as Hitler put it in one of his directives; he ordered his commanders to liquidate the bands in the east before the winter of 1942 'in order to avoid decisive disadvantages to Wehrmacht operations during the winter'.[1] But the Western Allies too were surprised that irregulars could operate so long and so successfully in so many theatres. The British were less sceptical than the Americans about the efficacy of partisan warfare: the British memory of South Africa had been refreshed by Ireland as well as Palestine and Lawrence had also not been forgotten, while the Americans had not met with guerrillas since the days of Pancho Villa in Mexico, just prior to World War I. Yet even Britain thought at first of partisans only in terms of small groups mainly engaged in Intelligence and sabotage tasks, followed perhaps later by guerrilla attacks on a larger scale when the front approached the partisan area.[2]

Indeed, partisan warfare appeared by any reasonable standard as an anachronism in an international conflict in which every modern weapon could be used against the partisans without restraint and every area be controlled by the occupying forces. Weapon developments had by-passed the partisans. While regular forces had acquired aircraft and tanks, bombs and rockets, motorized transport and self-propelled artillery, the guerrillas had added only a few light weapons and explosives to their armoury and still relied on the same tactics and techniques which had been used a thousand years earlier. Entire regular armies of country after country had proved no serious match in face of Germany's *Blitzkrieg* assaults; it was almost unbelievable that she could not succeed in annihilating the guerrilla forces of those countries with equal ease.

To think of partisans as a kind of modern highwaymen who hold up trains and convoys, or Red Indians who skilfully lay an ambush, is a conception which had become outdated early in the last war. Allied partisans stopped being bandits even in the eyes

[1] Führer Directive No. 46, dated August 18, 1942, reprinted in *Hitlers Weisungen für die Kriegführung 1939-1945*, edited by Walther Hubatsch, Frankfurt am Main 1962, p. 201.
[2] Cf. Professor F. W. D. Deakin, *Great Britain and European Resistance*. Paper read at the Second International Conference on the History of the Resistance, Milan, March 26-29, 1961.

of their opponents when Field Marshal von Weichs, the German C.-in-C. South-East (Balkans), directed his formations to refer in their reports to Tito's partisans not any longer as bands but to brigades, divisions and so on, and expressed himself to the effect that they had to be considered as the equivalent of the regular forces of Germany's other enemies.

Colonel C. M. Woodhouse has pointed to the tendency of irregular warfare to become more professional and high organized,[1] and this trend had become unavoidable when technical developments made it possible for partisan detachments to be handled in the last war almost like regular units.[2] That they were often led or advised by Army officers helped to reinforce this trend. Proper command structures and chains of command were laid down, assignments became more ambitious, specific missions at specified places and times could be given to partisans and, more important still, they showed themselves often capable of carrying them out.

On the other hand some of the Special Forces, particularly the Independent Companies and the Chindits, adopted guerrillaism. General Wingate has been taken to task for a variety of reasons and his critics have found an easy target in his plan for the capture of Hanoi and Bangkok by LRP brigades.[3] Indeed, if he was able to make this great leap forward, so were the Japanese. They would in fact have had to, if they had followed his precept that the answer to penetration is deeper counter-penetration, and by the time the LRPG had arrived in Hanoi the Japanese would have entered Delhi. But this plan in no way incorporated the essence of his thoughts, teachings and practice. His great contribution to military science was his demonstration that professional soldiers could profitably adopt guerrillaism, and we have drawn the conclusion that they could have disorganized and demoralized the enemy, as they were ordered to, had they been given the chance. The Independent Companies gave no less impressive proof of the value of guerrilla soldiers.

Thus a pattern was set in which partisans became more professional and the professionals in Special Forces acquired some

[1] Colonel C. M. Woodhouse in his Foreword to O. Heilbrunn, *Partisan Warfare*, op. cit., p. xiii.
[2] Cf. above Chapter 6.
[3] Cf. above Chapter 11.

partisan attributes. This combination of professionalism and guer-rillaism by civilians and soldiers has gained new significance with the advent of nuclear warfare.

In a nuclear war, regardless of whether nuclear weapons have been or will be used, we do not think of the battlefield as an area marked out on either side by enormously long front lines and *Schwerpunkte* for attack and defence. Larger concentrations of troops are ruled out, unless one side can compel the other to form them and thus present a target for nuclear weapons while avoid-ing concentrations of its own. Troops on either side will be more widely dispersed; more and wider areas will be left unoccupied.

Nuclear weapons may be used either right from the start or after a warning following the enemy conventional attack or in the course of the war, or they may not be used at all. The nuclear weapons may be strategic or tactical.

If an enemy decides to use strategic nuclear weapons he might not move out of his own country. He might stay there, secure his frontiers with strong forces and fire his nuclear weapons from his land bases, the sea and air into his opponent's country. In such a case there is little chance for the employment of forces of the rear, except perhaps for small parties of saboteurs whose evacuation would, however, raise considerable problems. The only effective reply to such an attack is the strategic nuclear counter-strike.

However, it is commonly accepted that if the enemy moves out of his country into the adversary's territory, there will be land battles. Both sides might use either strategic and tactical nuclear weapons, or tactical nuclear weapons only. In either case, mobile nuclear battle groups will operate in the field and endeavour to gain ground.

It is sometimes assumed that the aim of either side must then always be to compel the enemy to form concentrations so that he can be attacked with nuclear weapons. But this is not true. Prob-ably more frequently than not the enemy cannot be so compelled without exposing oneself, and sometimes it would be undesirable to so compel him if, for instance, his position is on the outskirts of a friendly city. It may on occasions be much easier to defeat him in the conventional way, provided he has first been forced to deconcentrate.

Nuclear warfare has added new weapons to the armoury but

it has not made all conventional weapons obsolete. It offers on the battlefield a choice of weapons, tactical nuclear and conventional ones. The commander has therefore also a choice in tactics: he may try to make the enemy concentrate and use tactical nuclear weapons against him, or he may try to force the enemy to deconcentrate and use conventional weapons. The more he succeeds in making the enemy deconcentrate, the smaller will be his own concentration required for the attack. If he is successful with either tactics he will achieve his objective, that is he will gain ground.

The tasks of the forces of the rear in a nuclear war can therefore be grouped under two headings:

1. They must try to prevent the use of nuclear weapons by the enemy or, if they have been fired, prevent him from exploiting the situation.

2. They must try to manoeuvre the enemy into concentrating or deconcentrating his forces, whichever is wanted by their own front.

As far as the first aspect is concerned, SAS and the US Special Force are trained to locate and, if at all possible, attack special targets, including nuclear targets. Since these targets will be heavily guarded on land and are inaccessible to a Special Force while they are on the sea or in the air, success will be limited. Likewise, the partisans have only a restricted chance to succeed. They too can sabotage only land-based installations; even then, the bases for strategic weapons are far behind partisan territory and so are the airfields of the Air Forces detailed for nuclear strikes. The partisans can at best interfere with tactical nuclear weapons; but their chances against battle groups so equipped must not be rated high.

Again, the capabilities of the forces of the rear are extremely limited when they try to prevent the enemy from exploiting the situation after he has fired nuclear weapons. He will probably use tanks for this purpose, and if they are assembled close behind the front, the forces of the rear can do little there in the way of sabotage or ambush. But they will report to their own front if enemy tank concentrations present a favourable target for destruction, possibly with nuclear weapons.

The forces of the rear will also try to draw the enemy's attention upon themselves in order to give their troops time to seal the breach. Yet again, their success will be restricted because the enemy will not allow his troops to be deflected by forces of the rear just when his nuclear attack has opened the way forward. Under the circumstances, Intelligence work will apparently be the rear's main contribution in such a situation.

But the forces of the rear can play a bigger part in making the enemy concentrate or deconcentrate his troops. As for concentrations, this task runs almost contrary to accepted ideas about their role because they usually tried in World War II to make the enemy disperse his forces.

How can the forces of the rear induce the enemy to concentrate his troops? Only, it appears, by making life so difficult for him that he decides on a large-scale action against them. We have seen that in the Fifth Offensive in Yugoslavia more than 100,000 German and allied troops fought against Tito's and Mihailovitch's guerrillas, and in the Fourth Offensive seven divisions and native units were marshalled against Tito's forces. But operations of this size require a substantial partisan force as bait. They do not therefore take place near the front where partisans are scarce, and the concentrated enemy formations would hardly be within range of tactical nuclear artillery. Furthermore, the enemy troops in these operations carried out an encirclement movement, with the guerrillas right in the centre of the battlefield, and this deployment is certainly not propitious for the use of nuclear ground or airborne weapons against the enemy.

The more likely role of the forces of the rear in this kind of operation seems to be a subsidiary one. Small parties in the rear can assist the front by channelling enemy movements in the desired directions. The rear forces will block his way here and keep it open there, force him on to one or two roads and allow movements in one direction while interdicting them in the other.

It is here that the indicated trend towards professionalism by guerrillas and guerrillaism by professional soldiers gains in significance. It means for the guerrillas enhanced military proficiency and for the professionals the adoption of guerrilla methods, particularly also the art of survival as practised by them. These skills might enable guerrillas and Chindit-type forces to operate in future nearer to the front than hitherto.

Nuclear warfare conditions seem to allow for such a shift of battlefield because wider areas will probably be left unoccupied by the enemy, and dispersed troops of his will be less capable of mounting operations against the forces of the rear in the area. It must not be overlooked, though, that the terrain must be favourable for the forces of the rear and that they must extricate themselves before their own side can fire nuclear weapons against the enemy. The main pressure on the enemy to concentrate must come from the front, but the rear can assist the front by canalizing the enemy's movements and closing or opening the sluice gates. The rear forces will also be required to report the enemy's reaction to the front.

The forces of the rear will help their own troops to exploit the nuclear attack by preventing the enemy from closing the resulting gap in his positions. They will block roads leading to the gap and attack rail and motorized transport in the area. Again, they will report the results of the nuclear attack and the enemy's counter-measures.

However, if the commander of their own troops decides to attack the enemy in the conventional way, the forces of the rear, in their more accustomed role, will try to weaken the enemy by making him disperse his troops before the attack. Their tasks in this context have been discussed before and there is no need to summarize them here.

In a nuclear war the forces of the rear may be the only large, purely conventional element in the theatre. It hardly seems practical to issue them with nuclear weapons. On the other hand, they are almost immune from nuclear attack, not only because the enemy will be reluctant to endanger his own hinterland by exploding nuclear weapons there, but also because they are usually dispersed and too small a target.

The presence of the conventional forces of the rear on the nuclear battlefield might then appear as anachronistic as guerrillas in an international conflict seemed to be just before they showed their usefulness in World War II. It is more realistic to realize instead that a commander without forces in the enemy rear fights his battle, be it nuclear or conventional, only on half the battlefield and, while exposing his rear areas to enemy interference, neglects the opportunities which the enemy rear offers him.

CONCLUSIONS

The forces of the rear, it is true, will not win the war for him. But they will make a great contribution towards the disorganization and demoralization of the enemy.

And that, after all, is the commander's strategic aim.

APPENDIX

TRAINING NOTES BY MAJOR-GENERAL O. C. WINGATE, COMMANDING LRP FORCES[1]

GENERAL RULES FOR THE EMPLOYMENT OF FORCES OF DEEP PENETRATION IN MODERN WARFARE

1. *What is Deep Penetration?*

The Japanese obtained considerable fighting experience in South-East Asia against the Chinese from 1935 onwards. This fighting taught them certain facts and the application of special tactics. This knowledge was not shared by us, and we failed to study Japanese methods. The result was that when our forces met the Japanese in different theatres of war, we were confronted by a new tactical method which we were in no way to meet. It was this factor more than any other which led to the various defeats we suffered. This new tactical method was penetration. The Japanese had realized that wherever dense forest or broken country existed in sufficient quantity, in mobile warfare (i.e. warfare where opposing armies are not sufficiently strong to hold a rigidly defended line from coast to coast, etc.) it was possible for bold and well-directed infantry, supported by aircraft, and with the widest initiative, to disregard fronts, flanks and other conventions of warfare, and to precede the main body by as much as seven days. The infantry uses this great mobility and independence of action to create road blocks in the rear of the enemy's positions, to deliver sudden surprise attacks on his reinforcements and columns and, generally, to attack him where he is not prepared for such attack and is unable to meet it.

The Japanese have always employed this method and usually with great effect. For this purpose they have used ordinary divisional infantry, and there is no doubt that where conditions exist

[1] The Training Notes are Crown copyright. Permission of the Controller of H.M. Stationery Office for the reproduction has been obtained.

that make such warfare possible that it is the ordinary function of ordinary infantry.

The Japanese, again unlike ourselves, ensured that their infantry would be amply provided with men for the firing line. A Japanese battalion in battle has even put as many men in the firing line as a British brigade. This again is a logical application of the Japanese understanding of the nature of warfare in the broken and forested areas of South-East Asia.

In this kind of country, supporting arms are not only of comparatively little value, but frequently constitute a grave embarrassment to the force of which they form a part. Needless to say, this is not true everywhere, or even throughout any given theatre. There are areas even in Burma where artillery and armour can be employed with effect. These are, however, in the minority (needless to say, artillery is always of use in static warfare wherever the terrain). The more mobile the operation, the harder it is to employ supporting arms with effect.

In their campaigns, the Japanese appeared to recognize that in aircraft lay their most effectual supporting arm. Our troops complained that frequently they had no sooner seen the Japanese infantry than the Japanese aircraft arrived and, by means of signalling more effective than our own, took action against our positions.

All these points are fully recognized, and have either been corrected or are in the process of being corrected. Nevertheless, we have yet to prove that we understand how to apply the principles we have learnt in practice.

The new tactics which the Japanese employed against us in their Malaya and Burma campaigns may be summed up by the term 'Short Range Penetration'. Their infantry were unable, as a rule, to precede their main force by more than a few days. They were not fed from the air, but obtained their supplies from the main forces at such times as they made contact with the latter. They are thus compelled to fight their enemy's forward troops in the field, and are not able to hit him in places where their blows would be most effectual. Their effect, in fact, is entirely tactical, not strategical; on the small scale, not the grand scale.

It remains for ourselves to improve this technique of the Japanese by the application of a method which we have already tried out elsewhere, and which may be summed up by the term 'Long Range Penetration'. This is strategical as opposed to tactical penetration. It influences not only the enemy's forward troops but his whole military machine, and his main plan. It is made possible by two factors comparatively new to war, whose full application is only beginning to be grasped during the present war. These factors are, firstly, the power of wireless to direct and control small or large bodies of troops in the heart of enemy territory, and, secondly, the power of aircraft to maintain such troops with essential supplies; to make physical contact with them where this is necessary; and finally, and most important, to employ them to make its own blow against the widely scattered and invisible enemy effectual.

To sum up, therefore, Deep Penetration means the operation of regular columns of high fighting calibre in the heart of the enemy's war machine; engaging targets which in the nature of things he is unable adequately to protect, and thus compelling him to alter his plan, thus creating the situation which our own main forces are able to take decisive advantage. These operations by columns are made possible only through the existence of thick forest or patriotic population, the full exploitation of wireless, and the support of aircraft.

2. Necessary Conditions for Deep Penetration

Deep Penetration is not at present possible under all conditions. Experience has proved that columns of penetration must be strong enough to slip through any net the enemy may attempt to draw round them. The method of Dispersal, which is at present in its infancy, may eventually permit the activity of columns in thickly-occupied territory where the inhabitants are friendly. The necessity, however, for concentrating to strike a blow, to receive rations, ammunition, etc, from the air, or to move any considerable distance, makes it very desirable that the column should, as far as possible, operate as one group, and only exceptionally, and when in distress, have recourse to the Dispersal procedure. Columns as at present constituted can, therefore, operate wherever there is either forested or thickly enclosed country covering areas occupied by the enemy, or where the friendly inhabitants are sufficiently numerous and warlike, and the enemy sufficiently thin, to permit the inhabitants taking the place of the friendly forest, etc. A combination of forest and friendly inhabitants is the ideal, and this permits in the highest degree the effectual operation of Columns of Deep Penetration.

In the course of the coming war with the Japanese, we are likely to meet both types of condition suitable for Deep Penetration. In the southern parts of South-East Asia the forest is universal and friendly : but the inhabitants are, in the main, hostile or indifferent. In China, on the other hand, there is comparatively little forest, but there is a dense population of patriotic Chinese, with a comparatively thin occupation of the enemy. From the borders of India, therefore, to the shores of the Yellow Sea lies territory suitable for the operations of Columns of Deep Penetration.

3. Factors governing the operation of Columns of Deep Penetration

From the nature of their employment, it is evident that these columns should never be embroiled with the enemy troops in the forward areas. Troops of short range penetration can carry out the reconnaissance and protective functions that their parent formation will require when it is engaged in active operations against the Japanese. In these forward areas, however, the enemy maintains his best troops, and at the greatest density on the ground. Consequently, operations under these conditions are not favourable to the lightly equipped troops of Deep Penetration. In fact, every blow struck 200 miles behind the enemy's lines may be stated to have ten times the effect of a blow of the same weight struck in the forward areas. To use a prize-fighting parallel, in the forward areas the enemy's fists are to be found, and to strike at these is not of great value. In the back areas are his unprotected kidneys, his midriff, his throat and other vulnerable points. The targets for troops of Deep Penetration may be regarded, therefore, as the more vital and tender portions of the enemy's anatomy. In the nature of things, even when he realizes the threat that these columns constitute to the tenderer parts, the enemy cannot provide the necessary protection and deal effectively with the column except by dropping his fists, i.e. withdrawing troops from the frontal attack against his main adversary. It is just this situation that his adversary, i.e. our own main force, has been waiting for, and is prepared to take advantage of.

In addition to bearing in mind the above principles and factors, the soldier of Deep Penetration must also realize to the full why it is that this method, which has never been practised in previous wars, is now possible. He must realize that it is due to the introduction into warfare of two comparatively new factors, the full application of which was not fully realized until the present war. These factors are Wireless Telegraphy and Aircraft. The aircraft makes possible the vertical supply line, and what is tantamount to artillery support for infantry columns deep in enemy occupied territory. It also facilitates the evacuation of wounded, of documents, prisoners, etc. Wireless telegraphy makes possible the effectual direction of columns, which are isolated in enemy occupied country, from the Army Headquarters which is conducting the major operation. These columns can by these means be kept regularly and fully informed of all that is known of the enemy or our own forces. They can be warned of enemy action which threatens their safety; directed to move and to act in such a way as to create the maximum effect against the enemy. In general, they can be kept in touch with each other, with the main force, and with the general situation. Never before in warfare has this been possible, and this fact alone will in time revolutionize modern methods of making war.

4. Nature of Target
Possibly undue emphasis has been laid in the past in my notes on this subject on the attack on the enemy's lines of communications. While this is an obvious and profitable type of target, Forces of Deep Penetration can and often will be used to attack enemy reinforcements, headquarters, aerodromes, rest camps, etc. The nature and locality of the target will be decided by the Army Commander, who will use the Force of Deep Penetration to create a situation of which he intends to take advantage. At the same time it is well to remember that Forces of Penetration can be used not only in one but in a large number of different ways simultaneously. In this type of warfare we have much to learn and little experience.

5. Command and Control
In any given major operation, there will be certain forces committed to the role of Deep Penetration. All these forces must

rationally be under one commander, who will himself be under the commander of the whole operation. In some cases, the operation will simply be that of an Army Corps, or even a Division, or it may be an operation involving the employment of an Army or even an Army Group. The operations of the Forces of Deep Penetration will be, however, *sui-generis*, and will be designed together to produce a certain effect on the enemy's main plan. These forces will, in every case, be widely separated from the main forces, and their problems and operations being all of the same nature, it is rational that their control should be in the same hands. In certain cases, Brigades may have to be handed over to Corps and even Divisions for control and direction.

6. *Principles of operation of Columns of Deep Penetration*
Columns of Deep Penetration when used across country have mobility, and the power to disappear into thick forest, etc.; and to inflict surprise blows on their enemy. In general, it may be said that they should not fight unless they have succeeded in obtaining surprise; although when two or more columns are engaged together in one task, individual columns must obviously be prepared to forgo this advantage. Surprise is the only way to beat the Japanese. But it is not enough to inflict an occasional surprise and then expect to be left alone while you recuperate from the effects of the battle. The momentum of surprise must be maintained. The need for this will sometimes knock hell out of a column, and make it necessary for the column to take a rest at its permanent rendezvous. Nevertheless, it is a vital principle which must never be ignored.

The British Officer is inclined to talk loosely about surprise, as though he fully understood what it was in war. But since 999 out of a thousand British Officers have never inflicted anything in the nature of a surprise in war upon an enemy, this complacent attitude must be abandoned. Careful and painstaking thought must at once be given to the problems connected with the infliction of surprise. Firstly, it is necessary for every officer to ask himself, 'What is surprise?' Surprise is being caught out; being confronted with a situation which you had never expected (this itself is not surprise) and which you are not prepared to meet owing to your not having given previous thought to the matter.

It is very satisfactory when surprise can be inflicted in a single motion, e.g. by a surprise march ending in the delivery of an attack while the enemy army is in bed. Such simple and satisfactory surprises are rarely possible in war, particularly against the Japanese. The Japanese act like lightning when surprised and invariably have a plan of action which they will operate whatever racket may be going on at the time. Surprise must therefore be gained, as a rule, by more subtle means. The officer should look upon every action as containing three phases, and he should reckon to obtain his surprise in the third phase. The side that retains the initiative retains the power to inflict surprise. The normal process may therefore be illustrated as follows:

A Column, etc., Commander will initiate a certain action against the enemy. Using his superior intellect, he will foresee the enemy's reaction to his action. He will therefore permit the enemy's reaction fully to develop; and will then take advantage of that development by a previously concerted plan. This is the third phase of the action, in which our commanders will normally reckon to achieve surprise. To take a case in point. The commander wishes to drive out an enemy company which he knows to be located in a certain village. He will therefore send a provocative force to within three-mile radius of the village. He will construct a dummy bivouac. As soon as his preparations are completed, a small patrol may enter the village and draw the enemy's attention to their proximity. Hubbub may be created in the dummy bivouac. The Japanese Commander will certainly debouch with considerable vigour, and approach the bivouac, usually in the latter stages, with caution. The Column Commander, well concealed in the forest, but observing through his scouts, will wait until the Japanese Commander puts down his mortar and MG crump upon the dummy bivouac and later proceeds to investigate the result. The column will attack by previously reconnoitred routes with every chance of completely discomfiting the enemy. That explains what I mean by the third phase of an action. Commanders will seldom reckon to obtain surprise in the first phase, i.e. by a rapid advance into the village in the hope of finding the Japanese asleep in their beds. Experience teaches that under these circumstances the Japanese, regardless of what may be happening, immediately rush to man their previously prepared defences, where they at once direct a heavy fire on fixed lines against their attackers.

7. *The meaning and use of Mobility*

I hope that every officer who has perused these notes has already asked himself what I mean by stating a column, which has to march laboriously every inch of the way with an average weight of 60 lb. per man on the backs of its unfortunate members, possesses mobility over an enemy less heavily laden and naturally agile, employing motor transport and other means of rapid progress from point to point. If the officer has not asked himself this question it should be apparent to him that he has not yet learnt how to think. And he should begin at once to practise this exacting occupation, as this alone would enable him to defeat the relatively thoughtless Japanese Commander.

The mobility to which I am referring is the power that a column possesses to move away from an enemy in such a way, and into such country, that the enemy will be afraid or unable to follow it. Experience has shown that the Japanese are normally no more anxious to commit themselves to the jungle than are our own troops. Columns of Deep Penetration, therefore, use the jungle as the screen which covers their deployment, gives them power to concentrate and disperse without observation, and which permits the construction of booby traps and ambushes of a nature (that makes) the enemy exceedingly chary in following them up.

The study and practice of these methods must be the unremitting care of every officer in Columns of Deep Penetration. Their precise application will be described elsewhere. It is, however, true to say that a column in this respect possesses an advantage which the enemy cannot interfere with, i.e. the power to move unimpeded. Without this power, the column would soon be run to earth and destroyed.

8. *Employment of Aircraft in the role of Supporting Artillery*

More will be found on this subject in my notes under the heading 'Air Co-operation with Columns'. It is enough here to say that one of the hardest tasks which confronts the soldier on the ground in mobile warfare is to make effectual use of the aircraft which are allotted him for his support. Coming down to brass tacks, we find this is due to the rarity with which he approaches dangerous targets, worthy of such support, sufficiently closely and intimately to be capable of indicating them with the degree of accuracy necessary to render the air attack of value. Careful thought and practice during the weeks of training will enable us to overcome this weakness. I consider that if we are able to master this problem, our efficiency will be increased manyfold, and we shall discover the means of driving the air blow home on the concentrated and minute targets presented by the enemy in Burma and elsewhere in South-East Asia.

To sum up, it is a matter of steeling ourselves to get right up to these targets and indicate them to the air with 100 per cent accuracy. On this subject again complacency must be cast out. Up to date we have not been able to employ the air forces which are likely to be put at our disposal up to 5 per cent of their potential advantage. This problem will be solved by thought and study before the operations begin.

BIBLIOGRAPHY

General Works

AUCHINLECK, Field-Marshal Sir Claude: Despatch 'Operations in the Indo-Burma Theatre from 21st June, 1943, to 15th November, 1943', *Second Supplement to The London Gazette*, April 27, 1948.

BRYANT, Sir Arthur: *The Turn of the Tide. Based on the War Diaries of Field-Marshal Viscount Alanbrooke*. London 1957.

—*Triumph in the West. Completing the War Diaries of Field-Marshal Viscount Alanbrooke*. London 1959.

CHURCHILL, Sir Winston: *The Second World War*, vol. ii, London 1949; vol. iv, London 1951; vol. v, London 1952.

CLAUSEWITZ, General Carl von: *Vom Kriege*. Berlin 1832.

CONNELL, John: *Auchinleck, A Biography of Field-Marshal Sir Claude Auchinleck*. London 1959.

EHRMAN, John: *Grand Strategy*, vol. v, August 1943—September 1944. London 1956.

FRANKE, General-Major Hermann (ed.): *Handbuch der neuzeitlichen Wehrwissenschaften*, vol. i. Berlin und Leipzig 1936.

GARTHOFF, Raymond L.: *Soviet Military Doctrine*. Glencoe, Illinois, 1953.

DE GAULLE, General: *War Memoirs. Unity, 1942-44*. London 1959.

GIFFARD, General Sir George J.: Despatch 'Operations in Burma and North-East India from 16th November, 1943, to 22nd June, 1944'. *Supplement to The London Gazette*, March 13, 1951.

GOERLITZ, Walter: *The German General Staff. Its History and Structure 1657-1945*. London 1953.

HART, B. H. Liddell: *Strategy. The Indirect Approach*. London 1954.

HOWARD, Michael: *The Franco-Prussian War*. London 1961.

HUBATSCH, Walther (ed.): *Hitlers Weisungen für die Kriegführung 1939-45*. Frankfurt am Main 1962.

HUTTON, Lt.-General T. J.: 'Report on Operations in Burma from 27th December, 1941, to 5th March, 1942'. *Supplement to The London Gazette*, March 5, 1948.

JONG, Louis de: *The German Fifth Column in the Second World War*. London, 1956.

LEVERKUEHN, Paul: *Der geheime Nachrichtendienst der deutschen Wehrmacht im Kriege*. Frankfurt am Main 1957.

LUDENDORFF, General Erich: *Der totale Krieg*. München 1940.

MANSTEIN, Field-Marshal Erich von: *Lost Victories*. London 1958.

McCARTHY, Dudley: *Australia in the War of 1939-45*. Series One, vol v. *South-West Pacific Area—First Year*. Canberra 1959.

MILITARY HISTORY SECTION, Headquarters, Army Forces Far East: *Japanese Preparations for Operations in Manchuria, January 1943—August 1945*. 1953.

MORISON, Samuel Eliot: *The Invasion of France and Germany 1944-5*. *History of US Naval Operations in World War II*, vol. xi. London 1957.

OMAN, Sir Charles: *A History of the Peninsular War*, vol. v. Oxford 1914.

POGUE, Forrest C.: *The Supreme Command, United States Army in World War II. The European Theatre of Operations*. Washington 1954.

Report to the Combined Chiefs of Staff by the Supreme Commander South-East Asia 1943-5. London 1951.

ROMANUS, Charles F., and SUTHERLAND, Riley: *Stilwell's Command Problems*. Office of the Chief of Military History, Washington 1956.
—*Stilwell's Mission to China*. US Army in World War II. Washington 1953.
SHERWOOD, Robert E.: *The White House Papers of Harry L. Hopkins*, vol. i, September 1939 to January 1942. London 1948.
SLIM, Field-Marshal Sir William: *Defeat Into Victory*. London 1956.
STRACEY, Colonel C. P.: *The Canadian Army 1939-45. An Official Historical Summary*. Ottawa 1948.
SUN TZU: *On the Art of War, The Oldest Military Treatise in the World*. Translated by Lionel Giles. London 1910.
TELPUCHOWSKI, B. S.: *Die sowjetische Geschichte des Grossen Vaterländischen Krieges 1941-45*. Herausgegeben und kritisch erläutert von Andreas Hillgruber und Hans-Adolf Jacobsen. Frankfurt am Main 1961.
TESKE, Oberst Hermann: *Die silbernen Spiegel*. Heidelberg 1952.
WAR DEPARTMENT: *Technical Manual. Handbook on Japanese Military Forces*. October 1, 1944.
WHITE, Theodore H.: *The Stilwell Papers*. London 1949.
WIGMORE, Lionel: *Australia in the War 1939-45*, vol. iv, *The Japanese Thrust*. Canberra 1957.

Special Forces and Guerrillas

ALLEN, W. E. D.: *Gideon Force*. In Irwin R. Blacker (ed.): *Irregulars, Partisans, Guerrillas*. New York 1954.
—*Guerrilla Warfare in Abyssinia*. London 1943.
AMERY, Julian: *Sons of the Eagle. A Study in Guerrilla War*. London 1948.
ANISIMOV, Oleg: *The German Occupation in Northern Russia during World War II: Political and Administrative Aspects*. Research Programme on the USSR. New York City 1954.
BARKER, Dudley: *Grivas, Portrait of a Terrorist*. London 1959.
BEKKER, C. D.: *K-Men, The Story of the German Frogmen and Midget Submarines*. London 1955.
BENYON-TINKER, W. E.: *Dust Upon the Sea*. London 1947.
BERRY, Brigadier-General: 'Statement by UK Representatives'. In *European Resistance Movements 1939-45*. Oxford 1960.
BERTHOLD, Will: *Brandenburg Division*. London 1961.
BONCIANI, Carlo: *'F' Squadron*. London 1947.
BOXALL, Jack: *A Story of 2/5 Australian Commando Squadron*. N.d.
BRAJUS-KOVIC, Lt.-Colonel: 'La Guerre de Libération en Yougoslavie 1941-45', in *European Resistance Movements 1939-45*. Oxford 1960.
BRAZIER-CREAGH, Brigadier K. R.: 'Malaya'. Lecture reprinted in *Royal United Service Institution Journal* 1954, p. 175.
BROOKS, General Sir Dallas: 'The Royal Marines'. Lecture reprinted in *Royal United Service Institution Journal* 1948, vol. 93, p. 260.
BUCKLEY, Christopher: *Norway. The Commandos. Dieppe*. London 1951.
BURCHETT, W. G.: *Wingate's Phantom Army*. Bombay 1944.
BURHANS, Robert D.: *The First Special Service Force*. Washington 1947.
CALLINAN, Lt.-Colonel Bernard J.: *Independent Company*. London 1953.
CALVERT, Brigadier Michael: *Prisoners of Hope*. London 1952.
CHAPMAN, Colonel F. Spencer: *The Jungle is Neutral*. London 1949.
CHURCHILL, Brigadier T. B. L.: 'The Value of Commandos'. *Royal United Service Institution Journal* 1950, vol. 95, p. 87.
CLARKE, Brigadier Dudley: *Seven Assignments*. London 1948.

BIBLIOGRAPHY

CLUTTERBUCK, Lt.-Colonel R. L.: 'Bertrand Stewart Prize Essay 1960', *The Army Quarterly*, January 1961, p. 164.

COLLIER, Basil: *The Defence of the United Kingdom. History of the Second World War.* London 1957.

COWLES, Virginia: *The Phantom Major. The Story of David Stirling and the SAS Regiment.* London 1958.

CRICHTON-STUART, Michael: *G-Patrol.* London 1958.

—'The Story of a Long Range Desert Patrol'. *The Army Quarterly*, vol xlvii, October 1943, p. 70, and January 1944, p. 197.

DAVIDOV, General Denis: *Essay sur la guerre de partisans.* Traduit du russe. 1841.

DEAKIN, Professor F. W. D.: *Great Britain and European Resistance.* Paper read at the Second International Conference on the History of the Resistance, Milan, March 26-29, 1961.

DEDIJER, Vladimir: *Tito Speaks.* London 1953.

DENNY, John Howard: *Chindit Indiscretion.* London 1956.

DEPARTMENT OF THE ARMY, Office, Chief of Information: *Special Warfare US Army*, Washington DC, 1962.

—*German Anti-Guerrilla Operations in the Balkans (1941-44).* Washington, DC, August 1954.

DIXON, Brigadier C. A. and HEILBRUNN, O.: *Communist Guerrilla Warfare.* George Allen & Unwin, London 1954 (3rd ed. 1961); Praeger, New York 1955 (4th ed. 1962); Paris 1956; Frankfurt am Main 1956.

DOUGHERTY, James E.: 'The Guerrilla War in Malaya'. *US Naval Institute Proceedings*, vol. 84, No. 9, September 1958.

DRYSDALE, Lt.-Colonel D. B.: '41 Commando'. *Marine Corps Gazette*, August 1953, vol. 37, p. 28.

DURNFORD-SLATER, Brigadier John: *Commando.* London 1953.

FALL, Professor Bernard: *Street Without Joy. Indo-China at War 1946-54.* Harrisburg 1961.

FARRAN, Major Roy: *Winged Dagger.* London 1948.

—*Operation Tombola.* London 1960.

FEDEROV, A.: *L'Obkom clandestin au travail.* Paris 1951.

FELLOWES-GORDON, Major Ian: *Amiable Assassins.* London 1957.

FERGUSSON, Brigadier Sir Bernard: *Beyond the Chindwin.* London 1945.

—*The Wild Green Earth.* London 1946.

—*The Black Watch and the King's Enemies.* London 1950.

—*The Watery Maze. The Story of Combined Operations.* London 1961.

—'Behind the Enemy's Lines in Burma'. Lecture reprinted in *Royal United Service Institution Journal*, vol. 91, August 1946, p. 347.

FLEMING, Colonel Peter: *Invasion 1940. An Account of the German Preparations and the British Counter-Measures.* London 1957.

FOLEY, Charles: *Commando Extraordinary.* London 1954.

48 Royal Marine Commando, The Story 1944-45. Published Privately, 1946.

GIAP, Vo Nguyen: *People's War, People's Army.* New York 1962.

GLASSMAN, Henry S.: *Lead the Way, Rangers—5th Ranger Bn.* 1945.

GREENE, Lt.-Colonel T. N. (ed.): *The Guerrilla—And How to Fight Him.* New York 1962.

GRIFFITH, Brigadier-General Samuel B.: Introduction to Mao Tse-tung: *Guerrilla Warfare.* New York 1961.

GUBBINS, Major-General Sir Colin: 'Resistance Movements in the War'. Lecture reprinted in *Royal United Service Institution Journal* 1948, vol. 93, p. 210.

GUEVARA, Ernesto: *La Guerra de las Guerrillas.* Havana 1960, New York 1961.

GUTHRIE, Captain Duncan: *Jungle Diary*. London 1946.
HACKETT, Lt.-General Sir John W.: 'The Employment of Special Forces'. Lecture reprinted in *Royal United Service Institution Journal* 1952, vol. 97, p. 34.
HAMLETT, Lt.-General Barksdale: 'Special Forces, Training for Peace and War'. *Army Information Digest*, June 1961, p. 2.
HANRAHAN, Gene Z.: *The Communist Struggle in Malaya*. New York 1954.
—'The Chinese Red Army and Guerrilla Warfare'. US *Army Combat Forces Journal*. February 1951.
HARRISON, D. I.: *These Men Are Dangerous. The Special Air Service at War*. London 1957.
HEILBRUNN, Otto: *Communist Guerrilla Warfare*; see DIXON, Brigadier C. A., and HEILBRUNN, O.
—*The Soviet Secret Services*. George Allen & Unwin, London 1956 (2nd. ed. 1957); Praeger, New York 1956; Frankfurt am Main 1956.
—*Partisanenbuch*. Zurich 1960.
—*Partisan Warfare*. George Allen & Unwin, London 1962; Praeger, New York 1962; Paris 1963; Frankfurt am Main 1963; Heimevernsbladet, Oslo, 1962.
HILLS, Lt.-Colonel R. J. T.: *Phantom Was There*. London 1951.
HOGARD, Commandant J.: 'Guerre révolutionnaire et pacification'. *Revue Militaire d'Information*, January 1957.
—'Guerre révolutionnaire ou Révolution dans l'art de la guerre'. *Revue de Défense Nationale*, December 1956.
HOWELL, Major Edgar M.: *The Soviet Partisan Movement 1941-44*. Department of the Army Pamphlet. Washington 1956.
HUEMMELCHEN, Gerhard: 'Balkanräumung 1944'. *Wehrwissenschaftliche Rundschau* 1959, 9. Jahrgang, p. 566.
IGNATOW, P. K.: *Partisanen*. Berlin 1953.
INSTITUT HISTORIQUE DE L'ARMEE DE LA REPUBLIQUE FEDERATIVE POPULAIRE DE YOUGOSLAVIE: *Les Efforts de Guerre de la Yougoslavie, 1941-45*. N.d.
KAPETANOVIC, Nikola: *Tito and the Partisans*. Belgrade, n.d.
KAY, R. L.: *New Zealand in the Second World War*. Official History, War History Branch: *Long Range Desert Group in Libya, 1940-41*, Wellington 1949, and *Long Range Desert Group in the Mediterranean*, Wellington 1950.
KEMP, Peter: *No Colour or Crest*. London 1958.
KIRBY, Major-General S. Woodburn (with C. T. Addis, J. F. Meiklejohn, M. R. Roberts, G. T. Wards and N. L. Desoer): *The War Against Japan*, vol. ii, London 1958, vol. iii, London 1961.
KITSON, Major Frank: *Gangs and Counter-Gangs*. London 1960.
KOVIC-DIMITRYE, Lt.-Colonel Brajus: 'La Guerre de Libération Nationale en Yougoslavie (1941-45)', in *European Resistance Movements 1939-45*. Oxford 1960.
KOVPAK, Major-General S. A.: *Our Partisan Course*. London 1947.
KRIEGSHEIM, Major Herbert: *Getarnt, Getäuscht und doch Getreu- die geheimnisvollen 'Brandenburger'*. Berlin 1958.
KVEDAR, Lt.-General Dusan: 'Territorial Warfare'. *Journal of the United Service Institution of India*, vol. lxxxix, April-June 1959, no. 375, p. 131.
LANDSBOROUGH, Gordon: *Tobruk Commando*. London 1956.
LARSEN, Colin R.: *Pacific Commandos, New Zealanders and Fijians in Action*. Wellington 1946.
LAYCOCK, Major-General Sir Robert: 'Raids in the last War and their Lessons'. Lecture reprinted in *Royal United Service Institution Journal* 1947, vol. 92, p. 528.
LLOYD-OWEN, Lt.-Colonel David: *The Desert, My Dwelling Place*. London 1957.

LOCKHART, Sir Robert Bruce: *The Marines Were There*. London 1950.
LODWICK, John: *The Filibusters. The Story of the Special Boat Service*. London 1947.
MACLEAN, Brigadier Sir Fitzroy: *Disputed Barricade*. London 1957.
MANUE, Georges R.: 'Le rôle de l'Armée en Algérie'. *Revue Militaire d'Information*. July 1956, p. 13.
MAO TSE-TUNG: 'On the Protracted War'. In *Selected Works of Mao Tse-tung*, vol. ii, London 1954.
—'Strategic Problems of Guerrilla War'. *Ibidem*.
—'Interview with the British Correspondent James Bertram'. *Ibidem*.
—*Aspects of China's Anti-Jap Struggle*. Bombay 1948.
—*Guerrilla Warfare*. With an Introduction by Brigadier-General Samuel B. Griffith. New York 1961.
MEAD, Lt.-Colonel P. W.: 'The Chindit Operations of 1944'. *Royal United Service Institution Journal* 1955, vol. 100, p. 258.
MEISTER, Jürg: 'Die sowjetrussischen amphibischen Operationen 1939-45'. *Marine Rundschau* Heft 4, 1955, p. 124.
MIERS, Lt.-Colonel Richard: *Shoot to Kill*. London 1959.
MIHAILOVIC, The Trial of. Stenographic Records and Documents. Belgrade 1946.
MIKSCHE, Lt.-Colonel F. O.: *Secret Forces. The Technique of Underground Movements*. London 1950.
MILLER, H. *Menace in Malaya*. London 1954.
MILLS-ROBERTS, Brigadier Derek: *Clash by Night*. London 1956.
MURRAY, Colonel J. C.: 'The Anti-Bandit War'. *Marine Corps Gazette*, January to May 1954.
MYERS, Brigadier E. C. W.: *Greek Entanglement*. London 1955.
NEY, Colonel Virgil: *Notes on Guerrilla War*. Washington, DC, 1961.
NOONAN, William: *The Surprising Battalion*. Sydney 1945.
OATTS, Lt.-Colonel Balfour: *The Jungle in Arms*. London 1962.
O'BALLANCE, Major Edgar: 'The Algerian Struggle'. *The Army Quarterly*. October 1960.
OGBURN, Charlton: *The Marauders*. New York 1956.
OSANKU, Franklin Mark (ed.): *Modern Guerrilla Warfare*. New York 1962.
OSBORNE, Lt.-Colonel W. L.: 'Shaduzup'. *Infantry Journal* 66, April 1950, p. 13.
OWEN, Lt.-Colonel Frank: *The Campaign in Burma*. Prepared for South-East Asia Command by the Central Office of Information. London 1946.
PARET, Peter, and SHY, John W.: *Guerrillas in the 1960s*. New York 1961.
PEACOCK, Geraldine: *The Life of a Jungle Wallah*. Ilfracombe, n.d.
PENIAKOFF, Lt.-Colonel Vladimir: *Popski's Private Army*. London 1950.
PLENCA, Dusan: *Le Mouvement de Libération Nationale en Yougoslavie*. Paper read at the Second International Congress on the History of the Resistance, Milan, March 26-29, 1961.
READ, Captain G. W. (ed.): *Raiding Forces. The Story of an Independent Command in the Aegean 1943-45*. Compiled from Official Sources and Reports by Observer Officers of No. 1 Public Relation Service, MEF.
REDELIS, Valdis: *Partisanenkrieg*. Heidelberg 1958.
REGIMENT COMMANDO. In *L'Armée, La Nation*, November 1947, vol. 2, p. 14.
RENDULIC, General-Oberst Dr Lothar: 'Der Partisanenkrieg'. In *Bilanz des Zweiten Weltkrieges*. Oldenburg 1953.
RENTSCH, Hellmuth: *Partisanenkampf—Erfahrungen und Lehren*. Frankfurt am Main 1961.
RICHTLINIEN *des Oberkommandos der Wehrmacht für die Bandenbekämpfung*, vom 6, Mai 1944.

RIGG, Colonel Robert B.: *Red China's Fighting Hordes*. Harrisburg 1952.
ROLO, Charles: *Wingate's Raiders*. London 1945.
SAMAIN, Bryan: *Commando Men*. London 1948.
SAUNDERS, Hilary St George: *The Green Beret*. London 1949.
SCHRAMM, Percy Ernst (ed.): *Kriegstagebuch des Oberkommandos der Wehrmacht (Wehrmachtsführungsstab)*. Erster Halbband, Band iv, Frankfurt am Main 1961, Zweiter Halbband, Band iv, Frankfurt am Main 1961.
SCHRAMM, Dr Wilhelm Ritter von (ed.): *Die Geschichte des Panzerkorps Grossdeutschland*, III Band, collected and assembled by Helmuth Spaeter. Duisburg-Ruhrort 1958.
SHAW, W. B. Kennedy: *Long Range Desert Group*. London 1945.
SKORZENY, Otto: *Skorzeny's Special Missions*. London 1957.
—*Skorzeny's Secret Missions*. New York 1950.
SLOMAN, Major J. G.: 'Guerrilla Warfare'. *Australian Army Journal* September 1954 and *Military Review* July 1956.
SOUYRIS, Capitaine André: 'Un procédé efficace de Contre-guérilla'. *Revue de Défense Nationale*, 1956, p. 686.
—*Les conditions de la parade et de la riposte à la guerre révolutionnaire*. *Revue Militaire d'Information*, February and March 1957.
STANDING, Percy Cross: *Guerrilla Leaders of the World*. London 1912.
STIBBE, Philip: *Return Via Rangoon*. London 1947.
STORY *of 45 Royal Marine Commando, The*. Written by the Officers and published privately, 1946.
STORY *of 'V' Force, The. Indian Army Review*, vol. 2, No. 12. October 1946.
SYKES, Christopher: *Orde Wingate*. London 1959.
TANHAM, George K.: *Communist Revolutionary Warfare—The Vietminh in Indo-China*. New York 1961.
TOBIN, Colonel P. A.: 'The Bertrand Stewart Prize'. *Army Quarterly*, vol. lxv, January 1953, p. 161.
TWOHIG, Lt.-Colonel J. P. O'Brien: 'Are Commandos Really Necessary?' *Army Quarterly*, vol. lvii, October 1948, p. 88.
WAR DEPARTMENT, Historical Division: *Merrill's Marauders (February to May 1944)*. Washington 1945.
WAVELL, Field-Marshal Earl: 'The Soldier as Citizen'. *Sunday Times*, August 26, 1945.
WILLET, John: *Popski*. London 1954.
WILLIAMS, Colonel R. C., Jr.: 'Amphibious Scouts and Raiders'. *Military Affairs*, vol. xiii, 1949, p. 157.
WOODHOUSE, Colonel C. M.: *Apple of Discord*. London 1948.
—'The Greek Resistance 1942-44'. In *European Resistance Movements 1939-45*. Oxford 1960.
XIMENES: 'La guerre révolutionnaire et ses donnés fondamentales'. *Revue Militaire d'Information*, February/March 1957.
YARBOROUGH, Brigadier-General William P.: 'Special Warriors in the US Army'. *The Airman*, November 1961, p. 41.
YOUNG, Captain Leilyn M.: 'Rangers in a Night Operation'. *Military Review*, vol. xxiv, July 1944, No. 4, p. 64.
YOUNG, Lt.-Colonel Peter: *Storm from the Sea*. London 1958.
YUNNIE, Park: *Warriors on Wheels*. London 1959.

BIBLIOGRAPHY

Air Force and Airborne Forces

ARNOLD, General H. H.: 'The Aerial Invasion of Burma'. *National Geographical Magazine* 86, August 1944, p. 129.

BRERETON, Lt.-General Lewis H.: *The Brereton Diaries*. New York 1946.

CHATTERTON, Brigadier George: *The Wings of Pegasus*. London 1962.

CRAVEN, W. F., and CATE, J. L.: *The Army Air Forces in World War II*, vol. iii. *Argument to V-E Day (January 1944 to May 1945)*. Chicago 1951.

DRUM, General Karl: *Airpower and Russian Partisan Warfare*. USAF Historical Studies: No. 177. USAF Historical Division, Research Studies Institute, Air University. March 1962, Alabama.

FOXLEY-NORRIS, Wing-Commander C. N.: 'The Use of Airpower in Security Operations'. *Royal United Service Institution Journal* 1954, p. 555.

V.D. HEYDTE, Professor Dr Freiherr: 'Die Fallschirmtruppe im Zweiten Weltkrieg', in *Bilanz des Zweiten Weltkrieges*, Oldenburg/Hamburg 1953.

MACKINTOSH, J. M.: 'Soviet Airborne Troops', in *The Soviet Air and Rocket Forces*, ed. by Asher Lee, London 1959.

MIKSCHE, Lt.-Colonel F. O.: *Paratroops*. London 1943.

NATTA, Colonel T. F. van: 'Airdrop Supply'. *Infantry Journal* 62, May 1948, p. 20.

NEHRING, General Walter K.: in *Russian Airborne Operations*, Office of the Chief of Military History, Ms. No. P-116, Washington 1952, p. 35.

PEIRSE, Air Chief Marshal Sir Richard: Despatch 'Air Operations in South-East Asia, 16th November, 1943, to 31st May, 1944'. *Supplement to The London Gazette*, March 13, 1951.

REINHARDT, General-Major Hellmuth: in *Russian Airborne Operations*, Office of the Chief of Military History, Ms. No. P-116, Washington 1952, p. 5.

ROMULUS: 'Future Employment of Airborne Forces'. *Royal United Service Institution Journal*, vol. 100, No. 598, May 1955, p. 239.

RUMSEY, J. R. L.: 'Air Supply in Burma'. *Army Quarterly* 1947, No. 55 (October), p. 33.

SAUNDERS, Hilary St George: *The Red Beret*. London 1950.

SCHWABEDISSEN, General-Leutnant Walter: *The Russian Airforce in the Eyes of German Commanders*. USAF Historical Division, Study No. 175, Research Studies Institute, Air University, Alabama, June 1960.

STUDENT, Colonel-General Kurt: 'Airborne Forces'. In *The Soviet Army*, ed. by B. H. Liddell Hart. London 1956.

TAYLOR, Dr Joe G.: *Air Supply in the Burma Campaign*. USAF Historical Division, Study No. 75, Research Studies Institute, Air University, Alabama.

WAR DEPARTMENT, Military Intelligence Division: *Japanese Parachute Troops*. Special Series No. 32, Washington, July 1, 1945.

WARREN, Dr John C.: *Airborne Missions in the Mediterranean 1942-45*. USAF Historical Studies, Study No. 74, USAF Historical Division, Research Studies Institute, Air University, Alabama, September 1955.

—*Airborne Operations in World War II, European Theater*. USAF Historical Studies, Study No. 97, USAF Historical Division, Research Studies Institute, Air University, Alabama. September 1956.

WEBSTER, Sir Charles, and FRANKLAND, Dr Noble: *The Strategic Air Offensive Against Germany. History of the Second World War.* Vol. iv, London 1961.

INDEX

9780367711849